Birds   THE ART OF ORNITHOLOGY

Illustrations on pages 1–4 & 25:

p.1: Goshawk Feather, *Accipiter gentilis*, by Margaret Bushby Lascelles Cockburn, c.1858.
pp.2-3: Bird of Paradise, *Paradisaea* sp. from *Raccolta di Uccelli*, by Giovanni da Udine, c.1580.
p.4: Fork-tailed Flycatcher, *Tyrannus savana*, by Prideaux John Selby, c.1788–1867.
p.25: Feather (detail) from Temminck's Tragopan, *Tragopan temminckii*, Anonymous, c.1822–29.

For my beloved Melanie

First published in the United States of
America in 2008 by
Rizzoli International Publications, Inc.
300 Park Avenue South
New York, NY 10010
www.rizzoliusa.com

Originally published in the United Kingdom
in 2008 by Scriptum Editions.
Created by Co & Bear Productions (UK) Ltd.
in association with the Natural History Museum, London.
Copyright © 2008 Co & Bear Productions (UK) Ltd.

2008 2009 2010 2011 / 10 9 8 7 6 5 4 3 2 1

ISBN: 978-0-8478-3134-0

Library of Congress Control Number: 2007934367

Printed in Italy

Birds

THE ART OF ORNITHOLOGY

BY JONATHAN ELPHICK

RIZZOLI
NEW YORK

P. J. Selby
Delt.

FOREWORD

*W*hen it was suggested that i write the foreword to this beautiful, erudite and accessible book, I was most happy to do so, more especially as it provided an opportunity to highlight the intimate and synergistic connections that exist between bird art and the huge, scientifically vital bird collections held by institutions such as The Natural History Museum. However, on reading the author's preface, I realised that he and I share a closer bond than I could have suspected, as we both grew up, not many years apart, in exactly the same part of the world and, apparently, were even influenced by the same family in our love of ornithology. While, unlike him, I never knowingly encountered the Corncrake there, I remember my father, a general practitioner of long-standing in the district, pointing out sites where he had heard them calling not long since and speculating as to the possible reasons for their disappearance.

Alongside the diverse aesthetic experiences it can engender, bird art has historically played a key scientific role. Until at least the end of the eighteenth century, long-term preservation techniques for bird specimen material were largely inadequate and institutions capable of looking after bird specimens indefinitely were essentially absent. Artistic representation of birds, in conjunction with the written word, has thus proved to have been the most important means of communicating scientific information and ideas concerning their identity and relationships from this period. Although many bird specimens were collected during the world-circling explorations of Captain Cook in the late 1760s and 1770s, relatively few of these have survived; instead, it is the paintings of such artists as Sydney Parkinson, William Ellis and Georg Forster, who accompanied Cook on his voyages, that have proved of most lasting scientific value. Similarly, whereas the specimens from the great Leverian Museum, on which John Latham depended heavily for his descriptions of new bird species, have long since been scattered and largely lost, important insight into its contents is still provided by the watercolours of Sarah Stone, many of which are held by the Natural History Museum. New ornithological revelations from old bird artwork continue to arise, perhaps most recently exemplified by the realisation that a painting of 1611 by the Dutch artist Roelandt Savery seems to provide the final piece of evidence necessary to prove that the enigmatic White Dodo of Réunion Island was actually based on the conflation of early travellers' accounts of a now extinct Réunion Ibis, with illustrations of an aberrantly coloured Dodo from Mauritius.

This book progressively illuminates how, throughout the nineteenth and twentieth centuries, a succession of brilliant artists have made accessible the discoveries of ornithology to an ever-growing general public eager for scientific knowledge in combination with aesthetic pleasure. Indeed, in the work of people like F. W. Frohawk, some went further in recreating scientifically sound representations of extinct species for which no complete specimen existed, an approach still being developed at the present time in the work of artist scientists such as Julian Hume. This is indeed an aptly titled book, whose contents will bring pleasure and understanding to many.

Dr Robert Prys-Jones

PREFACE

*O*n a shelf in my library, I still have a now rather battered book full of colour paintings I made of the birds I found in the gloriously unimproved farmland, hills, moorlands, woods, marshes, rivers, lakes and coasts of the north Wales countryside where it was my great fortune to grow up, accompanied by notes on their distribution and status. It emulated the handsomely illustrated bird books I was beginning to find on the shelves of libraries or was shown by my seniors at the local field club and ornithological society. I made this book as a teenager, over forty years ago, having been passionately interested in birds ever since early childhood, and now, as I enter later middle age, this love affair shows no sign of abating. Despite its rather pompous title – *Coloured Plates of Birds Observed in Flintshire, Volume I* – it is interesting to look at as a record of what I found, and make comparisons with then and now. Buzzards, for instance, were rare, due to zealous gamekeepers, while Corncrakes were still looking for mates in lush meadows – I watched one of the last noisily 'craking' males in awe, despite the huge discomfort borne of sitting inside a hawthorn hedge. Now the latter are long gone, while the former are numerous in the area.

At the same time as increasing my knowledge of the birds in the field, I developed my interest in bird art. Through my brothers Michael and Richard, I came to learn more of the work of British bird artists as they introduced me to examples such as the collection at the Hancock Museum in Newcastle-upon-Tyne by the great wood engraver Thomas Bewick, and books such as the Puffin picture books of paintings of estuary birds and birds of mountains and moorlands by Richard Talbot Kelly. I also saved much of my pocket money and any received as birthday and Christmas presents to put towards enlarging my own small library of bird books.

My 'adoption' in the 1950s as a fledgling birder by the remarkable Walton family led not only to a widening of my experience of birds and birding, but also a chance to explore the well-stocked library in their house. It included such gems as the idiosyncratic *Pirates and Predators,* written by that larger-than-life figure Colonel Richard Meinertzhagen and containing dramatic plates of birds of prey by the then very elderly but still very active George Lodge, and Witherby *et al's* superb five-volume *Handbook of British Birds,* whose plates I pored over at every opportunity.

Later I watched, from a respectful distance, the great wildlife artist Charles Tunnicliffe at work at Malltraeth, Anglesey – a place he loved greatly and adopted as his home, and a favourite birdwatching haunt of mine, too. These glimpses of what bird artists could achieve led me to a more detailed exploration of the subject. Ever since, I have lost no opportunity in seeking out and looking at bird art wherever I could find it. A career as a writer and editor has also led me to work with many fine modern bird artists.

So it is hardly surprising that, when I was invited by the publishers and the Natural History Museum to write this book, I was delighted to accept. Planning was at first relatively straightforward. Although the book could have been arranged in various different ways, all involved agreed that a chronological account would give the best idea of the development of the subject.

But then the main problem rapidly became apparent: who to include? More worryingly, who to leave out? Many equally worthy contenders (including personal favourites) jostled in my mind for a place, but for various reasons did not make it on board. The choice of artists, though not in any way a random one, is of necessity far from all-encompassing, as the field is so wide and rich: the collections of the Natural History Museum, from which the great majority of images in this book come, include some half-a-million natural-history illustrations on paper, and a million books. In the final choice, the aim has been to give an idea of the great range of bird art, from the more fanciful representations of exotic birds in earlier times to the accurate and detailed scientific illustrations of more recent years. It also includes a range of styles, and a wide variety of birds from different families, from tiny hummingbirds to huge pelicans.

I hope that as well as informing and entertaining, this book will encourage an appreciation of the riches of bird life and the will to help protect these wonderful creatures so that future generations of artists and others can continue to enjoy and celebrate their beauty.

JONATHAN ELPHICK

Beginnings

*A*s soon as our remote human ancestors started drawing, animals, including birds, figured in the exquisite designs they left on the walls of caves, such as the famous examples at Lascaux in the Dordogne region of south-central France, and Altamira to the south of Santander in north-eastern Spain. As well as perhaps serving as instruction manuals to teach novice hunters, they are likely to have had a symbolic significance, forming part of a prehistoric culture in which animals had great spiritual significance.

The great civilisation of Ancient Egypt made accurate portrayals of animals, including birds, that were hunted or domesticated. The fresco on the tomb of Atet at Meidum, not far south of present-day Cairo on the fertile banks of the Nile, includes images of three clearly distinguishable species of geese – the White-fronted Goose, the larger Bean Goose and the more colourful Red-breasted Goose. This was painted in about 2,600 BC. A relief carving from another Egyptian tomb, that of Mereruka at Saqqara, dating back some 4,000 years, shows geese and cranes being force-fed in a very early forerunner of the practice of *gavage* that is still used to produce the foie gras so important in French cuisine.

Ancient Egyptian images of birds also included more fanciful renditions in painting and sculpture of a symbolic nature. These were invested with huge religious importance (the images were often worshipped as being one and the same thing as the deity). Notable examples are the Sacred Ibis, chosen as the symbol of the god of wisdom and learning, Thoth, and a falcon, symbolising Horus, the most famous of falcon gods.

Later, in Ancient Greece, Aristotle (384–322 BC) made the first more-or-less scientific study of nature, setting down his thoughts on this and many other topics in hundreds of books, of which fewer than fifty survive, including some on animals. Aristotle included clear descriptions of many of the 140 kinds of birds he recognised. Today, by contrast, ornithologists separate birds into as many as 9,800 different species.

Aristotle, and later the Roman natural philosopher Gaius Plinius Secundus, better known as Pliny the Elder (c.20–79), dominated thinking and writing about natural history for the following millennium, and still exerted a considerable influence on many biologists in more recent times. Pliny was a voracious digester of the writing of others, and was said to have slept only briefly, spending much of his time poring over

Specht   H. fe.

PLINIVS secundus nouocomensis equestribus militiis industrie functus: procu
rationes quoq; splendidissimas atq; continuas summa integritate adminstrauit. Et
tamen liberalibus studiis tantam operam dedit: ut non temere qs plura motio scripserit.
Itaq; bella omnia que undiq; cum romanis gesta sunt xxxvii. uoluminibus comprehendit. Ite
naturalis historie. xxxvii. libros absoluit. Periit gadis campanie. Nam cum misenesi classi
pręesset & flagrante Veseuo: ad explorandas propius causas liburnicas prętendisset: neq;
aduersantibus uentis remeare posset: ui pulueris ac fauille oppressus est: uel ut quidam
existimant a seruo suo occisus: quę deficiens estu ut necem sibi maturaret orauerat hic in
his libris. xx. milia rey dignay ex lectione uoluminu circiter duum milium cő plexus est.
Primus aůt liber quasi index. xxxvi. libroy sequentium consumationem totỷ operis &
species continet tituloy.

P. Saluatoris Franceschini Notary

LIBROS NATVRALIS HISTORIAE
nouitiu cimenis qrititu tuoy opus natu apud me
proxima iętura licentiore epistola narrare cõstitui
ui ic udissime imperator. Sit enim hęc tui prę
fatio uerissima: dum maxime consenescit i patre.
Namq; tu solebas putare esse aliqd meas nugas:
ut obscere moliar Catullum conterraneu meum
agnoscis & hoc castrēse uerbum ille enim ut scis
pmutatis prioribus syllabis duriusculum se fecit
q uolebat existimari a uernaculis tuis & famulis.
Simul ut hac mea petulantia fiat q proxime non
fieri questuses in alia procaci epistola nostra ut in
quędam acta exeant. Sciantq; omnes qm exquo
tecum uiuat iperium triumphalis & censorius tu
sexieto cõsul ac tribunitię potestatis particeps: et
qiis nobilibus fecisti: du illud patri pariter & equeq
tri ordini prestas prefectus prętorii eius omniaq;
hęc rei publicę: et nobis quidę qualis incastrēsi contubernio. Nec qcq mutauit iste fortunę
amplitudo in bis: nisi ut prodesse tantundę posses ut uelles. Itaq; cũ ceteris sueneratione
tui pateant omnia illa: nobis adcolēdum te familiarius audatia sola supest. Hanc igit tibi
imputabis: et in nostra culpa tibi ignosces. Perfricui facie: nec tamē profeci quoniam alia
uia occurris: igens & longius etiam summouęs igentibus fascibus fulgorat in nullo unq;
uerius dicta uis ęloquętię tribunitię potestatis facundię: qto tu ore patris laudes tonas:
qto fratris amas: qtus ipoetica es. O magna secunditas animi quēadmodum frēm quoq;
imitareris excogitasti: sed hęc quis posset itrepidus extimare subiturus ingenii tui iuditiu
presertim lacessitum. Neq; eim similis & conditio publicantium & nosatum tibi dicantiu.
Tum possem dicere qd ista legis iperator humili uulgo scripta sunt agricolay opificum
turbę deniq; studioy ociosis quid te iudice facis: quia hanc operam cum dicerē nő eras in
hoc albo: maiorem te sciebam quam ut descensurum huc putarem. Pręterea est quędam
publica etiam eruditoy reiectio: utitur illa: et M. Tullius extra oēm ingēs italiam positus
etq; miremur per aduocatum defendit: nec doctissimum ōnium Persium hoc legere uolo
Lelium Congum uolo. Qs si hoc Lucilius qui primus condidit stili nasum legerit quasi
abusionem & uituperatione reputabit: primus enim satyricum carmen conscripsit i quo
utiq; uituperato uniuscuiusq; continet. Nasum autē dixit quasi uituperationis signu uel
maxime naso declarandum dicendumq; ē: si aduocatum sibi putauit Cicero mutuandum,
presertim cum de re publica scriberet quanto nos cautius ab aliquo iudice defendimur.

IVSTICIA IVDITM P PARATIO SEDIS TVE

his books or having others read to him. His huge work, comprising thirty-seven volumes, was essentially a compilation of information extracted from upwards of 2,000 books by other authors.

In the Far East, in China, Japan and Korea, the very long tradition of animal painting involved a major difference from Western artists: the artists painted only living birds, rather than dead specimens or trophies. Working as long ago as the early years of the Tang Dynasty (618–906), Chinese artists were superb at crystallising the essence of the living bird in their paintings, predating Western artists by centuries. By watching their subjects patiently and for long periods, they felt able to get inside them in their minds – almost to become the birds themselves – and create convincingly lifelike images.

The work of Chinese artists was informed by a lifetime of learning; as Christine Jackson describes in her superb *Dictionary of Bird Artists of the World* (1999), during their long apprenticeship they often came to specialise in one subject area, devoting their whole lives to improving their technique of painting subjects such as bamboo, horses or birds. And, again unlike bird painters in the West, at least until recently, some of them went even further in the direction of specialisation, painting just one particular kind of bird, for example geese, eagles or cranes.

Often, birds and flowers are combined in graceful designs, and different types have special symbolic meanings. For instance, the peacock and peony both symbolise beauty, and Chinese artists frequently combine them in a painting. This is not just a historic attitude, but continues in the work of recent oriental artists right up to the present day.

The representation of birds in the art of medieval Europe was largely symbolic, too, and on the whole was strictly tied to the Christian religion. Religious manuscripts from the seventh to the fifteenth centuries were illuminated with beautiful illustrations, each one painstakingly drawn and coloured by hand, using gold leaf as well as inks and paints. In these works, which included psalters, gospels, illustrated Bibles, missals and books of hours, birds decorate the margins either set among stylised foliage or as free-standing motifs. The birds, too, are generally stylised, although some are accurately drawn. As well as many depictions of recognisable bird species, such as Common Cranes, Common Peafowl, Hoopoes, Green Woodpeckers, Northern Ravens, Black-billed Magpies and Eurasian Jays, some of the figures are

PLATE 2.
Title page from *Historia Naturalis*
Pliny the Elder
1469. Incunabulum, illuminated with watercolour and gold paint.
400mm x 270mm
(15¾in x 10⅝in)

This beautiful example of an illuminated page comes from the famous thirty-seven volume work Historia Naturalis *('Natural History') by the great Roman natural philosopher and writer Pliny the Elder. This huge and rather rambling account originally appeared in Rome in 77 AD, and was thereafter published in numerous editions. The book from which this introductory page is taken is a first edition of one of the finest of the medieval editions, published in Venice in 1469.*

PLATE 3.
Junglefowl (male)
Gallus sp.

Giovanni da Udine
c.1550. Watercolour.
433mm x 315mm
(17in x 12⅜in)

*This painting of a spirited
cockerel is from
a book in the Natural
History Museum's
collection attributed
to Giovanni da Udine
(1487–1564). It is the
oldest collection of bird
paintings in the Museum.
The title,* Raccolta di
Uccelli, *can be translated
as 'A Collection of Birds'.
Da Udine was a pupil
of Raphael in Rome,
and later worked for
the Medicis in Florence –
although he was best
known for his botanical
paintings, he did also
paint birds. The Red
Junglefowl* (Gallus
gallus), *found from
northern India to
southern China and
parts of Indonesia, is the
ancestor of the world's
most abundant bird by
far – the domestic fowl.*

impossible to identify.

Some of the birds were doubtless drawn from nature – a good example is the European Goldfinch. This brightly coloured species is by far the most frequent of all small birds to appear in illuminated manuscripts. It was easily observed at close range, as it was commonly kept as a cage bird, and became valued for its complex symbolism, which refers to the resurrection of Christ and as a symbol of fertility and healing. Many of the avian subjects of the manuscripts, however, were copied from the work of other artists. As with other early images of birds in the centuries before printing, errors arose through the process of copying, both in the making of copies of a particular manuscript and in the copying of birds from one manuscript to another.

Another medieval invention was the bestiary. This was a collection of information and illustrations of animals, plants and minerals, much of it more concerned with myth and supposition than realistic observation of nature. It was reproduced in many different forms throughout the Middle Ages. These are all thought to have originated in a book called *Physiologus*, assembled long before, perhaps as early as the fourth century, and first appearing in Greek and then Latin. Each of its forty or so sections contained a religious or moral lesson to be drawn from the (invariably inaccurate) habits or appearance of the animal concerned.

One of the first real ornithologists, the Holy Roman Emperor Frederick II of Hohenstaufen, King of Sicily and Jerusalem (1194–1250), stood out at a time when knowledge of natural history had essentially stagnated. Books on the subject were for the most part compilations of work of classical authors, the perpetuation of numerous fanciful ideas and fables about birds and other animals or religious tracts in which the creatures were seen only through the distorting lens of religion. Frederick set out much of his knowledge of birds in the first part of an unfinished work. Despite its title, *De Arte Venandi cum Avibus* ('On the Art of Hunting with Birds'), this is much more than a manual of falconry, dealing as it does with many aspects of ornithology. For example, it includes a lengthy chapter giving a detailed analysis of bird flight that in many respects is still of value today. This important work contains marginal illustrations that are often remarkable for their time, showing birds of prey and their characteristic prey, as well as illustrating techniques used by falconers.

PLATE 4.
Medieval woodcut
illustration from
Hortus Sanitatis
1491. Hand-coloured
woodcut.
280mm x 210mm
(11in x 8¼in)

*This is a page from the
birds section of one of
the most important and
impressive of all medieval
natural history books. Its
Latin title means 'Garden
of Health', and it deals
mainly with the medicinal
uses of animals, minerals
and particularly plants.
Drawing heavily on the
work of earlier authors
and illustrators,
it was first printed in
German with the title
Ortus sanitatis … ein gart
der Gesuntheit, in Meinz
in 1485. This was
followed by several more
editions in German, some
with the woodcuts
coloured for the first time,
and then a greatly
enlarged edition in Latin
from whichthis picture
and the one on page 19
are taken, which was
published by Jacobus
Meydenback in 1491.*

The hostility of the church to Frederick's forward-thinking ideas ensured that his masterwork was banned and did not surface again until the close of the sixteenth century, almost 350 years after his death, and it was not until almost another 200 more years had elapsed that it came to the attention of ornithologists.

In the mid-fifteenth century, the invention of printing was of huge importance; the text and illustrations in books no longer had to be laboriously copied by hand. This development went hand in hand with the development of woodcuts for reproducing illustrations. Pliny's great work *Historia Naturalis* was first printed in 1469, and had a major influence out of all proportion to its tiny print run of only 100 copies. It was followed soon after, in 1475, by *Buch der Natur*. This was the first book to contain drawings of animals. The text was a translation, by the German cleric Konrad von Megenberg, of *De Animalibus*, a book by the German Dominican theologian, saint, philosopher and scientist Albert von Bollstädt of Cologne, usually known as Albertus Magnus or Doctor Universalis (c.1200–80).

Among the most impressive and beautiful of all the illustrations in early printed books on birds are those appearing in the works of the Swiss naturalist Conrad Gesner (1516–65), the Frenchman Pierre Belon (1517–64) and the Italian Ulisse Aldrovandi (Aldrovandus) (c.1522–1605). In many cases these were lively portrayals, full of action, that captured the characteristic features and postures of their subjects.

Born in the city of Zurich, Gesner was the son of a poor furrier and tanner. He was sent away as a child to live with his uncle when his father was killed in a battle. After studying in Paris, Zurich, Strasbourg and Bruges, he spent much of the rest of his life writing many books on natural history. His major work dealing with animals was his *Historium Animalium*, published in Zurich in four volumes between 1551 and 1587. The second volume, dealing with birds, appeared in 1555, with a woodcut illustrating each of the 217 species included.

One of the first naturalist-explorers, Belon travelled to many parts of Europe and the Near East, gathering information and accumulating specimens for his studies of the wildlife of the Mediterranean. Although by training a botanist and apothecary, he was one of the founders of comparative animal anatomy. Belon also had the distinction of producing the first work devoted completely to birds. Titled *L'Histoire de la nature des oyseaux*, this appeared in 1555, illustrated by fourteen woodcuts. His second bird book, *Pourtraicts d'oyseaux*, published in Paris in 1557, contained 174 woodcuts, many taken from the author's own drawings, which were coloured by hand. Nine years later, at the age of forty-seven, Belon was stabbed to death, probably by robbers, in the Bois de Boulogne in Paris.

Aldrovandus was born into a wealthy family in Bologna. He spent much of his inheritance on travelling to research his writing and on paying artists to make illustrations for his books. Although his writing is, on the whole, less stylish and accurate than that produced by Gesner, he adopted a more advanced classification of animals – although, like his contemporaries, he regarded bats as birds rather than mammals. Even though many still contained errors and fanciful features that seem bizarre to us today, the illustrations accompanying his texts were on the whole more accurate than those in Gesner's works. They included anatomical studies, including both the skeletons of whole birds and details, for example, of the muscles controlling the movement of the upper mandible of a parrot's beak, or the oviduct of a hen.

Although Aldrovandus started writing *Ornithology*, his great treatise on birds, when he was a young man, it was so detailed and required so much effort to produce that it was not published until he was in his seventies, the three volumes on birds appearing between 1599 and 1603. Much of the rest of his *Historia Naturalis* was not published until after his death.

A pupil of Aldrovandus, Volcher Coiter (1534–76), who was born in the city of Groningen in the northern Netherlands, was an unusually perceptive naturalist for his time, and included in his accounts of his studies many accurate observations. These include his ideas on the way that the different shapes of birds' bills suit each type to a particular diet, and the fact that the very long toes of birds living on soft marshy ground help to spread their weight and prevent them from sinking in. His papers also included some outstandingly accurate drawings: of the skeletons of various different birds, of the skull of a woodpecker and of changes apparent in the sections of the eggs he examined daily during the process of incubation.

The end of the sixteenth century roughly marks the beginning of the era when engraving had largely replaced woodcut as the main technique used

PLATE 5.
Medieval woodcut
illustration from
Hortus Sanitatis
1491. Hand-coloured
woodcut.
80mm x 60mm
(3in x 2¼in)

The Hortus Sanitatis
*appeared at a time when
illustrations in natural
history books were rare. It
was the first printed book
to contain pictures of
birds, in the third of its
seven parts, which is
entitled 'Tractatus de
Avibus'. Consisting of 122
'chapters', each decorated
with a woodcut, it
includes not only birds but
also other flying creatures,
including bats, insects and
various fabulous animals,
such as the one shown
here. The 1491 Latin
edition from which this
plate is taken seems to be
an amalgamation of the
original 1485 book
(ascribed to a Frankfurt
medical officer, Johanne
Wonnecke von Caub) and
another popular work in
German, Conrad von
Megenberg's popular* Buch
der Natur.

by bird artists, and careful observation gradually started to replace
reverence for the opinions – often wildly inaccurate – of earlier scholars,
in many cases dating back to the Ancient Greeks and Romans. As well as
the increasing number of books about birds that contained illustrations of
their subjects, there was a flowering of fine-art painting that featured
birds as the principal subject.

From the early sixteenth century onwards, paintings of still life by
classical artists had included birds. Popular and in demand, still-life
paintings were often the work of artists starting out on their careers,
enabling them to establish a clientele and gain experience while doing so.
By the mid-seventeenth century, a whole genre had grown up of such

paintings of birds. These were shown as dead, hanging from a butcher's hook or arranged, sometimes with other food or household objects, in the kitchen of a wealthy patron, or as living birds in formal arrangements, their postures stilted and unnatural and set against a background of an idealised landscape such as the Garden of Eden or the classical garden of a great house. Often, too, these paintings featured an unnatural assortment of different species from various parts of the world.

Still-life painting enabled the artists to show off their prowess at rendering different textures – the softness of a dove's breast feathers contrasting with the firm, smooth skin of a melon and the pliable, convoluted surface of a cabbage, for instance – as well as the effects of light and shade.

Leading genre painters during the seventeenth century were overwhelmingly Dutch or Flemish. Roelandt Savery (1576–1639) was the most noted member of a Flemish painting dynasty, and spent much of his life in Holland. He was the one of the first painters in the region to paint portraits of animals alone, and was also a skilful etcher as well as an accomplished painter. His works contain quite a few different kinds of bird, mainly colourful exotic species such as cassowaries, macaws and crowned cranes. He is most famous for his paintings of that symbol of extinction, the Dodo.

Other nature painters in the Low Countries at this time included such master craftsmen as the Dutchman Pieter Holsteyn the Elder (1580–1662). Working in his birthplace of Haarlem, he earned a living mainly as an etcher and glass painter, but also produced delicate miniature gouaches and watercolours. Holsteyn's son, also Pieter (1614–87), followed the family profession, studying under his father and engraving mainly portraits, although like his father also creating superb studies of birds, both familiar and alien.

The father's and son's surviving bird paintings include accurate and beautiful portrayals of European birds, including various wildfowl (Smews, Tufted Ducks and Garganeys) and waders (Pied Avocets and Eurasian Curlews), and songbirds such as the Eurasian Bullfinch, as well as exotic species that include a South American White-eared Puffbird and several portraits of Dodos – both the Mauritius species that was famously wiped out by humans by 1690, if not earlier, and the probably fictitious species known as the 'white dodo' from the nearby Indian Ocean island

PLATE 6.
Dodo
Raphus cucullatus

Roelandt Savery
c.1626. Oil on canvas.
1050mm x 800mm
(39⅛in x 31⅛in)

This is the most famous of all known contemporary illustrations of the Dodo, and depicts that symbol of extinction lifesize, surrounded by ducks, South American macaws and other birds. Presented to the British Museum by the early English ornithologist George Edwards in 1759, it was later used by the museum's Professor Richard Owen, the great comparative anatomist and first describer of the Dodo's anatomy, as a template to reconstruct the bird from scanty fossil material. It was this interpretation that has become the orthodox image of this giant flightless pigeon to the present day. Recently, though, the accuracy of the portly, squat form and horizontal posture has been questioned, and modern opinion suggests that the Dodo was a slimmer, more upright bird.

PLATE 7.
Portrait of Audubon
Lance Calkin
c.1859–1936. Oil on
canvas.
610mm x 750mm
(24in x 29⅛in)

*Although the English
artist George Lance
Calkin (1859–1936),
who painted this portrait
of the famous American
bird artist John James
Audubon, was not born
until eight years after his
subject died, he copied a
work by another British
portrait painter,
Francis Cruikshank
(who flourished from
1848–81). It is a mark
of Audubon's fame – and
his enjoyment of his
celebrity – that he sat
for portrait painters on
several occasions. This
portrait shows him in his
typical public garb of
cloak with a huge fur
collar; ever the showman,
he loved to play the part
of the intrepid American
woodsman and explorer,
adding the thrill of the
new and strange to the
beauty of his paintings
to provide an irresistible
appeal to his rich patrons.*

of Réunion.

Like other contemporary bird painters, the Holsteyns had not actually
seen many of their more exotic subjects alive in the wild, but relied on
earlier accounts or specimens preserved in alcohol or salt brought back
by explorers and seamen, or from observing live birds kept in captivity
in the growing numbers of menageries that were owned by their wealthy
patrons. As explorers penetrated further into previously uncharted
realms, they brought back more and more unfamiliar animals and plants,
both dead and alive.

The most accomplished as a portrayer of living birds in oils was
Melchior de Hondecoeter (1636–95). In contrast to many of his
contemporaries, his style was more robust and his subjects appeared
more lifelike. A painting by him typically set the usual wide array of
different species in an Italianate landscape decorated with classical urns
and ruins. Unlike many artists of the period, he ensured that the different
species were shown at their true relative sizes. He also imbued them with
vitality by showing them strutting about, calling or singing with wide-
open bills, preparing to take off, emerging from and arriving on the scene
with only part of their bodies showing at the edge of the picture, or in
flight – though the postures of his flying birds, like those of most painters
for hundreds of years to come, were not true to nature.

Some of the fine-art paintings of this period showed the ancient field
sport of falconry. A good example is found in the work of Ferdinand
Hamilton (1664–1750), one of three sons of a Scottish painter, James
Hamilton (1640–1720) of Fifeshire. The three boys were all born in
Brussels after their parents had been forced to flee to that city during the
British Civil War. Like his brothers, Ferdinand, the most accomplished of
the three, painted in the Dutch/Flemish still-life style, often including
birds in his compositions. In addition to various portrayals of dead birds
in game stores and a witty pairing of guineafowl and guinea pigs,
Ferdinand painted a spirited portrayal of a Grey Heron being attacked by
one of three Gyr Falcons – the largest and most powerful of all the falcon
family and traditionally regarded as fit for a king (only one step down
from eagles, which were reserved for emperors).

In 1688, Jakob Bogdani (1660–1724), a very fine painter who had
departed his native Hungary in 1683 to work in Amsterdam, left that city
to settle in England, becoming naturalised as an English citizen in 1700.

Dutch art was greatly appreciated there at this time, its popularity largely due to the fact that King Charles II had spent part of his exile in Holland, and a Dutchman, William II, ruled England with his wife Mary from 1688 until her death in 1694, and then on his own until 1702. Many of Bogdani's canvases are full of exotic birds, including parrots, numerous species of which had already been introduced from tropical regions to European menageries. As well as these birds from all over the world, at least forty different European species of birds can readily be recognised in his work.

As with other artists in the genre, the exotic and the more familiar species are occasionally shown separately, but more often they are together in combinations that look bizarre to anyone who knows about bird distribution. Typical Bogdani confections include the juxtaposition of parrots such as macaws and amazons from South America or the Caribbean, cockatoos from Indonesia, mynahs from India and Great Tits, Blue Tits, Eurasian Jays or Green Woodpeckers, familiar birds from the British countryside. He was very fond of including a red bird to add a patch of brilliant colour contrasting with the bright yellows, blues and other hues of the other birds – a Red Avadavat (a little finch-like bird from southern Asia popular as a cage bird), a Scarlet Ibis (a large waterbird from South America) or a male Northern Cardinal (a crested songbird from North America also kept as a cage bird in England, which was known at the time as the Virginian Nightingale, the name affectionately bestowed on it by homesick early settlers).

In addition to their artistic merit, these paintings of assortments of birds reveal a great deal about precisely which birds were known at the time. It is particularly intriguing to an ornithologist today to see that one of Bogdani's subjects was the Collared Dove – then it is likely to have been an exotic import as a preserved skin or as a living bird in a menagerie from its native southern Asia. It is rather undistinguished in appearance, with mainly greyish-buff plumage, but draws attention to itself by its calls, including nasal and mewing alarm and display calls, and especially by its endlessly repeated and monotonous cooing, which – despite consisting of three notes rather than two – is often erroneously reported as evidence of early Common Cuckoos.

A remarkable exception in both style and content to his many landscapes crowded with birds, is his fabulous painting *Two Icelandic Falcons*, which he most likely painted from different views of a single individual of the Icelandic race of the Gyr Falcon. These graceful but immensely powerful birds perch on the corner of a great column of some huge building in the classical style, but are ready for instant action. Their snowy-white plumage, adorned on the back and tail with a subtle pattern of dark chevrons, contrasts beautifully with the solid, sombre, stark permanence of the backdrop.

One of the most famous of all painters, Harmenszoon van Rijn Rembrandt (1606–69), included a number of still lifes featuring birds in his impressive output of paintings, made all the more compelling by his superlative rendering of light and shade that was such a hallmark of his style. These works depicted just one or two birds, often together with typical still-life objects or people.

Although he painted some live birds, such as a falcon with its knightly owner and a suitable imperious eagle, many of Rembrandt's avian subjects were dead game. Among these, the Great Bittern stands out as a favourite subject of his, being featured for instance in his superb study of the bird and a gun. The extremely secretive habits of this large member of the heron family, which spends almost all its life sequestered deep within large, dense reed beds, provided a challenge to the hunter and falconer who pursued it as an important quarry for serving at lavish banquets laid on for royalty and nobility. Its wonderfully subtle plumage, mottled and barred in shades of brown, buff and black, as well as camouflaging the bird against the background of reeds, ensured that it was equally challenging to paint as well as Rembrandt did. The same species also makes an appearance in one of the artist's many self-portraits, which shows Rembrandt hanging up a dead Great Bittern.

Rembrandt's mastery of line is well exemplified by some exquisite ink and chalk sketches of birds of paradise in the Louvre, Paris, which he made between about 1636 and 1638. As with the illustrations in Gesner's bird book and other early representations of these birds (which came from the strange, far-off land of New Guinea), they lacked feet. This is because the first dried 'trade skins' of these gorgeous birds, prepared by New Guinea natives and brought back by explorers in the 1520s as gifts for the King of Spain, had their legs and feet removed. They had been described by the local people as 'birds of the gods'. Back in Europe, the belief soon became firmly established that these were indeed heavenly creatures, which spent their entire lives floating in the sky, nourished only by the air or by dew, until they died and fell to earth. Although intact skins, complete with legs and feet, imported to Europe by the early 1600s refuted this notion, the more romantic version of their lifestyle was regularly referred to by artists and writers. Furthermore, the specific name of the Greater Bird-of-paradise, *Paradisaea apoda*, coined by the great biologist and 'father of taxonomy' Linnaeus in 1758, also alluded to this fable, for *apoda* comes from the Latin words meaning 'without legs or feet'.

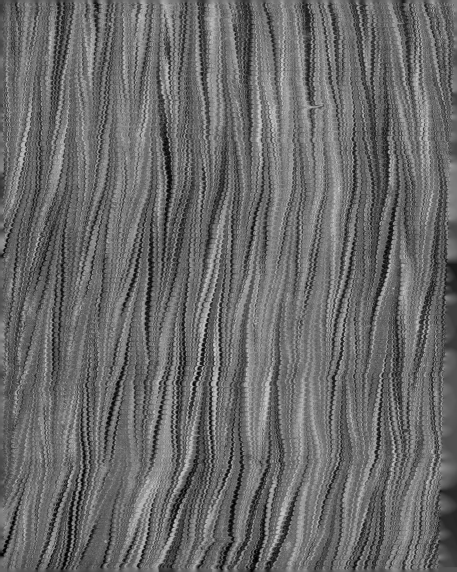

Chapter One { 1650—1800

PLATE 8.
Ruff *(female)*
Philomachus pugnax

Eleazar Albin
1737. Hand-coloured
engraving.
288mm x 222mm
(11¼in x 8¾in)

In his book A Natural
History of Birds *(1738),
thought to be the first
folio book to feature
hand-coloured
illustrations of British
birds, the German émigré
Eleazar Albin called this
medium-sized wader the
'Pool Snipe'. Although
this name was once in
general use for the
common and well-known
Redshank, Albin here uses
it to refer to the Ruff.*

$\mathcal{V}$ery different in style from the work of the still-life painters was that of the book illustrators and publishers of the period. The end of the sixteenth century roughly marks the beginning of the era when engraving had largely replaced woodcut as the main technique used by bird artists, and this was reflected in the output of a wide variety of enthusiasts such as the Merian family of Germany. The publisher Matthaeus Merian (1593–1650) and his engraver sons Matthaeus Junior (1621–87) and Kaspar (1627–86), are thought to have been jointly responsible for producing one of the first bird books to contain a large number of plates showing different species. Historiae naturalis de avibus (Natural History of Birds) was published between 1650 and 1653. Its author was the naturalist John Jonston, born in Poland though the son of a Scotsman who had emigrated to Silesia in the early 1600s.

Jonston's work was an example of the old-style attempts at an encyclopaedic coverage of birds (and the rest of the animal kingdom in five other companion volumes), drawing extensively on the often erroneous writings of earlier authors such as Gesner and Aldrovandus. However, despite the limitations of its text, its illustrations gave it great popular appeal, and it was published in many editions (including translations from the original Latin into English, German, Dutch and French) for more than a hundred years after its first appearance, the last one appearing as late as 1773. The illustrations in Jonston's book, though generally a little wooden, oddly proportioned and lacking in originality, are often good likenesses of the birds concerned, and are interesting in that they are laid out on the pages in a similar way to that of modern field guides, with similar-looking or related birds appearing on the same page.

Totally different in style, and much more animated and artistically accomplished, was the work of the Englishman Francis Barlow (1626- –1704). Although he spent most of his life in London, he made visits to the countryside, even venturing as far afield as Scotland, where he observed and sketched birds. Barlow's work spanned 1650–76 and includes some fine oil paintings of various birds, both native to Britain and exotic, although relatively few of these survive, and their colours

The Poole Snipe.

G. Albin Del. 1737.

have faded. Even when they were originally painted, though, they never had the glowing, vibrant colours of his Dutch contemporaries.

The main legacies of Barlow's work are his etchings, and also the preparatory sketches for these, which he generally outlined in brown ink and filled in with a grey wash. Although Barlow etched many of his own plates, he also used other craftsmen for the task, such as Wenceslaus Hollar (1606–77), an etcher who left his native Bohemia to settle in England. Hollar was a consummate craftsman, able to draw a line without having to waste much time stopping out and re-etching as did many other lesser practitioners of the art. Although he was well paid for his skill – he could command wages of as much as a shilling an hour from printmakers, a good wage at the time – he was a scrupulously honest man, using an hourglass to calculate the amount of time he spent on his work.

In his books, such as Barlow's *Birds and Beasts in Sixty-Seven Excellent and Useful Prints* (1655) and *Birds and Fowles of Various Species* (1658), the artist includes farmyard scenes with wild and domesticated birds, and an odd assemblage of an Indian Peacock with four peahens, a cock and hen Common Pheasant, an Ostrich, a cassowary, a couple of Barn Swallows and a monkey, set amid classical ruins in a grand garden. He is likely to have been able to draw all these from life. King Charles II allowed imported Ostriches, gifts from the Moroccan Ambassador, to roam free in his royal menagerie in St James's Park, and a cassowary, brought from New Guinea with the help of the English and Dutch East India Companies, excited great interest when it was exhibited at Bartholomew Fair. This was one of England's major national annual events, which was held at the time in West Smithfield, London, on 24 August, the feast day of Saint Bartholomew, one of Jesus' twelve apostles, and the patron saint of tanners.

Barlow's pictures are full of historical symbolism: the apparently odd inclusion of the monkey in the picture described above, often used by artists to represent human folly and pride, may serve as a sarcastic comment on the excesses of the royal court. Similarly, the swallows, which also appear in flight in many of Barlow's pictures, may be there to remind those who looked at them of the fleeting nature of our time in the world. They were observed to disappear with the onset of winter, and at this time and for up to a hundred or more years thereafter it was generally believed that birds now known in Britain as long-distance migrants to Africa or elsewhere died, hibernated or were transmuted into other species.

Barlow's portrayals of hunting scenes, including falconry and fishing, led to his being affectionately dubbed 'the real father of British sporting painting' and he was praised by such notable critics of the time as the diarist John Evelyn. Like other monarchs, Charles II greatly enjoyed field sports, and his falconers kept eagles as well as falcons and hawks. Many of Barlow's illustrations feature eagles, evidently his favourite birds since he includes at least one in many scenes. A good example appears in his best-known body of work, a series of etchings for a new translation of Aesop's Fables. These famous morality tales were said to have been created by the Ancient Greek storyteller who gave his name to them, and were probably passed on orally until they were popularised in a Latin translation by the Roman poet Phaedrus. They featured a cast of birds, insects and other animals, and were a perfect vehicle for Barlow's animated style. The book was first published in 1666 and was followed by numerous later editions. One of the most dramatic of these illustrations depicts a scene from 'The Tale of the Eagle and the Fox'. Barlow's picture shows the eagle at her nest in a tree betraying her friend the fox as she is about to feed one of the mammal's cubs she has caught to her own young, while the fox wreaks her revenge by holding in her mouth a flaming brand – which she has found by luck at an altar where villagers have been sacrificing a goat – to the base of the nest to set it alight, forcing the eagle to drop the cub. The moral of the story is 'False faith may escape human punishment, but cannot escape the divine'. In the original tale, the fox uses a piece of burning goat flesh to start the fire, and Barlow also modifies the details of the tale by showing two other foxes, one returning with a goose it has caught to the remaining cubs to find them being attacked by the eagle's mate, while the other gazes up at another nest with an eagle perched on it.

Eleazar Albin (c. 1680–1742) produced one of the most important illustrated English bird books of the first half of the early eighteenth century. In addition to an earlier work on insects (one of the first British books on natural history to be illustrated with coloured plates), and as well as paintings of other animals including spiders and fish, he is best known for his three-volume *Natural History of Birds*, published in 1731,

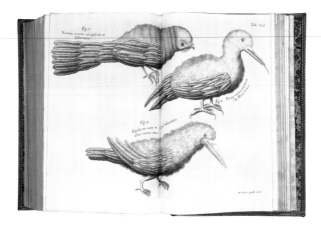

1734 and 1738. Each plate is dedicated to a subscriber to the books or to some well-known personality.

As with so many naturalists, artists and collectors, Albin benefited from the patronage of Sir Hans Sloane, the wealthy and influential doctor, naturalist and owner of a vast collection of plants and animals. Sloane bequeathed his collection to the nation, a collection that came to form the nucleus of the British Museum in Bloomsbury after his death in 1753. The natural-history collections, including those of Sir Joseph Banks and others as well as Sloane's huge one, were not transferred until 1881–83 to the new building in South Kensington housing what eventually became known as the Natural History Museum.

Albin coloured the background as well as the birds, and was one of the first artists to set each bird on a branch or other suitable perch, sometimes with the typical food of the species as well. Unfortunately, Albin's work, though pioneering in that the prints obtained by etching the drawings were individually coloured by hand, suffered the disadvantage of a limited palette of colours, some appearing rather muddy and dull in the finished work since they were obtained from plant, earth and mineral sources only. The colours also varied considerably from one print to another.

The importance of his books, however, lay not in the artistic quality of their illustrations, which made the birds look flat and rather lifeless, like paper cut-outs. Rather, his legacy lies in the fact that some of his illustrations and descriptions are the first of those particular species to appear and thus serve as 'type specimens'. A type specimen (often informally referred to simply as a 'type') is the original from which the official scientific description of that species is made and against which other specimens of the species can be compared. In ornithology, such type specimens are usually actual preserved specimens of the bird. In the past, there were many examples of illustrations being used as a record of the type in the absence of a specimen, and it was once common to base descriptions of species on published illustrations even when specimens did survive.

At the time of their publication, Albin's illustrations were not paintings of types – they gained this status only subsequently, when Linnaeus based his descriptions of some birds upon them. Unlike previous bird artists, in his little book with a long title, *A natural history of English song birds, and such of the foreign, as are usually brought over and esteem'd for their singing*, published in 1737 and designed to appeal to cage-bird enthusiasts, Albin painted the eggs of each species, as well as an adult male and female where these differed in appearance. This was helpful to Linnaeus in his work of bird classification.

But Albin's designs also received more unscrupulous attention, and were poached by pottery firms, including famous companies such as those in Meissen near Dresden, Germany, and Worcester, in England, which copied his images on to vases and other items.

Albin did not work alone. He shared the task of drawing, engraving and colouring the plates with his daughter, Elizabeth (c.1708–41). She has the distinction of being the first woman known to have worked as an illustrator of bird books, signing forty-one of the plates as having been her work alone. Her style, too, was distinctive, softer and more delicate than her father's, and she was evidently more painstaking, painting with lighter, shorter strokes of the brush.

In contrast to Eleazer Albin, who was first and foremost an artist, George Edwards (1694–1773) has been described as 'the father of British ornithology'. Born in West Ham (at the time little more than an Essex village to the east of London), Edwards was well described in 1966 by the great British ornithologist and prolific writer and broadcaster James Fisher as 'fat, cheerful, kindly and humble'. Like Fisher himself, Edwards

PLATE 9.
Jamaican Poorwill,
Jamaican Woodpecker
& Belted Kingfisher
Siphonorhis americanus,
Melanerpes radiolatus &
Ceryle alcyon
Sir Hans Sloane
1725. Hand-coloured
engraving.
325mm x 405 mm
(12¾in x 16in)

The great naturalist and museum and library creator Sloane spent fifteen months as a young man in the Caribbean, working as physician to the Governor of Jamaica, the Duke of Albermarle, and studied and collected many of the island's plants and some animals, too, including birds. The owl at the top of this plate was labelled as Noctua minor and called 'Small Wood-owl' by Sloane, but is in fact almost certainly a nightjar, the endemic Jamaican Poorwill; this is now either extinct or at best very rare. Sloane describes the whisker-like feathers around its bill as being 'like those of a Cat's Mustachoes'.

The Bill Bird

64

was a man of many interests: as well as being an avid student of natural history, he also read widely on such subjects as astronomy, antiquities, painting and sculpture. He had free access to a private library which a relative of his first employer had left him. He was also lucky to have parents with enough money to allow him to make several journeys abroad, though these were not without incident. In 1716, while in Sweden, he narrowly escaped being imprisoned as a spy by the Danish military; three years later, in France, he was lucky to avoid being transported to the American colonies.

On his return, Edwards decided to spend much of his time studying natural history, as well as learning to draw and paint animals, especially birds. Like Albin, he was fortunate in meeting Sir Hans Sloane, who in 1733 appointed him to the job of Librarian and Bedell (beadle) of the Royal College of Physicians on the death of the previous incumbent. He was given rooms in the college, and his salary, though not large, bought him enough time to continue his investigations into natural history, to work at his drawings – many of which he sold to clients – and to work his way through the natural-history titles among the 8,000 volumes in the library, many of them rare, valuable and otherwise difficult to obtain.

At the same time, Edwards embarked on a four-volume illustrated work, his *History of Birds* (also known as *A Natural History of Uncommon Birds*) which was published between 1743 and 1751. He followed this with the similar three-volume *Gleanings of Natural History* (1758–64). Edwards engraved and etched his own plates, having been taught to do so by the first real illustrator of North American birds, Mark Catesby, who had taught himself the craft. Edwards included a large number of North American birds in his books. He was an acute observer and skilled at accurately describing birds new to science: a mark of this is that Linnaeus used his descriptions to name about 350 bird species.

His illustrations were rather less impressive. Although his birds are more varied in posture, and more lively and rounded than those of Albin and his daughter, the style of engraving favoured by Edwards, with shading composed of many minute lines very close together, made them look as if they were clothed in fur rather than feathers.

Thomas Pennant (1726–97) was one of the best known and most popular authorities on natural history as well as a variety of other topics, gleaning information from wide reading and from his many travels both

PLATE 10.
Rainbow-billed Toucan
Ramphastos sulfuratus

George Edwards
1747. Hand-coloured engraving.
287mm x 208mm
(11¼in x 8¼in)

This coloured engraving appears as Plate 64 in Volume II of Edwards' A Natural History of Uncommon Birds, *which was published in 1747. The thirty-four species in the toucan family are restricted to the tropical areas of the Americas, from central Mexico south as far as Bolivia and northern Argentina, though not in the Caribbean, with the greatest diversity in the Amazon region. Their improbably huge bills are very lightweight, being hollow; they are strengthened within by an intricate system of bony struts.*

PLATE 11.
Yellow-crested
Cockatoo
Cacatua sulphurea

William Hayes
1780. Watercolour.
250mm x 310mm
(9¾in x 12¼in)

*This is one of many
watercolours of exotic
birds painted for wealthy
patrons by an English
artist whose life was so
different from theirs. All
but one of his ten
surviving children
remained at home.
Although helping him in
his work, they had to be
supported financially by
him, with the result that
the family suffered great
poverty, despite William
taking on a job as a
postmaster to supplement
his income from painting.
He used sixty of his
paintings to make the
plates, including this one,
for a book entitled* Rare
and Curious Birds
accurately Drawn and
Coloured from Specimens
in the Menagerie at
Osterley Park. *The
menagerie was an
important collection of
birds made by Sarah
Child, a member of a
wealthy banking family.*

in Britain and further afield, almost all of them on horseback. He was
fortunate to be born into a wealthy and very old Welsh family, inheriting
the family estate called Downing set in beautiful countryside in Whitford,
Flintshire, North Wales. He was a prolific writer and traveller, and (like
so many young men of means during the eighteenth century) made the
grand tour of Europe . He took detailed notes of birds he observed, and
wrote an account of his experiences in 1765.

Pennant was also an indefatigable correspondent, who seemed to know
everyone of importance in the fields of zoology, botany and a whole
range of other learned subjects – including such luminaries as Linnaeus,
Pallas, Fabricius, Buffon and Voltaire. He was one of the main
correspondents of that most famous of all British naturalists – and one of
the most famous naturalists in the world – the Reverend Gilbert White,
curate of the parish of Selborne, Hampshire. This resulted in a book, *The
Natural History and Antiquities of Selborne*, that is mainly a compilation by
White of his correspondence with Pennant and another eminent
zoologist, Daines Barrington, sharing his observations and discoveries
and seeking information. First appearing in 1788, it is one of the most
published books in the English language, with subsequent editions and
translations numbering well over 200. White's letters to Pennant are
among the most important documents available to students of natural
history but, sadly, Pennant's replies were lost long ago.

A prolific author, Pennant had his books illustrated by a total of over
800 different plates, drawn by various artists. Many were done by the
English artist Peter Paillou (c.1712–84), thought to be of Huguenot
descent, who spent some twenty years at Downing. He not only made
original watercolour illustrations from which the book plates were
engraved and did much of the hand colouring of the prints, but also
completed a set of paintings that hung in the house of scenes showing a
variety of different habitats, complete with typical birds and other
animals; four of these represented different climatic regions.

Pennant's first major book including birds, *British Zoology*, appeared
between 1761 and 1766. It was originally published in four volumes,
with an appendix forming a fifth volume appearing afterwards. The
second volume dealt exclusively with birds. Covering all the vertebrate
animals of Britain, the work was handsomely illustrated by 132 colour
plates, mostly painted by Paillou, 121 of which show birds. It was this

Cocatoo.

W. S. Sharp.

important work that partly inspired Gilbert White to write to Pennant after an introduction by his brother Benjamin, a bookseller and publisher. In turn, Pennant used information from many of White's letters to him in the second and subsequent editions of *British Zoology*.

Although Pennant intended his next major regional fauna, *Indian Zoology*, to be a multi-volume study, only the first volume ever appeared. The first edition, published in 1769, is now a rare and sought-after book. It contains twelve colour plates, all but one of which depict birds. Some were copied from drawings by Sydney Parkinson, who had in turn taken them from the original work of Pieter de Bevere. As with Pennant's other natural-history books, the plates were engraved by Peter Mazell, whose over-tidying and thickening of the lines drawn by the artists meant that the images lost some of the vitality and delicacy of the originals.

Ever the populist, Pennant also produced a small book, *Genera of Birds*, which he intended as an elementary text for the interested layman, aiming at the same market as many of today's bird books. Although the first edition, published in 1773, lacked illustrations, a new one was reissued in 1781, containing fifteen plates.

With the help of his many friends and correspondents, Pennant made great strides in accumulating knowledge of birds occurring in Britain, adding sixteen species to the list between 1751 and 1796 – approximately half the total of new British species for the entire eighteenth century. The newly recognised species included not only some rarities such as the Little Bustard, the Red-breasted Goose and the Cream-coloured Courser, but also the Grey Phalarope and Ortolan Bunting, which are now known as scarce though annual visitors, and species that breed locally like the Red-necked Phalarope and Dartford Warbler.

The most important of Pennant's many publications in terms of adding to ornithological knowledge was his *Arctic Zoology*, since it contained the first scientific descriptions of many species. Part of the first volume (appearing in 1784) and all of the second (published the following year) were devoted to birds. A supplementary volume (sometimes referred to as Volume III) was published in 1787.

Arctic Zoology remained the standard work on the region for fifty years. In fact, Pennant had originally planned to produce a work covering just the British colonies of North America, but the war between the settlers

PLATE 12.
Magnificent Riflebird
(male)
Ptiloris magnificus

Anonymous
Latham Collection
c.1781–1824.
Watercolour.
212mm x 200mm
(8¼in x 7⅞in)

This is one of the many artworks of birds collected by the long-lived medical doctor, ornithologist and museum-owner John Latham for his ten-volume A General History of Birds, *which was published between 1821 and 1828. As with many others, this illustration of one of the spectacular birds of paradise does not, in fact, appear in that work, due to the prohibitive costs of fine colour printing, which was then a very labour-intensive operation. There are over 800 plates in the Latham collection of the Natural History Museum; although most are by him, a good many are not attributed, and a few are signed by John Abbot, the soldier-artist Thomas Davies, Latham's daughter Ann, or Lord Stanley.*

PLATE 13.
Green Peafowl *(male)*
Pavo muticus

John Latham
c.1781–1824.
Watercolour.
160mm x 200mm
(6¼in x 7⅞in)

*In striking contrast to its
close relative, the much
more familiar Indian,
Blue or Common Peafowl,*
Pavo cristatus, *this is now
a scarce bird whose
extensive range in
southern Asia has
contracted and
fragmented due to its
vulnerability to hunting
and habitat deterioration.
The old name 'Japan [or
Japanese] Peacock' is a
misnomer, for it has never
occurred in Japan, the
word being erroneously
substituted for 'Java',
where one race still
hangs on.*

and the British that culminated in the Declaration of American Independence in July 1776 led him to change the emphasis away from a celebration of the wildlife of a newly independent, rival nation to include the Arctic region of Eurasia, north of 60° N.

One of Pennant's most important correspondents, and like him a Fellow of the Royal Society, John Latham (1740–1837) also has the distinction of having been one of the main founders of the Linnean Society of London. This world-famous scholarly institution, which still flourishes today, came into being in 1788, ten years after the death of the great Swedish naturalist and inventor of the binomial (two-name) system of classifying plant and animal species, whose name it commemorates. It was founded to promote his classificatory system, and also to house his large collection of specimens, manuscripts and books.

Latham was a notable ornithologist and skilled field naturalist. He built up a collection of birds and other specimens for his own private museum; he drew, etched and coloured all the pictures for his books himself; and he also worked as a doctor in general practice. The first ornithological masterwork of this remarkably industrious man was his *A General Synopsis of Birds*, published between 1781 and 1785 and containing 106 plates. This was followed two years later by a supplement with 23 plates and four years after that by a second supplement of 13 plates. Like all his illustrations, the plates in these books were workmanlike but not inspired, consisting essentially of flat depictions of single birds, with simple though clear rendering of their plumage patterns. They continued the tradition of predecessors such as Albin, with rather stylised settings of a truncated branch or a mound of grass on which the birds could perch.

Latham's main contribution to ornithology was in describing and naming species new to science. Many of these were from the little-known continent of Australia, which was being rapidly colonised. He had the benefit of new information from the expedition reports from Captain Cook's first voyage and specimens collected by naturalists after colonisation, as well as some of their drawings when skins were unavailable. Latham is justly regarded as one of the founders of Australian ornithology.

Although he used Linnaeus's classification system as a basis for his own, Latham did not use the Linnean binomial system of nomenclature until

1790, when he listed all known bird species of the world in his *Index Ornithologicus*. This sudden change of heart was prompted not necessarily by humility on Latham's part, but because he realised that without such formal naming, it was unlikely that any new species would be named in his honour.

Nevertheless, the importance of Latham's achievement and an indication of his energy and diligence is apparent from the fact that he listed a total of 3,000 known species of birds worldwide – an almost fourfold increase in just over thirty years on Linnaeus's list of 758. And although he has been criticised for a lack of rigour in his analysis of distinctive characters, and for the fact that

he described with different names what turned out to be the same species more than once, these are faults which were equally true of many contemporary ornithologists.

His medical practice had made Latham a very wealthy man, and he was able to retire in 1796 at the age of fifty-six. However, in 1819 he suffered a series of financial disasters, and to save himself from insolvency this apparently tireless worker embarked on his final great work, the *General History of Birds*. Published between 1821 and 1828, when he was in his eighties, this last great work ran to ten volumes and an index, with 193 colour plates, again all drawn, engraved and painted by the author himself. The illustrations included many American species. Despite failing eyesight, Latham was working up until his death in February 1837, at the age of ninety-six.

One of the colourists employed by John Latham to produce copies of his *A General Synopsis of Birds* was Sarah Stone (c.1761–1844), a remarkable example of that rarity in the past, a female natural-history artist. Born in the parish of St Giles, Ickenham, Middlesex, now part of Greater London, she married John Smith, a captain in the Royal Navy, in 1789. Sarah exhibited her work in the 1780s and 1790s at various London exhibitions, including those of the Royal Academy, and made meticulous drawings and paintings of birds and other creatures for the major naturalists of her day, such as Thomas Pennant. These included depictions of many new species brought back to England by collectors exploring colonial Australia and India.

Thomas Bewick (1753–1828) is among the most famous of all British bird artists, his work remembered – and used – to this day. The eldest of eight children, he had the good fortune for an ornithologist-to-be of growing up on his father's farm in the parish of Ovingham, which, although only a few miles from the regional capital of Newcastle-upon-Tyne, was then in the heart of the Northumbrian countryside. Although not rich, Bewick's father was comfortably off, owning a colliery on his land as well as the farm. Young Thomas was watching and sketching birds almost as soon as he could walk. His talent was evidently unstoppable.

Although possessed of a quick wit and lively mind, Bewick found school work tedious and often played truant to explore the countryside and indulge in perennially popular childhood games such as damming streams. But all was not idle play, for here he took in with his artist's eye

PLATE 14.
Greater Flamingo, American race
Phoenicopterus ruber ruber

Sarah Stone
c.1788. Watercolour.
477mm x 365mm
(18¾in x 14⅜in)

Sarah Stone painted this remarkable, almost caricatural, picture of a flamingo alarmed by a small snake from a specimen in the famous museum of the eccentric Sir John Ashton Lever (1729–1788). The cost of the Leverian Museum, containing a collection of 28,000 exotic animals and other curiosities, resulted in its creator's bankruptcy. A tragic result was that although the collection was offered to the nation twice, the government refused it and, following a public auction, most of the specimens, including rare and now extinct birds, eventually vanished. In many cases, Sarah's pictures remain the only record of the birds in Lever's collection, including some that are now extinct.

PLATE 15.
Tawny Owl
Strix aluco

Thomas Bewick
c.1797. Wood engraving.
47mm x 56mm
(1⅞in x 2⅛in)

*This delightful study of a
Tawny Owl is a pencil
transfer drawing for a
wood engraving Bewick
made for one of his
famous tailpieces. The
barest outlines only were
transferred onto the end
grain of a very small
block of hard boxwood,
and great skill lay in his
precision cutting. His
delicate technique allowed
him to render feathers,
foliage and other features
with extremely fine detail,
despite the miniature size
of the image.*

the details of birds and other creatures, wild and domesticated, and the
landscapes in which he roamed. Using these for inspiration – and also the
colourful and dramatic depictions of animals on the local inn signs – he
made sketches in chalk at every opportunity on all available surfaces.
After covering his school slate, books and so on with these drawings, he
continued on the stone floors of his home, the local church and even the
gravestones in the churchyard. Soon after, he graduated to sketching with
pen and ink, completing his works by using the juice of blackberries as a
wash when he did not have watercolours.

Apprenticed to the Newcastle engraver Ralph Beilby for seven years,
the young Bewick had a thorough education in the art of metal engraving,
working on material as varied as banknotes, letterheads, seals, stamps and
coffin plates. He made profitable use of his spare time by developing a
great technical ability in the medium of wood engraving. This was at a
time when the craft of engraving wood blocks had declined due to the
supremacy of engraving on copper plates. Using long-forgotten
techniques, however, he developed an intaglio printing process using 'end
wood' – blocks of wood cut across the grain – which enabled him to
produce lines of great delicacy and accuracy. His ability to depict light
and texture with unequalled subtlety was achieved by his use of this
'white-line' engraving technique. A mark of Bewick's supremacy in this
difficult medium is that to this day few others have achieved such fine and
characterful work; a notable exception is the twentieth-century bird
artist Charles Tunnicliffe.

The majority of Bewick's work on birds appeared in his *A History of
British Birds*. This he published in two volumes in 1797 (on land birds) and
1804 (on waterbirds), containing 208 and 240 wood engravings
respectively. These were among the most popular natural-history works
of their day, running to eight editions – six of them appearing in Bewick's
lifetime – of which the last appeared in 1847. As in all his work, Bewick
showed great skill, carefully positioning text and illustrations to ensure
the most pleasing appearance. As a consequence, his books appear far
more elegant than those of many earlier artists or, indeed, of many of
his contemporaries.

Some critics are of the opinion that Bewick's best woodcuts are those
of the birds in these famous volumes. But whereas the species (such as the
European Robin and Fieldfare) he knew and had observed from boyhood

PLATE 16.
'Chinese Long-tailed
Finch'
Hypothetical species

Anonymous
Latham Collection
c.1781–1824.
Watercolour.
210mm x 161mm
(8¼in x 6¼in)

*This puzzling bird is
mentioned by John
Latham in his ambitious
work* A General History of
Birds. *Latham describes
this bird as being known
only from a collection of
paintings owned by 'the
late Captain Broadley',
and, remarkably, fails to
give it a scientific name.*

were convincing likenesses, some of the less familiar birds look rather
unnatural to modern eyes. It is arguable that his superb little vignettes of
country life that adorn the spaces in between the illustrated accounts of
the birds and other animals in his books are even more accomplished and
remarkable. Although some of these represent such typical bucolic scenes
as the blacksmith working at his forge or a milkmaid carrying her pails on
a yoke, none are sentimentalised as in the work of so many other artists
of the day, and many pull no punches in portraying the harshness of life
in the countryside at the time.

Bewick was an acute observer of his fellow humans as well as birds and
other animals, and a true social realist who did not shirk from implying
criticism of the gap between rich and poor. As well as criticising the wars
against Napoleon for their waste of human life and the nation's wealth,
he observed that 'the gentry whirled about in aristocratic pomposity'.
One vignette shows a beggar hanging himself from a tree, another a
weary, crippled soldier, cast off after fighting in the Napoleonic wars,
desperately gnawing on a bone, watched by an emaciated dog, its ribs
clearly protruding. But it is not all unmitigated gloom: Bewick's
illustrations are often full of humour, too, as in the scene of a would-be
nest-robber falling into a river as the branch he is grasping breaks off.

Bewick was greatly appreciated in his own time, as he still is to this day.
The great English poet William Wordsworth lauded the Northumbrian
engraver in a poem appearing in his *Lyrical Ballads*; in *Jane Eyre*, Charlotte
Bronte refers to her eponymous heroine reading Bewick's bird books and
being thrilled by the vignettes. The great British art critic John Ruskin –
himself a lover of birds but as a highly educated, sophisticated, urban
aesthete far removed from Bewick's forthright countryman's
appreciation of them – eulogised the latter's 'magnificent artistic power,
the flawless virtue, veracity, tenderness, the infinite humour of the man'.
He characteristically qualified this praise by uncharitably regretting that
since Bewick was not an educated gentleman, he did not depict 'more
elevated subjects' than those appearing in his vignettes, and saying that he
demonstrated a 'love of ugliness which is in the English soul'. More
recently, Beatrix Potter, who wrote and illustrated not only the tales of
rabbits, mice and other creatures for children that made her famous, but
also painted many superb realistic images of British fungi, animals and
plants, praised the Northumbrian artist's abilities.

As well as being justly renowned for his wood engravings, Bewick is commemorated to this day in the names of two birds. The first was the smallest of the three species of northern swan. Shorter-necked and more gooselike in appearance than the Whooper and Mute Swans, and with more musical calls, Bewick's Swan nests further north, in the Arctic tundra of Siberia and, like the Whooper, appears in Britain and Ireland as a winter visitor. The artist was commemorated in its scientific name, too – *Cygnus bewickii* – after the famous English ornithologist William Yarrell (1784–1853) distinguished Bewick's Swan from the Whooper and presented the first scientific description of the 'new' species in 1829.

Recently, Bewick's name has been lost from the scientific species name, since the bird was demoted to the rank of subspecies. Bewick's Swan is now regarded merely as the Eurasian race of the newly named Tundra Swan (*Cygnus columbianus*), which also includes its North American counterpart the Whistling Swan. But it lives on in the subspecific name *Cygnus columbianus bewickii*, and British birdwatchers still know this lovely bird as Bewick's Swan.

The other bird that bears Bewick's name lives far from his native Northumberland, being one of the many species of wrens found in the Americas (all seventy-nine species of this bird family live exclusively in the New World, apart from the familiar little bird known in the British Isles simply as the wren, which the Americans call the Winter Wren). Bewick's Wren (*Thryomanes bewickii*) ranges from the Canadian border to Mexico. But how did the Northumberland engraver's name come to be attached to this far-off bird? The answer relates to the esteem in which Audubon, the famous painter of North American bird life, held the then elderly Bewick when he paid him a visit only a year before his death at the age of seventy-five – and to the fact that the old man found eight new subscribers for Audubon's lavish life's work *The Birds of America*. Referring to him as 'at all times a most agreeable, kind and benevolent friend', Audubon later bestowed Bewick's name on the wren in question.

To this day, Bewick's woodcuts are frequently used in a variety of books, magazines and other printed works, typically as headpieces and tailpieces. But Bewick's bird books are not in themselves important contributions to the advancement of ornithological knowledge; the bird illustrations, despite their skilful execution and pleasing design, do not add new details, while the texts are largely poor copies of others' work.

PLATE 17.
Pompadour Green
Pigeon
(male and female)

Treron pompadora

Sydney Parkinson
c.1767–8. Watercolour.
324mm x 257mm
(45in x 23in)

*Parkinson's painting of a
pair of this lovely bird,
one of a large group of
species known collectively
as green pigeons, is a copy
of a painting by Pieter
Cornelis de Bevere from
the collection of the
Dutch Governor of Ceylon
(now Sri Lanka). The
male, distinguished by his
chestnut wings, is on the
upper branch, the female
on the lower. In this
version the birds' primary
flight feathers at the tip
of the wings are missing;
these would have been
clipped (as with waterfowl
and other birds in park
collections to this day) to
prevent the bird from
flying away. The bird in
the original drawing in
the Loten collection has
its wing feathers entire.*

(The first volume, on land birds, was written by Beilby; the second, on waterbirds, by Bewick himself.) His great achievement, apart from the superlative artistic quality of his technique in a difficult medium and his skill as a designer, was to popularise the growing science of ornithology in Britain.

Meanwhile, in France, some major bird books with colour engravings were being produced, reflecting the splendour of her growing empire. These included the works of the great French zoologist George-Louis Leclerc, Comte de Buffon (1707–88). He was a vehement opponent of Linnaeus's inspired and detailed scheme of binomial classification, believing that it was a sterile attempt at forcing disparate groups of species to be lumped together into artificial assemblages. He remarked that 'nature, from the midst of limits that we think prescribe it, is richer than our ideas and vaster than our systems'.

A mark of Buffon's renown is that he is one of the few naturalists in the world to have had a street named after him, in Paris. Voltaire famously described Buffon as having 'the mind of a sage in the body of an athlete', while Rousseau is said to have admired him so much that he kissed the threshold of his study. Buffon himself wrote extremely well on natural history. The pinnacle of his published works was his vast *Histoire naturelle, générale et particulière* (1749–1804), a compendium of all that he knew and could discover about the subject. This forty-four-volume encyclopedia included no less than ten volumes devoted solely to birds. It was made even more popular by the thousands of coloured plates issued separately as *Planches enluminées* (1765–73), 1,939 of which depicted birds. Many of these were created by the prolific artist François Martinet (c.1731–90), who supervised a team of more than eighty other artists and assistants (including members of his family) in this huge task. Although these were reasonably accurate in their portrayal of each species' plumage, many of the birds looked stiff and unlifelike.

By far the best of all French bird illustrations of this period were those that accompanied the books written by energetic traveller and prolific author François Levaillant (1753–1824), a disciple of Buffon. Levaillant was one of the first naturalists to make long voyages to study their subjects at first hand in the wild, rather than relying on second-hand stuffed birds, drawings, descriptions or birds in captivity.

The plates in his books were the work mainly of Jacques Barraband

(1768–1809), who had trained as a designer of porcelain and tapestry. His drawings were not only remarkably ornithologically accurate for their day, but also magnificent representations of beautiful exotic birds. Compared with many of the efforts of his contemporaries, the paintings showed their subjects in lifelike postures: instead of being flat and imprisoned on the page, they have a wonderful solidity as they regard the viewer with eyes animated by accurate highlights, while the texture and arrangement of their feathers is outstandingly realistic, aided by fine engraving and colour printing.

Histoire naturelle des oiseaux d'Afrique appeared as six volumes between 1796 and 1808. It contained 300 Barraband plates printed in colour and retouched by hand. There followed a series of two-volume monographs that are among the finest of all bird books of the late eighteenth and early nineteenth centuries. The *Histoire naturelle des perroquets* (1801–05), with 145 plates, covered the parrot family, but left out a significant proportion of the species, those from the jungles of New Guinea and from inland Australia and New Zealand being little known to science at this time. Although it was to be over thirty years before John Gould and others opened up these largely unexplored territories and revealed a wealth of new birds, including many parrots, some of the gaps were filled in after Levaillant's death with the publication between 1837 and 1838 of a supplementary third volume.

The birds of paradise and other spectacular species in the roller, toucan and barbet families were celebrated in *Histoire naturelle des oiseaux de paradis et des rolliers, suivie de celle des toucans et des barbus* (1801–06) with 114 plates, all drawn from skins. The final title Barraband illustrated for Levaillant, *Histoire naturelle des promerops et des guêpiers*, concerned sugarbirds and bee-eaters, as well as turacos and cuckoos.

Levaillant used non-travelling artists back in France to portray the exotic birds about which he wrote, but other natural-history artists were beginning to journey to far-off lands to draw birds in their native environments. This emphasis on making drawings of new birds reflected the difficulty of preventing specimens from decaying on long sea voyages, with preservation techniques still poorly developed. One such 'artist-naturalist' was the Scotsman Sydney Parkinson (1745–71), who was employed as a naturalist on Captain James Cook's first great voyage across the Pacific from 1768 to 1771 on the *Endeavour*.

The British Admiralty sent Cook on this circumnavigation of the globe to play Britain's part in the observation of the transit of the planet Venus across the face of the Sun. Cook was to observe from the island of Tahiti, and the main motive behind the experiment was that precise measurements of this event from different points would allow astronomers to calculate the true distance of the sun from the earth. At the same time, Cook was charged with finding and claiming for Britain any important lands he came across – in particular the unknown land mass known as Terra Australis Incognita, which was believed to occupy much of the southern ocean. As it turned out, Parkinson was the first professional artist to set foot on that great island continent, at first called New Holland, but later to be named Australia.

He was chosen to embark on this great voyage as an illustrator of plants and animals because his impressive work as a botanical artist had come to the notice of the famous and wealthy botanist Joseph Banks (1743–1820), who commissioned him to make drawings for him in London. Banks paid an estimated £10,000 to sail with Cook, with the proviso that he could take with him not only Parkinson, but also another Scottish artist, Alexander Buchan, to draw the landscapes and people that they would encounter, his Swedish secretary Herman Spöring and the Danish botanist Carl Solander, as well as four servants, two dogs and a huge amount of luggage. Together with Cook, his crew of eighty-five officers and men and the official astronomer, these additions made for crowded quarters on the small ship.

Along with the others, Parkinson found it trying working under such conditions, especially when the cabin in which he drew was full of specimens. But he evidently bore the burden with admirable stoicism. Different stages of the voyage presented their own problems. In Tahiti, he complained that he constantly had to keep the swarms of local flies off the specimens, and even that they ate the paint as he worked. And after Cook had navigated with his customary skill around New Zealand and was continuing his remarkably accurate charting of land as they sailed up the entire east coast of Australia, the sheer number of new specimens brought aboard every day threatened to overwhelm Parkinson. It is to his great credit that he managed to make 36 drawings of birds, let alone 148 of fishes and over 400 of plants. The total for the whole voyage was at

PLATE 18.
Common Kingfisher
Alcedo atthis

Pieter Cornelis de Bevere

c.1754–57. Watercolour.
350mm x 214mm
(13⅗in x 8⅖in)

The Singhalese–Dutch painter Pieter de Bevere made many fine watercolours of animals, mainly birds, for Gideon Loten, the Dutch Governor of Ceylon from 1752 to 1757, who was a keen amateur naturalist. This portrait of a kingfisher is typical of de Bevere's work, which combined delicate artistry with scientific accuracy. All the more remarkable is that the artist was completely self-taught.

PLATE 19.
Long-tailed Duck
Clangula hyemalis
William Ellis
1779. Watercolour.
162mm x 235mm
(6¼in x 9¼in)

This painting by Dr
Ellis, one of two official
surgeon–naturalists
on Cook's third voyage
in search of the north-
west passage, shows
one of the most
characteristic Arctic
birds. Known in North
America as the
Oldsquaw, this dainty
duck breeds by lakes
in the tundra, but
spends most of its life
at sea, where it is at
home far out in the
roughest seas. The
deepest diver of all
ducks, in winter it
feeds mainly on
molluscs and
crustaceans on the sea
bed, grinding up the
tough shells with the
aid of its short, stout
bill powered by
strong muscles.

least 1,300. These artistic records are of particular importance because
they are the only records of bird sightings on the voyage; no bird
specimens appear to have survived from Cook's first voyage – it is
thought that many of them were eaten, while the others perished as a
result of poor preservation techniques.

Tragically, Parkinson was never to see home again, since he was one of
thirty of the ship's company to die before the *Endeavour*'s arrival in Cape
Town in January 1771, chiefly from malaria and dysentery. This talented
artist is commemorated in ornithology in both the common and
scientific names of a seabird – Parkinson's Petrel (*Procellaria parkinsoni*) –
which breeds only in New Zealand.

Other eighteenth-century artists who made important illustrations of
the new birds being discovered in the region include William Ellis
(D.1785). He was an English doctor who enlisted as a surgeon's mate
aboard HMS *Discovery* under the captaincy of Charles Clerke during
Captain Cook's third great voyage of 1776–80. The purpose of this
voyage was to seek a north-west passage by finding an opening in the
Bering Sea, visiting New Zealand and various Pacific islands including
Hawaii, on their way to discover the Bering Straits. He was a fine
draughtsman, and his paintings include good likenesses of several New
Zealand land birds, such as the Red-crowned Parakeet (now called the
Red-fronted Parakeet), the South Island race of another much bigger
parrot, the aerobatic Kaka, and the New Zealand Falcon. Like Parkinson,
Dr Ellis met an untimely end, falling from the main mast of a ship in
Ostend, Belgium, en route to Germany in preparation for another
voyage of exploration.

George Raper (C.1767–97) served as a midshipman on HMS *Sirius*
which accompanied Arthur Phillip's first fleet to Australia that sailed from
Portsmouth, England, in May 1787, bearing a human cargo of convicts
sentenced to transportation to the nascent colony of New South Wales.
The convoy arrived after their long sea crossing at the settlement of Port
Jackson (now the city of Sydney), New South Wales, in January 1788.
Raper's attractive watercolour paintings of the landscape and wildlife he
encountered when he went ashore on the New South Wales mainland and
later, in March, on Norfolk Island are quite skilfully executed – an
achievement made more remarkable by the facts that he is likely to have
had only the basic midshipman's training in the elements of

W: W: Ellis ad viv: delin: t

Anas hyemalis

draughtsmanship, and he was only a young man in his early twenties when he carried out this work. Among Raper's work from the voyage of the *Sirius* is a painting of the extinct Lord Howe Island Pigeon, which lived only on the Pacific Ocean island off the east coast of Australia after which it was named. Raper's painting appears to be the only illustration of this species from life: a second portrait is almost certainly a copy of Raper's painting. The scientific description of this lost species was based on this important artwork.

Another member of this group of early painters of Australian birds was the Scottish painter Thomas Watling (c. 1762–1806). In complete contrast to Raper, he sailed to Australia not as a crew member but as one of the group of convicts arriving in Port Jackson in October 1792 on a small convoy of ships. Also, compared with Raper, he had received considerably more training as an artist, and his work is more sophisticated. He overcame an inauspicious start to his life in New South Wales, for he had used his drawing and engraving skills to forge Scottish banknotes and as punishment for this crime was sentenced in Dumfries in 1789 to be transported for fourteen years to the new British colony. Fortunately for him – and for appreciators of bird art – he was pardoned in 1796 after serving just half his sentence. Watling's output was impressive, and his work was infused with a combination of scientific accuracy and a highly developed sense of design. John Latham recognised superlative work when he saw it, and used many of Watling's accurate depictions to help him write his descriptions of Australian birds he knew otherwise only from museum skins.

By far the most talented of all these early painters of Australian birds was the Austrian artist Ferdinand Bauer (1760–1826). The son of the official court painter to the prince of Liechtenstein, he is, perhaps, best known as a botanical painter. He produced some of the world's most beautiful paintings in this genre, but he also made some exquisite watercolours of birds. Bauer accompanied the English explorer Matthew Flinders as official expedition artist during his circumnavigation of Australia to map the continent's coastline between 1801 and 1803 aboard HMS *Investigator*. When Flinders set sail for Britain, Bauer remained behind in Sydney and took part in expeditions in New South Wales and to Norfolk Island.

Of course, it was not just in Australia that a record was made in paint

PLATE 20.
Hooded Parrot
Psephotus dissimilis

**Ferdinand Lucas
Bauer**
c.1801–05. Watercolour.
335mm x 505mm
(13¼in x 20in)

Although better known as one of the world's finest botanical painters, Ferdinand Bauer was also a skilled animal artist. The eleven watercolours of parrots held by the Natural History Museum include this fine study of an uncommon Australian parrot, painted with Bauer's typically meticulous accuracy and precision. The Hooded Parrot (formerly known as the Hooded, or Black-hooded, Parakeet) has a very local distribution, being found only in the western part of Arnhem Land in Australia's Northern Territory.

of the new birds being observed and collected in the rapidly growing colonial territories. Pieter Cornelis de Bevere (c.1722–81) was a painter of mixed European and Asian ancestry (most of his relatives were Singhalese, but his grandfather was Dutch) who worked for the Dutch governor of Ceylon, J. G. Loten, during the 1750s, painting mainly birds (as well as plants, insects, fish and other marine life, and mammals) from life. Untutored in art, he had a natural gift for drawing and painting. George Edwards made extensive use of his paintings in the preparation of his *Gleanings of Natural History*, and some were also copied by Sydney Parkinson for illustrating Thomas Pennant's *Indian Zoology*. Loten's entire collection of de Bevere's watercolours is in safe hands in the Natural History Museum, London.

Although born in Suffolk, England, Mark Catesby (1683–1749) is often referred to as 'the father of American ornithology'. In 1712, he sailed to North America to stay with his sister Elizabeth and her husband, who had emigrated to the flourishing British colony of Virginia, settling in the town of Williamsburg. His second sojourn in America, from 1722 to 1726, was financed by Sir Hans Sloane and other English botanists.

Although he worked mainly as a plant collector, Catesby was such a good all-round naturalist that his book was regarded as a standard work on American birds and other wildlife until the end of the eighteenth century. Further editions appeared between 1748 and 1756, in a revision of the work by George Edwards, and in 1771, and editions with text in both Latin and German were published in Nuremberg in 1750 and 1777.

Similarly, John Abbot (1751–1840), though born in London and spending his youth in England, became one of the most important bird artists working in America in the late eighteenth and early nineteenth centuries. Building on a boyhood passion for natural history, which saw him making detailed sketches of insects and spiders, he improved his technique by taking up an offer of art lessons from Jacob Bonneau, an engraving and drawing master. Soon he had developed his skills sufficiently to exhibit two of his watercolours of butterflies at the Society of Artists of Great Britain in London. This was in 1770: three years later, when he was just twenty-two years old, he was regarded as a good enough naturalist to be sent by the Royal Society to observe, collect and draw specimens of flora and fauna in Virginia, Britain's first permanent colony in North America. He soon proved that his sponsors had made a

Smilax lævis Lauri folio non serrato, baccis nigris

Pica cristata caer
The crested Jay

Great Heron.

wise decision, and that he was an assiduous collector: within two months, he had amassed no fewer than 570 species.

But there was a dark cloud on the horizon: the impending War of American Independence, which broke out in 1775. To escape the resulting political turmoil, Abbot left early the following year to make the then long journey to Georgia. On arrival, he settled first some thirty miles (48km) south of the city of Augusta, in what is now part of Burke County. In 1806, he moved to Chatham County, and stayed in Georgia for the rest of his long life, studying, collecting and drawing from life the insects, plants and birds of the Savannah River Valley region along the border with South Carolina. Abbot coloured his detailed and sensitive pencil drawings with delicate watercolours.

Abbot's artistic skill and accuracy of observation meant that his work was appreciated by ornithologists and other naturalists on both sides of the Atlantic, and he was able to earn his living by exporting specimens and drawings to Europe. Despite his prolific output – he is known to have made over 5,000 watercolour sketches of flora and fauna – only some 200 of his paintings were published. No less than 104 of these were contained in a two-volume treatise on the rarer butterflies and moths of Georgia which appeared in 1797. Alexander Wilson (1766–1813), like most eighteenth-century ornithological naturalists and artists observing, describing and painting the birds of America, was a native of the British Isles. Born in Paisley, near Glasgow, Scotland, he was evidently a complex man. He was at times resourceful and generous, but also could, by all accounts, be obdurate and hot-tempered. As a young man, Wilson had been apprenticed to the weaving trade, but left to roam Scotland as a pedlar. While on the road, he used his skills as a composer of popular verse to foment doubtless justifiable resentment against the masters among the weaving community he had left. It is said that he sold 100,000 copies of one of his poems in just a few weeks. So savage were his satirical ballads attacking the masters that he was arrested and spent time in Paisley jail, and after being convicted of blackmail for threatening a mill owner with publication of a libellous poem had to flee Scotland. He decided to try his luck in America, and was joined in this venture by his nephew, William Duncan.

Wilson arrived in the New World in 1786, with only the minimum of possessions, including a few shillings, a flute, and a gun. No stranger to

PLATE 22.
Great Blue Heron
Ardea herodias

John Abbot
c.1775–1840.
Watercolour.
305mm x 197mm
(12in x 7¾in)

Standing about four feet (1.2m) tall, the Great Blue Heron is one of the biggest members of the heron family. This impressive wading bird has long been a favourite subject for bird painters in North America. Abbot's picture emphasises the long, sinuous neck. This contains specially modified vertebrae that enable the patiently standing or slowly stalking bird to coil its neck into an S-shape like a spring, and then suddenly shoot it forward with lightning speed so that it can seize a fish or other prey in its formidable dagger of a bill. Although feeding mainly on fish, it is an opportunist predator, capable of killing rats and other small mammals.

long journeys on foot, he walked from New York to Philadelphia, where he worked at a variety of menial jobs before gaining a position as a schoolmaster. At this stage in his life, two friends had a vital influence on him. To combat Wilson's black moods, his friend Alexander Lawson, a fellow Scot and a skilled engraver, persuaded him to take up drawing and taught him all he knew about etching and colouring. Another friend also had a major influence on Wilson: the American naturalist, artist and fellow schoolmaster William Bartram (1739–1823) encouraged his budding interest in ornithology.

Unlike Wilson and Abbot, Bartram was born in America, the son of the renowned Quaker farmer, nurseryman, plant collector and botanist John Bartram (1699–1777), who created North America's first real botanic garden at Kingsessing, Philadelphia. With an unrivalled collection of native plants, this attracted famous naturalists from Europe as well as America, and Bartram senior built up a thriving business shipping the plants he propagated to British horticulturalists; he was appointed 'King's Botanist' by George III of England. The money he made from this work enabled him to fund his extensive travels in search of new plants, and he took the teenage William, already trained as an engraver, with him on one of his major expeditions. Afterwards, William made further plant-collecting journeys. By the age of sixteen, he had become a careful observer of birds and a skilful preparer of skins, some of which he sent to the English ornithologist and artist George Edwards, together with his own bird drawings. Published in 1791, the book that brought him fame was his *Travels through North and South Carolinas, Georgia, East and West Florida*. This contained a catalogue of 215 bird species, forming the most complete list of North American birds until the work Wilson was later to produce.

Soon, with the help of Bartram's encouragement, Alexander Wilson began to dream about producing his own definitive work describing and illustrating all the birds of North America, and made long journeys on foot to observe and sketch birds which would later be engraved by Lawson. In 1804 he set off with his nephew and a friend to walk to the Niagara Falls, covering some 1,250 miles (2,000km) in just two months. In 1805, a year after taking American citizenship, Wilson began to realise his great ambition when he started work on the first volume of his

PLATE 23.
Purple Finch *(male)*
Carpodacus purpureus

William Bartram
[c.1773]. Watercolour.
239mm x 293mm
(9⅜in x 11½in)

Breeding in northern and western North America, the Purple Finch has an attractive rich warbling song. The northernmost populations, nesting in Canada, migrate into the USA for winter, while those breeding in north-eastern and western USA are largely resident all year round. The branch that Bartram has provided as a perch for his bird belongs to the Florida Anise Tree, a relative of the star anise, whose fruits are used to provide a strong aniseed flavour in Oriental cooking.

magnum opus, which he decided to call *American Ornithology*. His would be the first book devoted to birds with coloured plates to be published in America. Although the plates have a certain stiffness and the settings are stylised and not nearly as attractive as those of Catesby, Wilson was a superb, amazingly patient and observant field ornithologist and a very good writer. He was justly commemorated by having several birds named for him including a storm petrel, a plover, a phalarope and no less than three different species of wood warbler.

Following its publication three years later, he set out on a great trek across eastern North America to find new subscribers to fund the considerable cost of producing his great work, and to continue making his studies of birds in the field. It was on this long and tiring journey that the slim, birdlike Wilson, with his piercing eyes and aquiline nose, met the dashing, handsome and flamboyant artist Audubon, who was destined to become the most famous of all bird artists – and Wilson's greatest rival.

PLATE 24.
Grey Peacock-pheasant
(male)
Polyplectron bicalcaratum
George Edwards
1747. Hand-coloured
engraving.
287mm x 208mm
(11¼in x 8¼in)

*As the common name
implies, the seven species
of peacock-pheasant that
live in the forests of
south-east Asia are close
relatives of the more
familiar peafowls.
Although the males are
not so brightly plumaged
as male peafowls
(peacocks), there is a
subtle beauty in their
browns and grey feathers.*

PLATE 25.
Great Bustard *(male)*
Otis tarda
George Edwards
1747. Hand-coloured
engraving.
287mm x 208mm
(11¼in x 8¼in)

*The male Great Bustard,
is one of the world's
heaviest flying birds. By
1831 it was extinct as a
British breeder. It has
recently been reintroduced
from Europe into one of
its former strongholds,
Salisbury Plain.*

PL. 26.

PLATE 26.
'Crimson Hornbill'
'Buceros ruber'

Anonymous
Latham collection
c.1781–1824.
Watercolour.
175mm x 240mm
(7in x 9½in)

PLATE 27.
'Black-necked Thrush'
'Turdus nigricollis'

Anonymous
Latham collection
c.1781–1824.
Watercolour.
200mm x 160mm
(7¾ in x 6¼in)

These birds are further examples of Latham's probably hypothetical species. His account of them in A General History of Birds mentions that they were known only from drawings, in this case a collection of illustrations of mostly Indian birds. Although the bird in plate 26 has some plumage features of a female Tickell's Brown Hornbill (Anorrhinus tickelli), and the bird in plate 27 resembles a Black-collared Mynah (Gracupica nigricollis) many identifying characteristics are wrong, or absent.

9. h. 60

PLATE 28.
Jackass Penguin
(juvenile)
Spheniscus demersus

John Latham
c.1781–1824.
Watercolour.
210mm x 200mm
(8¼in x 7¾in)

*Named the Jackass
Penguin (from its loud,
braying calls), this sturdy
seabird breeds along the
coast of southern Africa.*

PLATE 29.
Secretary Bird
Sagittarius serpentarius

John Latham
c.1781–1824.
Watercolour.
195mm x 125mm
(7¾in x 5in)

*Although Latham
considered it as a species
of vulture, this highly
unusual bird of prey,
found only in Africa,
mainly on grasslands, is
now placed in a family of
its own. Its specific name
serpentarius refers to its
fondness for eating snakes,
which form part of its
wide range of ground-
dwelling prey. It deals
with them, including
poisonous ones, by
stamping hard on them
with its powerful feet.*

PLATE 30.
American Black Vulture
Coragyps atratus

John Latham
c.1781–1824.
Watercolour.
196mm x 155mm
(7¾in x 5in)

In his classification scheme, Latham lumped all the vultures together. Today, New World vultures (including the two condor species) are regarded as forming a separate family, more closely related to the storks than to birds of prey, which include the Old-World vultures. The latter have evolved a very similar appearance and adaptations to their New World counterparts, having adopted the same lifestyle.

PL. 30.

PLATE 31.
Great White Pelican
Pelecanus onocrotalus

John Latham
c.1781–1824.
Watercolour.
140mm x 185mm
(5½in x 7¼in)

In some individuals of this species, the plumage is suffused with a rosy tinge, due to the bird using its bill to spread secretions onto its feathers from its preen gland at the base of its tail, although the painter has greatly exaggerated this effect. Contrary to what is often believed, pelicans do not store fish in their pouches, using them instead solely as a fishing net and swallowing their catch quickly afterwards, having allowed the large amount of water taken in with it to drain away.

PL. 31.

PLATE 32.
Ostrich
Struthio camelus

Sarah Stone
c.1788. Watercolour.
350mm x 248mm
(13¼in x 9¾in)

*This characterful portrait
of an immature Ostrich is
far more invested with
life, and more accurate,
than the work of many
of Sarah Stone's
contemporaries. Sarah's
work compares most
favourably, especially
when one considers that
she painted her subject
from a preserved
specimen, rarely having
had the opportunity to
see the living birds.*

PLATE 33.
Ruff *(male)*
Philomachus pugnax

Sarah Stone
c.1788. Watercolour.
350mm x 248mm
(13¼ x 9¾in)

*The name of this species
of wader (traditionally
restricted to the male, the
female being known as a
'reeve') refers to the
remarkable erectile ruff
of feathers in its breeding
plumage that billows out
around the bird's head.*

PL. 32.

PL. 34.

PL. 35.

PLATE 34.
Hawfinch
Coccothraustes coccothraustes

Sarah Stone
c.1788. Watercolour.
248mm x 350mm
(9¾in x 13¾in)

PLATE 35.
Pied Water-Tyrant
Fluvicola pica

Sarah Stone
c.1788. Watercolour.
248mm x 350mm
(9¾in x 13¾in)

PLATE 36.
Orange-winged Pytilia
(*male, upper*) & Orange-
breasted Sunbird (*male,
lower*)
*Fringilla afra (upper) and
Nectarinia violacea (lower)*

Sarah Stone
c.1788. Watercolour.
350mm x 248mm
(13¾in x 9¾in)

PLATE 37.
Lark variety
Alaudidae sp.

Sarah Stone
c.1788. Watercolour.
350mm x 248mm
(13¾in x 9¾in)

*Sarah Stone painted the
perches for her birds in a
distinctive style, helping
researchers to recognise
paintings as authentically
hers. As here, the trunks
often had broken ends.
The Hawfinch (Plate 34)
is one of the biggest
members of the finch
family. Found throughout
much of Eurasia, it has a
massive bill powered by
big muscles. This enables
it to crack very hard
cherry and olive stones,
exerting a force of over
50kg (110lbs) —*

*equivalent to 60 tonnes
in a human! The striking
little Pied Water-Tyrant
(Plate 35) is a familiar
sight around wetlands in
the northernmost parts of
South America, and also
on the island of Trinidad
and extending into
eastern Panama. As with
the work of other early
bird artists, it is not
always possible to make a
definite identification
with some of Sarah
Stone's illustrations. The
lower bird on Plate 36 is
one of the colourful little
tropical nectar-feeding
birds called sunbirds,
which are in many ways
the Old World
counterparts of
hummingbirds. The
plumage pattern of this
male is typical of many*

*species. The bird perched
above is certainly a
member of the estrildid
finch family; it looks most
like an African species,
the Orange-winged
Pytilia, Pytilia afra. The
lark (Plate 37), too, is of
an uncertain species. The
painting of this bird in
particular shows well the
artist's skilful use of
shadow to give an illusion
of solidity to her subjects,
a technique rarely used by
her contemporaries. She
painted the plumage with
particular care, using
delicate strokes of a very
fine brush.*

PL. 36.

PL. 37.

PL. 38.

PLATE 38.
Chestnut-bellied
Cuckoo
Hyetornis pluvialis

Sarah Stone
c.1788. Watercolour.
248mm x 350mm
(9¾in x 13¼in)⁹

*This is one of two cuckoo
species endemic to the
island of Jamaica. Called
by Sarah Stone the 'Rain
Cuckow', and still known
by this name in Jamaica,
it is also known locally as
'Old Man Bird', referring
to its hoarse cackling
calls and the silvery-grey
'beard' on its chest. The
other endemic species, the
Jamaican Lizard-Cuckoo,
is called 'Old Woman
Bird', due to its longer,
sharper beak and higher-
pitched cackle!*

PLATE 39.
White-throated Toucan
Ramphastos tucanus

Sarah Stone
c.1788. Watercolour.
248mm x 350mm
(9¾in x 13¼in)

*The specimen of this bird
in the Leverian Museum
was acquired by Lord
Stanley for his museum
at Knowsley Hall, near
Liverpool, England. This
is a relatively common
toucan, found across a
huge area of northern
South America, and is
an important 'indicator
species', whose declines
locally can alert
conservationists to
habitat degradation
and fragmentation.*

PL. 39.

PLATE 40.
Guianan Cock-of-the-
Rock *(male)*
Rupicola rupicola

Sarah Stone
1788. Watercolour.
474mm x 360mm
(16¼ in x 14¼in)

*Many artists have tried to
do justice to the splendid
male of this species, which
is restricted to part of
north-east South America;
for its time, Sarah Stone's
attempt is impressive,
conveying well the beauty
of the glowing orange
plumage and
extraordinary half-moon
crest. As with the Ruff
(page 71), this finery is
used to impress females at
communal mating 'leks'.*

PLATE 41.
Western Crowned
Pigeon
Goura cristata

Sarah Stone
1788. Watercolour.
474mm x 360mm
(16¼ in x 14¼in)

*This is one of three
species of Crowned
Pigeon, found only in
New Guinea. These
beautiful birds are
the biggest of all living
pigeons, the size of
a turkey.*

40.

PLATE 42.
Small Minivet *(male)*
Pericrocotus cinnamomeus

Sydney Parkinson
1767. Watercolour.
323mm x 257mm
(12¾ in x 10in)

PLATE 43.
Crimson-throated Barbet
Megalaima rubricapillus

Sydney Parkinson
1767. Watercolour.
327mm x 262mm
(12⅞in x 10⅜in)

The two paintings on these pages were made by Parkinson in 1767. They are included in an album in the collections of the Natural History Museum containing forty drawings of Sri Lankan birds and mammals, most - if not all - of which are the work of this talented young artist, who set sail with Captain Cook the following year on the explorer's first great voyage round the world. They appear to have been painted from drawings or specimens brought home by J. G. Loten, Governor of Ceylon, on his return from the East. The string by which the Small Minivet is suspended is likely to be a snare, probably demonstrating the local bird-catching technique, which Parkinson may well have observed.

PLATE 44.
Banded Woodpecker
Picus miniaceus

Sydney Parkinson
1767. Watercolour.
324mm x 257mm
(14in x 12¼in)

*This thrush-sized
woodpecker occurs in
parts of Thailand, Burma,
Sumatra, Borneo and
Java. Parkinson has chosen
to show his bird on a
decaying tree trunk – a
typical place to see this
often rather unobtrusive
species. It forages at all
levels of the forest, from
fallen logs to the bases of
epiphytic plants high in
the canopy.*

PLATE 45.
Indian Scops Owl
Otus bakkamoena

Sydney Parkinson
1767. Watercolour.
325mm x 258mm
(12⅞in x 10⅛in)

*This little owl is quite
common throughout
much of the Indian
subcontinent. The
feathery tufts above its
eyes, although referred
to as 'ear-tufts', have
nothing to do with
hearing, but are likely
to be used in courtship
and other displays.*

PLATE 46.

Oriental Dwarf Kingfisher
Ceyx erithacus

Sydney Parkinson
1767. Watercolour.
324mm x 254mm
(12¾in x 10in)

This little bird flies down to jungle streams to hunt small fish, frogs and invertebrates. It also takes its prey from the ground or in mid-air.

ALCEDO Erithaca.

brachyura, dorso cærulea, abdomine luteo, capite uropygioque purpureis, gula nu-chaque albis. Habitat in Bengala & Zeylonica. Linnæus syst. nat.

PL. 47.

PL. 48.

PLATE 47.
Malabar Pied Hornbill
Anthracoceros coronatus

Sydney Parkinson
1767. Watercolour.
468mm x 325mm
(18⅜in x 12¾in)

A striking study of this species, in which the female uses mud, her own droppings and food remains to seal herself inside the nest cavity.

PLATE 48.
Tailorbird
Orthotomus sp.

Sydney Parkinson
c.1768–1771. Watercolour.
411mm x 293mm
(16¼in x 11½in)

The fifteen species of tailorbirds are tropical warblers with remarkable nesting habits. They fold over and then stitch

together two leaves or part of a single leaf, using plant fibres as thread. In the funnel thus formed they build the actual nest cup of vegetable down and other soft material. The artist has painted the young peering out expectantly.

PLATE 49.
Cotton Pygmy Goose
(female)
Nettapus coromandelianus

Sydney Parkinson
1767. Watercolour.
257mm x 322mm
(10in x 12¾in)

*Despite the name, the
three species of pygmy
goose are classified with
the ducks rather than the
geese and other wildfowl.
The African species is, on
average, the smallest of
all ducks — indeed of all
wildfowl — but the species
shown in Parkinson's
drawing is little larger.
Formerly known as the
Cotton Teal, it is
widespread throughout
tropical Asia, and also
occurs in parts of north-
eastern Australia.*

W: W: Ellis ʒ viv: delin: et pin
1779.

Oriental Falcon *Lath. p. 34* *i. 7*

28.

Lo.V. p 703. n 4

PL. 51.

PLATE 51.
Lesser Akialoa (or
'Akialoa')
Hemignathus obscurus

William Ellis
1779. Watercolour.
203mm x 177mm
(8in x 7in)

*In striking contrast to the
very widespread Peregrine
Falcon, this little member
of the Hawaiian
honeycreeper family is
now sadly extinct, having
been last recorded in
1940. Like many other
members of this family, it
is likely to have been
wiped out by a triple blow
from deforestation, the
damage done by
introduced mammals such
as pigs and goats and
disease carried by
introduced mosquitoes.*

PLATE 50.
Peregrine Falcon
(juvenile)
Falco peregrinus

William Ellis
1779. Watercolour.
258mm x 195mm
(10¼in x 7¾in)

*As with the rest of Ellis's
paintings shown on the
next four pages, the artist
drew this lively study of a
juvenile Peregrine Falcon
while serving as a
surgeon's mate and
official artist on Cook's*

*third great voyage.
According to Dr. A. M.
Lysaght, who catalogued
the bird paintings made
on all three of Cook's
circumnavigations, the
falcon apparently 'flew
on board off Japan'.*

PLATE 52.
Apapane *(male)*
Himatione sanguinea

William Ellis
c.1779. Watercolour.
252mm x 182mm
(10in x 7¼in)

*This Hawaiian
honeycreeper was more
fortunate than many of
its relatives in that it still
survives, in contrast to
over half the species in
the family known to have
suffered extinction in
historical times, many
of them since the time
when Ellis and others
on Cook's third voyage
encountered them.*

PLATE 53.
Green Rosella
Platycercus caledonicus

William Ellis
c.1779. Watercolour.
238mm x 187mm
(9⅜in x 7⅜in)

*As well as painting the
plumage of his avian
subjects with great
accuracy, Ellis was a good
portrayer of their correct
anatomy, as the careful
(preliminary) drawing of
the bird's head on the
right shows. The Green
Rosella is found only on
the island of Tasmania.*

flaviventris

PLATE 54.
Red-necked Phalarope
(male, left, and female)
Phalaropus lobatus

William Ellis
c.1779. Watercolour.
155mm x 270mm
(6in x 10⅝in)

PLATE 55.
Crested Auklet
Aethia cristatella

William Ellis
c.1779. Watercolour.
155mm x 260mm
(6in x 10¼in)

These attractive little waders (Plate 54) are quite at home swimming in the roughest seas, aided by their lobed toes. They feed typically by spinning round and round to stir up small invertebrates, which they then pluck deftly from the water surface. Breeding in the far north, they are also unusual in that the female is more brightly plumaged than the male, takes the lead in courtship, and leaves him to incubate her eggs and

rear the young alone. This striking-looking little relative of the puffin and the extinct Great Auk lives in the Bering Sea region of the North Pacific. Both side and plan views in Ellis's painting (Plate 55) clearly show the jaunty forward-pointing crest, as well as the orange-red bill, which becomes dull yellow in winter. The bill is well adapted for scooping up tiny plankton creatures, which the bird carries back to its young in a special throat pouch.

Alca cristatella

No.91

PL. 57.

PLATE 56.
Golden eagle
Aquila chrysaetos

William Lewin
c.1789–1794. Bodycolour
213mm x 175mm
(8⅜in x 7in)

PLATE 57.
Northern Hobby
Falco subbuteo

William Lewin
c.1789–1794.
Bodycolour.
218mm x 178mm
(8⅝in x 7in)

*One of three bird artist
sons of an English natural
history painter, William
Lewin had a bold,
confident style, well
illustrated in these
paintings of an immature
Golden Eagle, and a
Hobby. One of the most
elegant members of the
falcon family, the Hobby
is a superb flier that
catches fast-moving, alert
dragonflies as well as
swallows, swifts and other
aerobatic prey in mid-air
in its talons; it often
deftly transfers insect
prey to its bill to eat
on the wing.*

PLATE 58.

PLATE 58.
Yellow-tailed Black Cockatoo
Calyptorhynchus funereus

George Raper
1789. Watercolour.
480mm x 320mm
(19in x 12⅝in)

*This is a typical example
of the work of George
Raper, a sailor on HMS
Sirius, one of the ships
that sailed from England
to Australia in 1787
carrying convicts and
supplies to found the new
penal colony at Port
Jackson (now Sydney).
The large cockatoo shown
here is one of five species
of black cockatoo, and
can still be seen in the
Sydney area today.*

PLATE 59.
Glossy Black Cockatoo
Calyptorhynchus lathami

George Raper
1789. Watercolour.
495mm x 315mm
(19⅛in x 12⅜in)

*Smallest of the black
cockatoos, this species is
less common than the
Yellow-tailed Black
Cockatoo. The bird Raper
has figured here is a
female, distinguished by
the yellow blotches on her
head, and dark-barred red
tail panels with yellow
inner feathers.*

BIRD and FLOWER of PORT JACKSON. *Natural Size. G. Raper 1789*

PLATE 60.

Australian White Pelican
Pelecanus conspicillatus

George Raper
1789. Watercolour.
480mm x 330mm
(19in x 13in)

This interesting composition shows Australia's only pelican species. The huge pouch briefly acquires pink, scarlet and dark blue courtship colours in the breeding season. It is fluttered to help the bird cool down by evaporation on the sun-baked islands where it likes to breed.

PLATE 61.

Laughing Kookaburra
Dacelo novaeguineae

George Raper
1789. Watercolour.
495mm x 330mm
(19½in x 13in)

This is one of the largest members of the kingfisher family, and one of many species that eats few fish, feeding instead on a wide variety of mainly terrestrial prey. Despite its specific Latin name, it does not occur in New Guinea, which is home to three other, smaller kookaburra species.

PLATE 62.

Lord Howe Rail
Gallirallus sylvestris

George Raper
1790. Watercolour.
495mm x 322mm
(19¾in x 12¾in)

*Like the other member of
the rail family found on
Lord Howe Island, the
extinct White Gallinule
(see page 101), this
species is flightless, and
thus vulnerable to
humans and their
introduced animals which
degrade the habitat or eat
adults, young or eggs.
When Raper visited the
island, it was widespread,
but by 1853 it had been
driven to the mountain
tops, and in 1930 a mere
thirty or so birds
survived. Management
and captive breeding has
now increased the
population to more than
one hundred individuals.*

PLATE 63.

Emu
Dromaius novaehollandiae

George Raper
1791. Watercolour.
480mm x 318mm
(19in x 12½in)

*This huge flightless bird
was of considerable
importance to the early
settlers to Australia, who
killed it for its nutritious
and tasty beef-like meat
and for its oil, used to
provide fuel for lamps.
They also eagerly
collected its large eggs,
up to fifteen or more of
which may be found in
a single nest.*

GROUND-BIRD *of* LORD-HOWE-ISLAND *by ⅔ of its Natural size.*

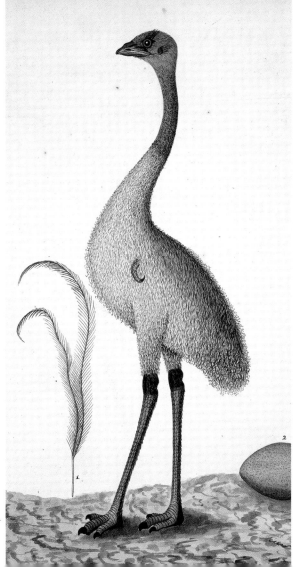

PLATE 64.
Black Swan
Cygnus atratus

**Port Jackson
Painter**
c.1792. Watercolour.
242mm x 192mm
(9½in x 7½in)

*Many of the pictures in
the Natural History
Museum from the early
Australian colony that are
signed by Thomas Watling
are, in fact, the work of
one or more (probably
three) other anonymous
artists, collectively known
as the 'Port Jackson
Painter'. This is the
world's only species of
swan that is almost all
black; only its flight
feathers are white.*

Three stages of this Bird taken at Lord Howe Island
before it arrives to maturity
Three changes of the white Gallinule / Latham Syn Supp 2. p. 327.

PLATE 65.
White Gallinule
Porphyrio albus

**Port Jackson
Painter**
1797. Watercolour.
199mm x 175mm
(7¾in x 7in)

*This painting is of
particular interest, as it
shows a bird that is now
extinct. Also known as the
'Lord Howe Swamphen',
this large member of the
rail family was quickly
exterminated by the first*

*human visitors to Lord
Howe island, 298 miles
(480km) east of the
Australian mainland.*

Great headed Goatsucker
Latham Syn Supp ii. p. 262.

PL. 67

PLATE 66.
Tawny Frogmouth
Podargus strigoides

Port Jackson Painter

c.1788–97. Watercolour.
275mm x 246mm
(10⅞in x 9¼in)

PLATE 67.
Maned Duck *(male)*
Chenonetta jubata

Port Jackson Painter

c.1788–97. Watercolour.
203mm x 234mm
(8in x 9¼in)

The early colonists of Australia were amazed by the unfamiliar birds they found there, including swans and cockatoos that were black instead of the familiar white, and this bizarre-looking 'goatsucker' was no exception. The same name was given to the related European Nightjar of their homeland. A member of the related frogmouth family of southern Asia and Australasia, its bill

has an even larger gape than the nightjar's, for grabbing small animals from the ground or a branch. Also known as the Australian Wood Duck, the Maned Duck has evolved a goose-like grazing lifestyle in open woodlands, wetland margins and farmland.

PLATE 68.
Merops orientalis

Pieter Cornelis de Bevere
c.1754–57. Watercolour.
246mm x 382mm
(9⅝in x 15in)

This painting of a beautiful bird is typical of the attempts of many early bird artists to tackle the difficult task of illustrating a bird in flight, with very unlifelike results. Despite this, the bird is painted by de Bevere with his usual sensitivity.

PLATE 69.
Asian Paradise-
Flycatcher *(male)*
Terpsiphone paradisi

Pieter Cornelis de Bevere
c.1752–57. Watercolour.
382mm x 251mm
(15in x 10in)

The female and young lack the stunning tail streamers of the male, and have a chestnut back and wings; in the Sri Lankan race the male never acquires the almost all-white plumage of some other races.

PL. 71.

PL. 70.

PLATE 70.
Hoopoe
Upupa epops

Pieter Cornelis de Bevere

c.1754–57. Watercolour.
246mm x 381mm
(9¾in x 15in)

Classified in a family of its own, the distinctive Hoopoe has a very wide distribution right across the warmer parts of the Old World. Both its common name and the generic name Upupa refer to the lovely, mellow 'hoop-hoop-hoop' song of the male during the early part of the breeding season in spring.

PLATE 71.
Indian Roller
Coracias benghalensis

Pieter Cornelis de Bevere

c.1754–57. Watercolour.
248mm x 385mm
(9¾in x 15¼in)

This illustration of another gorgeously plumaged Asian bird, shows it as de Bevere would have seen it, freshly killed. Although painting from such a specimen can have its advantages, it requires imagination to invest the subject with life – a feat de Bevere often achieves in no small measure.

PLATE 72.
Common (or Asian)
Koel *(female)*
Eudynamys scolopacea

**Pieter Cornelis de
Bevere**
c.1754–57. Watercolour.
214mm x 350mm
(8½in x 13¾in)

*De Bevere would have
heard as well as seen this
common bird regularly in
Sri Lanka, for it is one of
the noisiest of all the
birds of the region during
the breeding season. The
male's song, uttered all
day and often into the
night, is a monotonously
repeated sequence of shrill
'koel' notes that rise in
pitch to reach a frantic
climax. One of a number
of species in the Cuckoo
family that lays its eggs
in the nests of other birds,
leaving them to rear its
young as their own. The
female Common Koel
chooses House Crows or
Jungle Crows as its hosts.*

26

PLATE 73.
Greater Flameback
Chrysocolaptes lucidus

Pieter Cornelis de Bevere
c.1754–57. Watercolour.
350mm x 214mm
(13¾in x 8½in)

Here, de Bevere has painted a female of the Sri Lankan race stricklandi of this striking south Asian woodpecker, which lives up to its common name by largely having deep red wings. Widespread in all types of more open woodland, it can be quite tame and approachable.

PLATE 74.
Brown Fish-Owl
Ketupa zeylonensis

Pieter Cornelis de Bevere
c.1754–57. Watercolour.
350mm x 214mm
(13¾in x 8½in)

This rather doleful-looking bird is one of a small group of owls that specialise in feeding on fish. Unlike those of other owls, their legs are unfeathered — an adaptation that avoids the plumage becoming soiled with fish scales and slime.

PL. 75.

PLATE 75.
Little Green Bee-eater
Merops orientalis

Anonymous
Impey Collection
c.1780. Watercolour.
297mm x 483mm
(11¾in x 19in)

PLATE 76.
Black-headed Oriole
(male)
Oriolus xanthornus

Sheik Zayn al-Din
c.1780. Watercolour.
345mm x 486mm
(13½in x 19½in)

The two paintings from the collection of Lady Impey clearly illustrate the influence of traditional Mughal miniature painting in which the artists employed by her were trained. After she returned to England from Bengal with the paintings, they were examined by John Latham, who used some as a basis for his descriptions of species new to science. This makes them of considerable scientific importance, as they effectively became the type specimens of the species concerned (the ones from which the first scientific descriptions of the species were made) rather than the usual preserved skin of the actual bird.

PL. 76.

PLATE 77.
Tern
Sternidae sp.

Sheik Zayn al-Din
1781. Watercolour.
614mm x 845mm
(24¼in x 33¼in)

In 1777, Lady Mary
Impey travelled to India
to join her husband, Sir
Elijah Impey, who served
as the chief justice of the
Supreme Court in
Calcutta from 1774–83.
Here she established a
large menagerie of Asian
birds and mammals,
many of which were

unknown at the time to
western science.
Fortunately, Lady Impey
employed Indian artists
to make watercolour
drawings of these from
life. Terns have webbed
feet; this bird may have
lost its webs due to
disease in captivity.

PLATE 78.
Green Heron
Butorides virescens

William Bartram
[1774]. Pen and ink, and
watercolour.
377mm x 245mm
(14⅞in x 9⅝in)

*Bartram's drawings are
typically full of life, as
with this depiction of a
Green Heron patiently
waiting to seize prey with
a sudden extension of its
long neck. If patient
standing or stalking fails,
this common wetland
inhabitant of much of the
USA will stir up mud or
aquatic vegetation in an
attempt to flush out prey
hiding there.*

PLATE 79.
Bobolink
Dolichonyx oryzivorus

William Bartram
[1774/75]. Pen & Ink,
Watercolour.
256mm x 202mm
(10in x 8in)

*This little bird's odd
name comes from a
fancied resemblance to a
phrase of the male's loud,
bubbling song. It was
persecuted in huge
numbers in the past by
farmers for its
depredations on rice and
other grain crops during
its long migration south
to South America, mainly
Argentina. An alternative
name is 'Ricebird', and
the connection is also
made in the specific
name: oryzivorus means
'rice-eating'. Bartram has
also referred to this habit
by having his bird
perched on a rice stem.
He often added other
animals to the main
subject, as with the tree
frog and rat snake here.*

PL. 79.

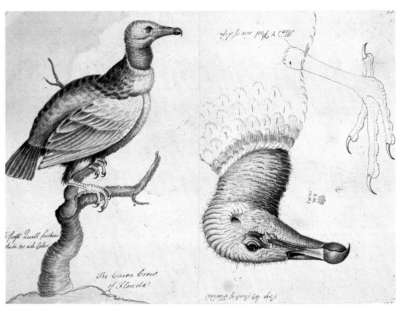

The Carion Crow of Florida

PLATE 80.
American Black
Vulture
Coragyps atratus

William Bartram
1774. Pen & Ink,
Watercolour.
242mm x 319mm
(10in x 12⅛in)

*Referred to by Bartram by
the American name of
'Carrion Crow', this bird
is not at all related to the
crow family, being one of
the New World vultures. It
is interesting to compare
this drawing with that
done by John Latham
(page 68).*

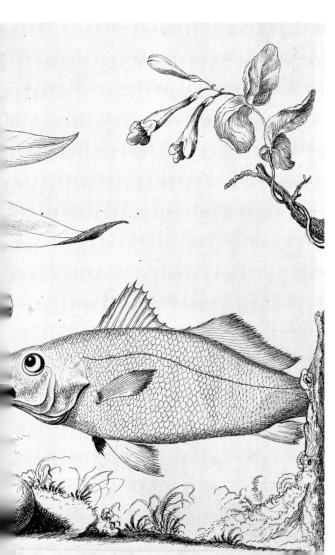

PLATE 81.
Northern Cardinal
Cardinalis cardinalis

William Bartram
1772. Pen and ink.
181mm x 304mm
(7¼in x 12in)

This drawing shows an odd assemblage of a bird, a shrub and a fish, the latter seemingly swimming through the air. The bird was well known to the settlers in eastern North America, as it is to people today, where it is a familiar visitor to bird feeders. Bartram referred to it as the 'Red Bird of America' and 'Red Sparaw', as well as by its more familiar contemporary name of 'Virginia Nightingale'. It is neither sparrow nor nightingale, being a member of a family of birds, the cardinals, most closely related to the tangers and buntings. The shrub is Devilwood, Osmanthus americanus, with intensely fragrant flowers, and the fish, that appears to be swimming in mid-air, is an Atlantic croaker, Micropogonias undulatus.

Chapter Two { 1800—1850

{ AUDUBON TO THE FIRST LITHOGRAPHERS 1800–1850

ℰARLY IN 1810, ALEXANDER WILSON SET OUT on one of his many voyages to collect new bird species and find subscribers for his *American Ornithology*. One of the many places he visited to sell his work was the small frontier town of Louisville. On arriving there in March, he soon learned of a storekeeper who lived nearby and gave drawing lessons. Hopeful that he might interest this promising-sounding person in subscribing to his great work, Wilson decided to pay the man a visit. What he did not know was that the storekeeper, John James Audubon (1785–1851), was himself a far more skilled painter of birds than Wilson could ever be, and moreover was destined to become the most famous bird painter of all time.

Audubon examined the two volumes of Wilson's work that his visitor spread before him, and expressed approval. According to Audubon's journal, he was on the point of agreeing to his visitor's request and had picked up his pen to sign as a subscriber, when his friend and business partner Ferdinand Rozier, who was also present, asked Audubon in French why he was going to subscribe, adding that his own work and his knowledge of birds was far superior to Wilson's. As Audubon later recorded in his journal, 'Vanity and the encomiums of my friend prevented me from subscribing'. Stung by this sudden reversal, Wilson asked Audubon if he had any drawings of his own of American birds and, on gazing at the splendid selection that Audubon showed him, was astonished to learn that his host had no intention of publishing them.

On returning to Philadelphia from New Orleans, Wilson added four more volumes of his *American Ornithology* to the two he had already published, completing the work in just two years. Although he originally intended the work to consist of ten volumes, he decided to reduce this to nine; he also cut short his collecting trips and worked day and night to speed up publication. It is to his credit that Wilson managed to complete all but the final volume before his death from dysentery in 1813 at the early age of forty-seven. It was left to Wilson's friend, the wealthy naturalist George Ord (1781–1866) to edit the Scotsman's eighth volume and write the ninth and, as Wilson's literary executor and

Great American Cock Male. VULGO (WILD TURKEY.) Meleagris Gallopavo

admirer, to champion his cause by attacking Audubon in print at every opportunity. Ord remained a thorn in Audubon's side throughout his life, with particularly vituperative support on the English side of the Atlantic from the eccentric Yorkshire naturalist Squire George Waterton (1782–1865), though Audubon himself wisely refused to rise to the bait.

John James Audubon was born on 26 April 1785 on the island of Hispaniola, in what was then a French colony called Saint Domingue (now Haiti). He was the illegitimate son of the Frenchman Jean Audubon, a former sea captain who had become quite wealthy as a sugar and wine trader, planter, and slave-dealer, and who had already fathered two illegitimate daughters by a Creole woman. The boy's mother, Jeanne Rabine, a French chambermaid who worked for a French family on the island, died of a fever when her son, named Jean Rabine, was just six months old. In August 1788, when he was three years old, his father took him back to France together with one of his half-sisters, Rose, to live with him and his wealthy and evidently very understanding wife, Anne Moynet, in their family home near the village of Couëron, a few miles west of Nantes in Brittany.

The following year, just before his fourth birthday, his parents legally adopted him. Now named Jean Jacques Fougère Audubon, he was cared for mainly by his stepmother, who spoiled him, his father being away for much of the time after joining the French navy as a lieutenant. He avoided school, preferring to roam the fields observing nature and collecting birds' eggs, nests and flowers; he also received home tuition in various subjects, including fencing, dancing and drawing. In 1796, when he was eleven, he was sent for four years to a naval training institute at Rochefort about 100 miles to the south of Nantes.

In the summer of 1803, when Audubon was eighteen, his father sent Jean to the United States to study English and to manage a farm that he had bought as an investment fourteen years earlier, sight unseen, at Mill Grove near Philadelphia. He was given yet another new name, and was known for the rest of his life as John James Laforest Audubon. Despite his reservations about the English – he had been brought up by his father, a fervent supporter of Napoleon, to despise and distrust them – Audubon became engaged to Lucy Bakewell, the daughter of an English couple who owned the property next to Mill Grove.

In 1805, wishing to persuade his father to overcome his objections to his marrying Lucy, Audubon decided to return to France. He remained there for a year, and made his earliest surviving ornithological drawings there: pencil and pastel studies of typical European birds such as Long-tailed Tits and European Greenfinches. These barely hint at the skill Audubon was to develop: they are stiff profiles, much like those of most other bird artists of the day. In April 1806 Audubon sailed back to America, accompanied by Ferdinand Rozier, chosen as a business partner by his father.

Instead of settling down to manage the business of the farm, the two young men led a carefree life. They went hunting, fishing and exploring, and Audubon spent much of his time watching and collecting birds and filling pages with sketches and notes. With the failure of the farm enterprise, they gradually sold the land and worked as clerks before deciding to seek their luck in Kentucky. Arriving at Louisville on the Ohio River in September 1807, they bought the general store where the meeting with Wilson was to take place. In the spring of 1808, Audubon returned to Philadelphia and married Lucy on 5 April. The couple then journeyed back together to Louisville.

As before, Audubon's heart was not in his business, and after little more than two years, he and Rozier decided to move on again to seek their fortune elsewhere. They opened another store about 120 miles (193km) west of Louisville in the little settlement of Henderson. In December 1810, Audubon, accompanied by Rozier, left the store to travel down the Ohio and Mississippi rivers with a cargo of gunpowder and whisky, bound for the settlement of Ste Geneviève. Rozier found this largely French frontier post much to his liking, and decided to stay there; in April 1811, he and Audubon decided to dissolve their unproductive partnership.

Audubon's misfortunes were not restricted to his business ventures. In 1812, the year that the United States declared war on Britain, and the year Audubon became an American citizen, he suffered one of the frequent temporary setbacks to his artistic career that were such a feature of his chequered life. While on one of his many journeys, he had his entire collection of bird paintings, at least 200 in number, entrusted to a relative, stored in a wooden box. He returned only to discover to his horror that the whole lot, containing almost 1,000 images of birds, had been shredded by rats to make a snug nest. His reaction shows his strength of character and his ability to see his glass as half full rather than

half empty. He recorded in his journal, 'The burning heat which instantly rushed through my brain was too great to be endured … I slept not for several nights … until I took up my gun, my notebook and my pencils and went forth to the woods as gaily as if nothing had happened. I felt pleased that I might now make better drawings than before …'.

In 1819 Audubon was arrested for debt and briefly imprisoned; he was released only after declaring himself bankrupt. This was a major turning point in his career: he gave up his vain attempts to succeed in business, and decided to work full time on his ambitious project of producing the finest book on all the birds of America. In 1820 he travelled to Cincinnati to work at the Western Museum as a taxidermist and scene painter, and Lucy and their two sons soon joined him there.

In October 1820 he was off again on an expedition, travelling down the Ohio river on a flatboat together with his dog Dash and a gifted disciple, the eighteen-year-old botanist and artist Joseph Mason, to increase his collection of American birds. The two paid their way by working on the boat. This was the first of many journeys in search of birds. At this time, the American frontier was formed by the Mississippi river. The land to the west was essentially uncharted territory, often populated by hostile Indian tribes, with few roads and vast tracts of virgin forest. Audubon explored many thousands of miles by river and on foot.

He was often dogged by hardships and bad luck, but he overcame these setbacks with admirable fortitude. However, it is doubtful that he would have been able to achieve so much without the unflagging help of his wife Lucy. She proved a tower of strength in his long absences, supporting him steadfastly by working as a teacher and providing for their two sons, Victor Gifford, born in 1809, and John Woodhouse, born three years later. She also dealt with correspondence, laboriously made copies of Audubon's writings in longhand, and accompanied him on some of his research trips, at times helping him to collect birds and plants to draw. Even the two boys were trained from a very young age to assist their father and mother in their goal of producing the finest bird book the world had ever known.

In 1824 Audubon went to Philadelphia to try and interest influential people in helping him publish his work. Stacked against Audubon were the expense of the undertaking, the fact that a sequel to Wilson's *American Ornithology* was being prepared by the young and gifted Charles

PLATE 83.
Eggs of 1. Song Thrush; 2. Golden-crested Wren (now Goldcrest); 3. Chimney Swallow (now Barn Swallow); 4. Common Wren (now Northern Wren); 5. Jay (now Eurasian Jay); 6. Kingfisher (now Eurasian Kingfisher)
1. Turdus philomelos 2. Regulus regulus 3. Hirundo rustica 4. Troglodytes troglodytes 5. Garrulus glandarius 6. Alcedo atthis

James Hope Stewart
c.1835. Watercolour. 106mm x 172mm (4⅛in x 6¾in)

This talented Scottish natural-history artist painted many of the watercolour illustrations of birds that appeared in his neighbour Sir William Jardine's attractive and extensive series of compact books entitled The Naturalist's Library. This example shows a selection of eggs of common British birds. Stewart was an amateur, working at his art in the spare time left over from his job as manager and farmer of a 2,000-acre estate.

PLATE 84.
Purple Martin
Progne subis

**John James
Audubon**
c.1827–30. Hand-
coloured aquatint.
658mm x 525mm
(26in x 20⅝in)

*This painting shows two
pairs of one of America's
most-loved birds at their
nest sites in a couple of
hollow gourds hung in a
tree to attract them. This
habit is a very old one,
first recorded from native
Indians and later southern
plantation slaves; few
martins in the eastern
part of North America
use natural nest sites in
holes in trees, cliffs or
other places, in contrast
to those in the west of
country. Today, most nest
in special, often multi-
occupancy, 'martin houses'
provided by humans.
Like many people today,
Audubon would have
welcomed the return
of these migrants
each spring.*

Bonaparte (nephew of the Emperor Napoleon) and the general coldness of the reception granted to a newcomer by scientific society, including George Ord's downright hostility. As a result, Audubon failed to find any backers and was persuaded by advice from Bonaparte and others to try his luck in England or France.

To finance the expensive trip to Europe, he worked hard for over a year, teaching French, music, dancing and drawing, while Lucy augmented his funds considerably by giving him the money she had saved from her work as a teacher and governess. In 1826, now forty-one years old, Audubon sailed to Liverpool bearing several letters of recommendation to important figures in British society. In Liverpool he met Lord Stanley, an MP and keen amateur naturalist with a large collection of birds and other animals. He was later to become one of the subscribers to Audubon's planned work.

Audubon made his way to Edinburgh to continue his quest for a printer who could do justice to his huge and detailed paintings, and to meet anyone of influence who could give him publicity. Through his meetings with the city's eminent naturalists, Audubon was introduced to William Home Lizars (1788–1859), then Edinburgh's leading engraver. The two hit it off splendidly and Lizars, full of admiration for the American's paintings, agreed to produce his life's work. Audubon was fortunate in being a great showman and self-advertiser. He capitalised on his natural assets. These included his striking looks, shoulder-length chestnut hair (which shone because he oiled it with bear fat) and unusual garb of a long, black frock coat or fringed buckskin jacket and baggy pantaloons – one wit commented that his clothes must have been made by a Wild West tailor rather than a West End one. All this helped to ensure that he was the talk of the town wherever he went. And, adding drama to his image, Audubon carried his drawings about slung over his shoulder in a huge, heavy portfolio.

As well as exhibiting his paintings in Liverpool, Manchester, Edinburgh and later in London, Audubon was wined and dined and invited to speak to scientific societies and other gatherings of cultured society. The 'American Woodsman', as he soon became known, thrilled them with graphic accounts of his adventures in search of birds across the wildernesses of America. Though many of the exploits he recounted to his eager audiences were true, from tales of encounters with native

American Indians to surviving an earthquake, Audubon could not resist embellishing some of them, and at times told downright untruths. As with others prone to such exaggeration, it is hard to tell whether he repeated intentional lies or came to believe his own tall stories. These began with the details of his birth. At times he said that his father's first wife on Haiti, a beautiful Spanish Creole woman, was in fact his mother; he also elevated his father from a lieutenant to an admiral of the French navy. On another occasion, he declined to scotch a rumour that suggested he was in fact the legendary dauphin, the lost son of Louis XVI and Marie Antoinette.

After signing a contract for the work with Lizars in November 1826, Audubon left Edinburgh at the beginning of April the following year, ending up in London in May. Meanwhile, back in Edinburgh, Lizars had completed only ten plates when Audubon received news from him in June 1827 that his colourists had gone on strike and he was unable to produce finished plates; he suggested that Audubon look for another printing company in London to do the colouring. It was a great stroke of luck that the firm he found after just three days was that of the Havells, a partnership between Robert Havell (1769–1832) and his son, also Robert (1793–1878). They agreed to redo the ten plates from Lizars and to take on the rest of the work.

Like Lizars, the Havells used the aquatint process to print the plates. This printing method ensured that the finished plates were usually as good as Audubon's original paintings; in some cases, where Robert Havell had made improvements, they were even better. Although Havell senior attended to the final detailed colouring, the assistants who did the washes were not always consistent, and complaints came in from some subscribers of inferior colouring, and in one case a slice of beef had found its way in between the plates, presumably from someone's meal! This proved costly to Audubon when the subscribers returned such plates for the colours to be washed off and the work redone. Things improved markedly after the elder Havell retired and his son Robert took over the work entirely. Not only was he a superb craftsman and a thorough overseer of his assistants' work, but his calm and unruffled personality was a good foil to Audubon's volatile temperament as the project inevitably hit problems. His skill and understanding of the quality of work Audubon wanted to achieve, together with his belief in the viability of the project, played a major part in turning Audubon's dream into reality.

As time passed and the pressure of work mounted, Audubon left more and more of the detailed work safely in Havell's expert hands. The artist would often make rough pencil sketches of backgrounds for his bird paintings, leaving Havell to interpret them and work them up into the desired result. Production pressures also led to the use of collage, rarely seen in bird paintings of this period. Audubon or his assistants would, for instance, paste in an improved painting over an earlier effort, or a missing male or female. And in a rare example of compromise, when Audubon realised his subscribers would not bear the expense of even more parts to include the new birds he was finding, he was forced to cram several species on the same plate.

In the end, each copy of *The Birds of America* contained 435 huge colour plates, comprising 1,065 figures of birds representing 491 species, from the first, a huge, proud Wild Turkey cock, to the final plate of a pair of plump little American Dippers. In total, the Havells may have produced as many as 100,000 hand-coloured plates for the 175–200 complete, and 120 or so incomplete, copies of *The Birds of America*. Using as many as fifty colourists to finish the plates by hand, they completed this mammoth task in eleven years, the last plate emerging from the press on 20 June 1838. During the protracted process of the plates being printed, Audubon returned to America three times to obtain further bird specimens, make new drawings and add to his tally of subscribers.

Artistically, Audubon's paintings are superb; ornithologically, they have some serious limitations. These were partly connected with his usual method of drawing not from life – which he often claimed to do – but from birds he had just killed. He pinned the specimen on a board on which he had placed a grid ruled off in small squares. He drew similar squares on his drawing paper so that he could accurately portray the creature's correct proportions. Though often an improvement on using badly stuffed specimens, this method allowed Audubon to force the birds into dramatic poses which were artistically exciting but sometimes untrue to life. To be fair to the artist, however, by angling a neck or raising a head here, and raising, or twisting a wing or a tail there, Audubon could show all the areas of the bird's plumage and their identifying markings.

Ornithologists looking at his work in later years frequently criticised Audubon for his lack of scientific training and pointed to errors in his paintings to support their views of him as an inaccurate observer. An example of such an error seized upon by Audubon's detractors is his 'bird of Washington'. Rather than being the new species of eagle he thought he had discovered and proudly named for the first president of the United States, this proved to be an immature Bald Eagle. Other errors included mistaking the Sandhill Crane for the young of the rarer Whooping Crane.

However, although Audubon did not make any major contributions to the science of ornithology, he was often a perceptive observer of bird behaviour in the field, and much of what he saw he put into his paintings. He was one of the first American naturalists to conduct experiments on homing abilities by inventing an early form of bird ringing. He attached 'a light silver thread' to the leg of each one of a brood of nestling Eastern Wood Pewees in their nest, 'loose enough not to hurt the part, but so fastened that no exertions of theirs could remove it'. The following year, he found two of the marked birds, now adults, occupying nests near where they had been raised. He also watched this species carefully over long periods, drawing the conclusion that it migrates only at night.

An accusation often levelled at Audubon by commentators long after his death was that he delighted in killing the birds he purported to love so much. Indeed, in an oft-repeated quotation, he did write to a friend, 'You must be aware that I call birds few when I shoot less than one hundred per day'. And as one of his biographers, the American naturalist Edwin Way Teale, put it with blunt humour, 'probably the most terrifying sight a bird could see was the approach of John James Audubon'. But this was true of all ornithologists before binoculars — let alone cameras and telephoto lenses — were available. Unlike many wealthier collectors, Audubon, often hard up and short of provisions, ate many of the birds he had killed. Nevertheless, as time passed, his eagerness to kill purely as a hunter as well as for his drawing waned; he became concerned about the wanton destruction of birds and other wildlife and his writings include

PLATE 26

Carolina Parrot

PSITTACUS CAROLINENSIS.

Plant Vitis. Cockle Burr.

criticism of clearance of woodlands and other habitats and the persecution of birds and their eggs.

Among the many species so carefully illustrated by Audubon were several that are sadly now extinct: his accurate depictions of their plumage provides a poignant record of their past glory, and are also valuable to science. A famous example is his often reproduced and superbly designed painting of a feeding flock of seven Carolina Parakeets painted in Louisiana, probably in 1825. Once common, this handsome little species was the only native member of the parrot family to breed in North America, but by the mid-1800s it had become much scarcer as a result of wholesale slaughter, mainly because of its fondness for orchard fruit. On 21 February 1918, the sole remaining captive Carolina Parakeet died in Cincinnati Zoo, Ohio, and by 1920 the last wild individual in the world had been recorded.

Audubon's approach to depicting birds represented a quantum leap forward. In contrast to many of the static images of previous bird artists, his birds are full of life: his hawks, kites and eagles swoop down on prey or rip it apart; songbirds reach up to pluck berries or snatch butterflies; others are shown stretching, preening, fighting and singing. A major aspect of Audubon's genius was not only to be able to create an arresting focus in the main subjects of the birds, but also to include plants and prey that were as beautifully drawn and painted as the main bird subjects, and that formed an integral part of the stunning overall design. The background was also carefully designed, and often showed the bird's typical habitat in detail, as with the rice plantations of Carolina in his painting of the Snowy Egret, the marshland haunts of the King Rail or the rocky seashore off which his Razorbills swim.

Unusually, in his portrayal of a Golden Eagle rising into the air from a towering mountain range clutching its prey, a Snowshoe Hare, firmly in its talons, Audubon included a human figure. In the bottom left-hand corner of this dramatic painting, which was very much in the Romantic style, a hunter – very probably intended to represent the painter himself – sits astride a fallen tree spanning a mighty chasm, carefully inching his way across and chopping off obstructing branches with a hand-axe. Slung round his back, the man bears the corpse of a huge eagle.

For some unknown reason, when engraving the picture Havell removed the little human figure from the final print, though he left the tree trunk

PLATE 85.
Carolina Parakeet
Conuropsis carolinensis

John James Audubon
c.1827–30. Hand-coloured aquatint. 853mm x 600mm (33⅛in x 23⅝in)

One of Audubon's most brilliant designs, this colourful scene is bursting with life as the birds feed on the seeds of the spiky fruits of cocklebur. These beautiful little parrots – the only parrot species native to the USA – were once abundant in the eastern United States, but were persecuted by humans, for food and their feathers, as agricultural pests and as cage birds. They also suffered from deforestation and competition for nest sites with introduced bees. The last wild specimen was shot in 1904, and the last captive individual died in 1918.

in place. It is intriguing to speculate whether Audubon himself had any part in this decision. If so, it may have had a great deal to do with the way in which he treated the unfortunate creature that served as a reluctant model for this powerful image. Having purchased a live Golden Eagle from a trapper on 24 February 1833, Audubon, so used to sketching from dead birds, found it impossible to create the image of the eagle to his high standards. After an agony of indecision in which he considered giving the noble bird its liberty, he decided, with some misgivings, to kill it using a method that would inflict 'the least pain to him'.

He records confining the eagle in a small room and attempting to suffocate it by covering it for hours with a tent of blankets into which he had placed a pan of lighted charcoal to produce copious fumes. The next day he added sulphur to the charcoal, but the choking sulphur dioxide gas this yielded only had the effect of driving Audubon and his son John out of the house, the eagle being still very much alive. Eventually he chose a method 'always used as the last expedient, and a most effectual one.' This was to 'thrust a long piece of pointed steel through his heart, when my proud prisoner fell dead, without even ruffling a feather'.

The poor bird's ordeal was over, but Audubon's was just beginning. He worked with such manic intensity on the drawing, and for so long (he describes the time variously as two weeks or sixty hours) that he experienced some kind of seizure that he intimated nearly killed him and required treatment by three doctors. The art historian Carole Anne Slatkin muses, 'Did he wonder, at the time, whether some higher force was seizing him, as he had seized the eagle, and the eagle had the rabbit?' Certainly Audubon often wrote of feeling akin to the birds of prey he painted: they shared with him the powerful hunting impulse, an impulse that had led him to kill the eagle and capture it for posterity in paint. It is hardly surprising that, so imbued was he with guilt and shame, Audubon should feel insecure about representing himself in the painting as a heroic figure hunting an eagle as an equal – and he was even afraid of heights!

One of Audubon's outstanding achievements as a painter was his willingness to experiment with many types of medium to produce the effects he wanted, and to portray the colours and textures of the birds' plumage and skin as accurately as he could. Far from being simple watercolours in the usual sense of the term, Audubon's paintings for *The Birds of America* are complex creations using various combinations of

PLATE 86.
Golden Eagle
Aquila chrysaetos

John James Audubon
1833. Hand-coloured aquatint.
970mm x 656mm
(38¼in x 25¾in)

As published in The Birds of America, *this dramatic portrayal of a mighty Golden Eagle carrying off a Snowshoe Hare in its powerful talons omits the little figure of the hunter inching his way across the huge tree that has fallen across a chasm at the bottom right of the picture – a detail that was in the artist's original painting. It is likely that the figure symbolises the artist himself, in his role as a brave and intrepid hunter of birds. The reason for this curious omission may be that Audubon instructed his engraver Robert Havell to do so out of a sense of inadequacy or guilt.*

PLATE 87.

Black-winged Stilt
Himantopus himantopus

Anonymous
Reeves Collection
c.1822–29. Watercolour.
590mm x 477mm
(23¼in x 18¾in)

This careful, accurate drawing of a freshly killed specimen of the wader that has the longest legs in relation to body size of any bird was made by an unknown hand. It is the work of one of the Chinese artists working for John Reeves (1774–1856), a tea inspector employed in China by the British East India Company. Reeves spent most of his nineteen years there mainly in the Portuguese settlement and port of Macao, near Hong Kong; he was allowed to visit Canton only when the British merchant fleet was present. A Fellow of the august scientific Royal Society in London, Reeves sent the drawings, birds and plants (both living and dead) that he accumulated back to the East India Company's head office and the London Horticultural Society, as well as to other contacts in England.

graphite pencil, pastels, oil paints, white gouache, chalk, ink, glazing and collage, as well as watercolour. He developed great skill in using hundreds of short pencil lines over the dried watercolour image of a bird to create plumage effects, with the shining, metallic graphite of the pencil catching the light to create iridescence. The watercolours themselves were often heavily applied to produce lifelike renditions of intensely coloured plumage; black feathers were often painted using blues, greens, browns and purples as well as black. Whereas watercolours often fade with exposure to light, these have survived intact.

Audubon used opaque white gouache in several ways: to depict intensely white plumage, to add highlights to the eyes and occasionally to correct mistakes. Thin films of oil paint were added to parts of a few of the watercolours, while transparent gum or gelatine glazes were used to intensify the colours and add gloss to areas of plumage. Other subtle plumage effects were achieved by applying black pastel or chalk over layers of glazed and unglazed black water-colour, producing a range of blacks, from matt to gloss. Collage was employed mainly in adding birds Audubon had painted earlier to new drawings, but sometimes it was used to make corrections or improvements.

Audubon also used metallic paint – probably made of bronze rather than gold leaf – on three paintings in *The Birds of America*, depicting the male Wild Turkey, the Ruby-throated Hummingbird and the Mallard, all painted in 1825. In the last two the paint has discoloured, but microscopic traces are still detectable in the turkey painting.

Mark Catesby had been the first to use a folio size for his volumes to allow space to do the birds justice, but Audubon's masterwork was even bigger. They are the largest bird books ever produced; Audubon had chosen the huge double elephant folio size – 39½ x 26½ inches – the same size as the paper on which he made his original drawings, so that he could paint even the largest species, the Wild Turkey, and the tallest, the Whooping Crane, at life size. Although the big birds are breathtaking in their impact, the paper size presented difficulties in designing the plates of smaller birds. Audubon's incorporation in his designs of plants to fill the space, often entwined about the birds in the most subtle way, more than overcame this problem.

Audubon had deliberately planned *The Birds of America* to contain plates only: Lizars had warned him that under English copyright law a copy of every book published in the country that contained text had to be donated to each of nine libraries, and he could ill afford the considerable additional expense involved. However, he realised that the book would be far more successful if accompanied by a good, detailed text. Although he had always kept copious notes in his journals, and dashed off letters of several thousand words to Lucy, the idea of sitting down and writing a book filled him with alarm, and his English was plainly not good enough. He also knew that with his lack of formal training in ornithology, he was ill placed to write with authority on the relationships and anatomy of the birds he was depicting, many of them new to science. Clearly he had to enlist the help of another more skilled in these areas.

In one of his many strokes of good luck, just when Audubon was despairing of finding a suitable ghostwriter, one of his acquaintances from Edinburgh, Professor James Wilson, recommended that he approach the highly regarded Scottish ornithologist William MacGillivray (1796-–1852) with his proposal. To his delight, MacGillivray, who was struggling to keep his wife and six children on the small income he received as a teacher, editor, translator and journalist, readily accepted.

The two men hit it off admirably, and MacGillivray became one of Audubon's staunchest supporters as well as greatly improving his text. Soon they were working almost round the clock in Edinburgh to meet Audubon's punishing self-imposed deadline, with Lucy as their copyist. The five volumes of *Ornithological Biography* appeared between 1831 and 1839, published in Edinburgh by Adam Black. MacGillivray's role was to correct Audubon's often poor English, supply or add to scientific facts and help sort out nomenclature. He did this skilfully, without too much watering down of Audubon's lively style. The accounts are a mix of descriptions of the bird and its behaviour in the field, technical details, tales of Audubon's adventurous travels and musings on a variety of subjects.

After his great work was complete, having made a total of four return journeys between America and Britain, Audubon returned to America for good in the autumn of 1839, taking with him Havell's aquatinted copper plates. Despite all his efforts aimed at securing subscribers for his expensive venture, only 151 committed themselves to buying every instalment of the work at the price of £182. 14s. ($1,000 in America) a set – far higher than the average annual income at the time. (Alexander

*This composite picture
showing different
plumages of one of the
most attractive members
of the auk family neatly
distils the development
of the bird, from the black
downy chick on the rock
through the breeding-
season adult swimming
on the sea in its summery
finery to the winter adult,
in which the pattern of
black and white are
reversed. Like most of his
contemporaries, and many
who followed after,
Audubon did not paint
flying birds convincingly:
the bird at the top looks
rather as if it has been
hurled across the sea.*

Wilson, by contrast, had managed to find over 450 subscribers, although the subscription to his nine volumes had been just $120.) As a result, the magnificent first edition of *The Birds of America* made little profit, with the costs of its production having ballooned to the huge figure for the time of over $100,000 (£18,000).

Although *The Birds of America* was not a successful commercial venture for Audubon, he had long ago realised that he could use its contents in a different way to produce a far more affordable work. Just as publishers often do to this day, he made use of his precious image bank of artwork by having a much smaller seven-volume edition produced, with text attached to the illustrations, in royal octavo size. At 10 x 6¼ inches, this was less than one-sixteenth the size of the great, unwieldy double elephant folio, and was sold at just $100 (£18.20). It also contained seventeen extra species which had been discovered since completion of the original edition.

Work on this compact edition started in America in 1839, with Audubon's son John reducing the great folio prints using a camera lucida. The printing was not done by engraving and aquatint, but by the new process of lithography. These lithographed plates were decidedly inferior to the subtle, gorgeously coloured original aquatints, but the printing method helped make the book affordable to far more subscribers. The last volume was completed and published in 1844. It was an instant success, and the first print run of 300 sold out in weeks. Just a year later, some 1,200 copies had been sold, and towards the end of the century it was available in ever-cheaper editions, making it easily affordable to middle-class families.

Although even this venture did not bring him great wealth, Audubon was now comfortably off, and he could at last afford to fulfil his promise to Lucy that he should one day keep them in comfort and provide for his extended family. Soon, eager to leave the city and return to the countryside he loved, Audubon bought 25 acres (10 hectares) of land at Carmansville (later called Washington Heights) on the Hudson River, at that time open country lying to the north of New York. The fine wooden house he had built there was named Minnie's Land in honour of the faithful and hard-working Lucy, the name Minnie being the Scottish version of his wife's name.

Audubon still worked with his customary manic energy, drawing for up

to fourteen hours a day, helped by his sons, for the three volumes of a book he had been planning on mammals, *The Viviparous Quadrupeds of America*, and in September 1842 he travelled to Canada and New England in search of subscribers to what was to prove his last major work. The two volumes of this work, containing 150 lithographed plates, were published in imperial folio size – 22 x 15 inches – in 1845 and 1846. His sons did much of the work, John painting more than half of the animals and Victor most of the backgrounds.

For one who had lived such an adventurous and active outdoor life, it is especially poignant that Audubon's health declined rapidly in his last years. By 1846, when he was just sixty-one, his eyesight had deteriorated so badly that he was unable to paint with any accuracy. His once handsome face was transformed as a result of his losing most of his teeth; but a more serious matter was that, unable to seek birds and paint, he was losing interest in life. Slowly but surely he became senile, and a stroke in 1847 did nothing to improve matters.

By 1849, the money that he had made was beginning to run out, and Audubon's son John chanced his luck by joining the California gold rush. Unfortunately his expedition proved a financial disaster, and the family once more experienced hard times. Two years later, on 27 January 1851, Audubon died, having worn himself out at the age of sixty-five. He died before the publication of the last of the three volumes of texts to his mammals book. Written by Reverend John Bachman, it appeared in 1854.

By 1869, Lucy's financial situation was so precarious that she was reduced to having to offer the remaining printing plates of her husband's great book for sale. After a Boston publisher had refused them, she sold them to a scrap metal dealer: copper fetched a good price at the time, and the plates weighed several tons in total. Luckily, a fourteen-year-old worker realised their value just after some had already been loaded into the smelter to produce bars, but only seventy-eight plates are thought to have survived. A few were donated to various American museums. Today only 120 complete copies of *The Birds of America* survive intact, about half of them in Europe and the rest in America. And if proof of their rarity and reputation were needed, a recent sale of a complete copy on 10 March 2000 at Christie's auction house, New York, was sold for the staggering figure of $8,802,500 (about £5.5 million), making it one of the most expensive books ever sold at auction. Even individual prints from cannibalised copies currently command prices upwards of $100,000 (£56,000).

William MacGillivray, the Scotsman who made such improvements to the text accompanying Audubon's masterwork, deserves far more credit than he received for his own work, both as an ornithologist and an artist. A man of robust opinions, and not afraid to air them, he did not suffer fools gladly, and in marked contrast to Audubon, who had a natural charm and a great talent for self-advertisement and flattery, he could often appear stiff and unyielding. His forthrightness could easily be mistaken by the sensitive for arrogance, his bluntness for rudeness; on the other hand he could be very kindly and helpful to those – such as Audubon – whom he respected as his equals. He was also revered by many of the students he taught.

Like Audubon, MacGillivray, who was born in Old Aberdeen in 1796, was illegitimate: his father was an army surgeon who was killed during the Peninsular War between Napoleon's occupying force and the British at the Battle of Corunna in north-west Spain in 1809. At the age of three, young William was sent to live with his uncle Roderick MacGillivray and his family at their farm on the windswept island of Harris in the Outer Hebrides. He studied at the parish school at Obbe, but also spent much time outdoors. He was skilled with a gun, and before he was eleven years old he had shot his first eagle, a Golden Eagle accused of attacking lambs. He later described the event with a characteristic blend of accurate observation and drama in his first book, *Descriptions of the Rapacious Birds of Great Britain*, published in 1836.

In 1807 the boy bade farewell to his uncle and moved to continue his studies at a boarding school in Aberdeen. After a year, the combination of good schooling and MacGillivray's natural intelligence enabled him to secure a place at Aberdeen University when he was only twelve years old. He regularly walked home across the very rough, mountainous country of the Highlands to Harris for the long vacations, a distance of some 180 miles (290km), including the boat crossing from the mainland.

After gaining a general MA at the university in 1814, MacGillivray went on to study medicine for almost five years but abandoned this course, deciding 'to devote the rest of [his] life to the study of natural history'.

On 7 September 1819 he set out on the greatest of all his walks. He wanted to see for himself the famous bird collections at the British

PLATE 89.
Channel-billed Toucan
Ramphastos vitellinus

Nicholas Aylward Vigors
1831. Oil on canvas.
340mm x 460mm
(13½in x 18in)

The Irishman who made this rather quaint, simple oil painting was a renowned zoologist, but unlike his friend Audubon not a professional bird painter. After interrupting his studies at Trinity College, Oxford, to serve in the Peninsular War (during which he was badly wounded), he became one of the founders and the first secretary of the Zoological Society of London, in 1826. Two years later he returned to Ireland to take over his family's estate and became a member of parliament for Carlow. He was one of the originators of the controversial and later discredited quinary system of bird classification, so avidly taken up by William Swanson (see page 157). It was Vigors who helped the young John Gould on his path to glory by appointing him as the Zoological Society's taxidermist.

PLATE 90.
Peregrine Falcon
Falco peregrinus
**William
MacGillivray**
1839. Watercolour.
750mm x 545mm
(29⅛in x 21⅛in)

*MacGillivray's bold
compositional style has
many similarities with
that of Audubon, whose
work he greatly admired.
The compliment was
amply returned, and is
fully justified. This is a
fine study of two Peregrine
Falcons. These are the
world's fastest birds when
they hurtle through the
air in a power dive, or
'stoop' at speeds that may
exceed 150 mph (250
kmh) on almost closed
wings like a living
arrowhead. They kill their
prey with one of their
powerful feet, striking
it with tremendous force,
the blow sometimes
knocking the victim's
head clean off.*

Museum and other institutions, and had decided to make the journey from Aberdeen to London entirely on foot. He chose a round-about route so that he could see as much of the country on the way as possible, and make observations of its natural history. In all, he tramped over 800 miles (1,288km). He completed the journey in six weeks, covering an average of just over 133 miles (214km) a week, or 19 miles (30km) a day. Eager to reach his destination, he walked 51 miles (82km) at one stretch and 58 on another. After only a week in the capital, which he characteristically filled with activity, sightseeing as well as examining collections in various museums, MacGillivray allowed himself the luxury of returning to Aberdeen by sea.

This adventure helped MacGillivray decide that he wanted to become a professional ornithologist. In his account of his marathon journey in his journal, he also reveals his uncompromising attitudes towards illustrating nature, observing that, 'If I were to be a painter by profession my aim would be to copy nature with the scrupulous, yea, even servile attention; instead of displaying a genius that scorned control by a masterly dash, which would produce the likeness of nothing on earth'.

Soon MacGillivray moved to Edinburgh, where he lived from late 1820 (after marrying his aunt's younger sister on Harris) to 1841. He secured a position at the university as assistant to Robert Jameson, Regius Professor of Natural History, but had to supplement his meagre pay by writing and editing. In 1830 he met Audubon and worked with him to improve and add to *Ornithological Biography*. The following year, while engaged in this absorbing task, he was appointed conservator of the museum of the Edinburgh College of Surgeons, where he carried out his duties with great skill and diligence.

His first task was to transfer the collections from three separate buildings to a new one, and this huge job he tackled with his customary zeal and attention to detail. He found many items in the collections in poor condition or badly displayed, so he had them cleaned and thenset about rearranging the whole lot. This laborious task included re-labelling some 4,000 specimens in his own neat handwriting. MacGillivray characteristically remarked that he had to do almost all the work himself 'as no benefit would be derived from the interference of others'. The man's output of work was astonishing: in a period of just ten years, between 1830 and 1840, he wrote thirteen of his own books as well as

PLATE 91.
Northern Raven
Corvus corax

**William
MacGillivray**
1832. Watercolour.
478mm x 683mm
(18¾in x 27in)

*Like the subject of this
picture, MacGillivray
loved the wild uplands.
Often the only sound he
would have heard on his
prodigious walks across
the Highlands would have
been the deep croaking of
this the largest of the crow
family, calling to its mate
as they soared high above
the crags. The Raven was
much persecuted by sheep
farmers and game
preservers in
MacGillivray's day, and he
has chosen to show this
bird atop the carcase of a
sheep. In fact, it sometimes
kills sickly lambs, but feeds
mainly on carrion.*

working on the synopsis and five volumes of the *Ornithological Biography*
with Audubon (the second volume alone containing over 300,000 words)
and a condensed version.

MacGillivray resigned from the museum in Edinburgh in 1841 to
become professor of natural history and lecturer in botany at Marischal
College back in Aberdeen. While attending to the many duties that went
with his new position, he also found time to produce a huge output of
writing – some of it, at least, driven by the necessity of providing for his
growing family (he had eleven children altogether, although some died in
infancy). However, despite his labours and his salary from curating and
teaching, he spent much of his life in relative poverty.

Essentially self-taught as a naturalist, MacGillivray despised those who
never ventured out of their museums to observe living nature for
themselves. He was a careful observer and scrupulously accurate
recorder of what he saw, from the 2,379 feathers he laboriously counted
in the beautiful little purse-shaped nest of a Long-tailed Tit, to the more
than 600 insects he obtained by dissecting the stomach of a dead Green
Woodpecker, or the effect of different weather conditions on the length

of the song of the Skylark. This accuracy is reflected in his beautiful watercolour drawings of birds, as well as mammals and fishes. Doubtless inspired by Audubon's masterpiece – and encouraged by the man himself – MacGillivray produced some of the finest natural-history watercolours of the period. As with Audubon's work, the birds were shown against a background of their characteristic habitat, and included equally carefully drawn and appropriate plants and other natural features.

The two men were great admirers of one another's work. Audubon was fulsome in his praise of his Scottish collaborator and friend, responding to his request to give him an honest opinion of some of his bird illustrations by averring, 'In short, I think them decidedly the best representations of birds I have ever seen'. He also named two American birds in his honour. For his part, MacGillivray honoured the American by naming one of his sons Audubon and dedicating *Descriptions of the Rapacious Birds of Great Britain* to him 'in admiration of his talents as an ornithologist and in gratitude for many acts of friendship'.

MacGillivray intended that the bird drawings should be used for plates to illustrate his *A History of British Birds*, but unfortunately this did not come about as he could not afford to have them engraved. This was just one of the reasons that the book was far from being a success in his own time. In addition, his touchiness and bristling attacks on those he believed inadequate, however eminent they might be, did not help endear him to the ornithological establishment. Predominantly English, it did not take kindly to this upstart Scotsman who challenged, confounded and threatened their neat compartmentalisation of their subject. For them, the only ornithologists worthy of the name were either museum researchers into bird classification, or those who studied bird anatomy; field naturalists were regarded as of no consequence, their work unscientific. Not only had MacGillivray effectively married his anatomical work with his studies of birds in the field, but his high academic standing as an anatomist meant that his new approach presented a clear threat to the status quo.

In autumn 1850, MacGillivray spent six strenuous weeks exploring the natural history and geology of Deeside in north-east Scotland, and worked up his usual detailed notes into a manuscript for publication. His fondness for exertion may have finally proved his downfall: after the Deeside expedition he became so ill that he was unable to return to the

university. He was, however, only fifty-four years old, and it is equally likely that the constant stress of a huge workload necessitated by his inadequate salary had much to do with his decline. In autumn 1851 he decided to move with his eldest daughter to Torquay, Devon, where he hoped that the warmer climate would be beneficial to his health. While he was there, his wife died suddenly in February 1852.

While he was mourning his loss, the fourth volume of his great bird book was finally published, with the fifth appearing at the end of July, shortly after he returned to Aberdeen. On 8 September, MacGillivray died at his house in the city. By this time, his great work was largely ignored; indeed it took more than sixty years after the last volume was published for ornithologists to appreciate just how good it was. His last book, *The Natural History of Deeside and Braemar*, was published posthumously when Queen Victoria, who had been a patron of his *A History of British Birds* and was especially fond of spending time at Balmoral Castle in the Deeside region, obtained the manuscript from his family. It was printed at her command for private circulation.

Author of the books that overshadowed MacGillivray's, William Yarrell (1784–1853) was one of the most successful of all producers of illustrated bird books in the first half of the nineteenth century. Like so many other Victorian naturalists, he was not a professional scientist, but he was one of the best of the amateurs despite coming late in life to the serious study of ornithology in his early forties.

Born in London, he spent a brief period as a young man working as a bank clerk, then joined his father in the newspaper wholesale business. He managed to spend much of his spare time fishing and shooting birds. He was soon elected a fellow of the Linnean Society in 1825, and was one of the founders of the Zoological Society of London.

With his love of the sport of angling, Yarrell became an authority on fishes as well as birds, and became well-known for his *A History of British Fishes* (1836). In the following year, he started to bring out a three-volume work with the same title as MacGillivray's, *History of British Birds* (1837–43). Unlike the Scotsman's thorough but unpopular series, Yarrell's work managed to be at the same time scholarly and popular, with the result that it became a best-seller. Yarrell's books benefited not only from his thorough and accurate texts, but a great part of their appeal was that they were illustrated with attractive and accurate wood

PLATE 92.
Grey Heron
Ardea cinerea
William MacGillivray
c.1835. Watercolour.
965mm x 735mm
(38in x 29in)

In his watercolours of birds, MacGillivray combined an artistic flair for creating a dramatic design with scientific accuracy in detail, and this spirited study of a Grey Heron is an excellent example. The alert posture of the bird dominating the foreground is echoed by the little figure of another individual on the island behind, keeping its distance, as befits a solitary hunter. This was one of the most noticeable of all big waterside birds in Britain, as it still is today: in Volume IV of his sadly often neglected masterwork, A History of British Birds, *MacGillivray wrote '… go where you will, in summer or in winter, to the shores of the sea or the far inland lake … you may here and there find a solitary heron.'*

PLATE 93.
Long-billed Sunbird
(juvenile, above, and male)
Cinnyris lotenius

Khuleelooddeen
c.1830–40. Gouache.
126mm x 122mm
(5in x 4¾in)

Here, the artist has chosen to illustrate the less dramatic plumages of a young bird and a non-breeding male of this elegant little species of sunbird, which is generally common in parts of southern India and Sri Lanka. An alternative common name, Loten's Sunbird, and also the specific name lotenius commemorate Gideon Loten, the Dutch Governor of what was then Ceylon (see also caption, page 51). Another common name, Maroon-breasted Sunbird, refers to the male's very different breeding plumage, in which its front half is glossy-greenish and purplish-black, separated on the breast by a maroon band from the dull, black underparts – at least when seen in sunlight; in dull light it looks all black.

engravings, many of them by John Thompson (1785–1866). A mark of the popularity of Yarrell's work was that his *A History of British Birds* was published in many different revised editions and became the standard work on the subject for over sixty years.

Another naturalist who unwittingly helped to consign MacGillivray's worthy British bird books to unjust near-oblivion was Sir William Jardine (1800–74). Like both MacGillivray and Yarrell, he was a fine ornithologist, but unlike them was born with the proverbial silver spoon in his mouth. At the age of twenty-one he inherited the family seat, Jardine Hall, about ten miles (16km) from the market town of Dumfries in south-west Scotland.

After studying medicine in Edinburgh and Paris, the handsome young squire returned to Jardine Hall where his privileged position enabled him to devote much of his time to the study of natural history, and to drawing birds. Between 1826 and 1843 his *Illustrations of Ornithology* were published jointly with Prideaux John Selby. Another landmark in his career was the publication between 1833 and 1843 of *The Naturalist's Library*, for which the plates were made by William Home Lizars in Edinburgh – Jardine's brother-in-law and the man who had failed Audubon as an engraver. The idea for this successful venture was a joint one between Jardine and Lizars. This ambitious series contained no less than forty pocket-sized volumes, of which fourteen dealt with birds. Each volume also contained, as a preface, a well-written biography of a famous naturalist, and the entire series ended with a tribute to the father of scientific classification, Linnaeus. The volume on parrots was the last major British ornithological work to contain illustrations engraved in metal. The text was well illustrated with delightful and accurate engraved portraits of the birds set against a background of their typical habitat. The difficulties of scale presented by the small plates were overcome by having only the birds hand coloured, while the foliage or landscapes were left uncoloured. Most of the drawings were the work of the Scottish illustrator James Hope Stewart (1789–1856), though some were done by Selby, Jardine and Lear.

What was so different about this series of books was that it was aimed squarely at the educated non-specialist and the growing number of amateur naturalists, with a relatively affordable price of six shillings for each compact volume. This was in complete contrast to the works of

N. cotenia
1. Young
2. Non-breeding

220

Audubon, Gould and other artists (including Selby and Jardine) who produced huge books that only the rich could afford to buy. In effect it was a forerunner of the wealth of relatively inexpensive popular natural-history titles available today.

Over the years, Jardine built up a large and important collection of about 9,000 specimens of birds from many parts of the world, containing some 6,000 species of birds. It included a good number of type specimens. Unfortunately, much of this valuable resource was lost to science after Jardine's heir, who did not understand its value, instructed the collection to be sold at auction in London in 1886, twelve years after Jardine's death.

Like his friend Jardine, Prideaux John Selby (1788–1867) was a wealthy landowner. He inherited a large estate in Northumberland, inland from the coastal town of Bamburgh. Here, at Twizell House, he led the life of a respected country squire, serving as a high sheriff and deputy lieutenant of the county of Northumberland, and often entertained the leading naturalists and wildlife artists of the day, providing them with a welcome break on their long journeys between Edinburgh, Newcastle or London to attend scientific meetings or visit museums.

Appearing in parts from 1821 to 1834, Selby's finest work, *Illustrations of British Ornithology*, contained a total of 218 life-sized illustrations of British birds, usually bound in two great folio-sized volumes – the first contains 89 plates of land birds, and the second 129 plates of waterbirds. All were done by Selby, apart from a few that were drawn by Jardine and some by Selby's brother-in-law Robert Mitford, a naval captain who later rose to the rank of admiral. Selby produced his own copper etchings of his drawings and had these completed in colour by William Home Lizars in Edinburgh, Scotland. Representing a brilliant combination of varied talents, the results are among the finest of all bird illustrations created with metal plates. Although drawn from mounted specimens, the birds are portrayed in life-like poses. The plates have a classical beauty all of their own, thanks largely to Selby's skilful drawing and etching techniques. These feature strong outlines and detailed and highly distinctive line work to create subtle plumage details.

The timing of Selby's work was unfortunate, however, for its appearance was largely overshadowed by Audubon's even larger *The Birds of America*. Selby and Jardine met Audubon and, deeply impressed by his

PLATE 94.
Beautiful Sunbird
(male)
Cinnyris pulchellus

William Swainson
c.1835. Watercolour.
164mm x 115mm
(6⅜in x 4½in)

The typically plain background against which this lovely little nectar-eating African bird is set shows off Swainson's skilled draughtsmanship to advantage. The crisp lines with the short strokes that suggest the feathers are more typical of engraving than of lithography with which the artist was experimenting. Much of the beauty of this and many other nineteenth-century bird illustrations is due to the often unsung skill of the hand colourists.

PLATE 95.
Blue-bellied Roller
Coracias cyanogaster
William Swainson
c.1835. Watercolour.
170mm x 125mm
(6¾in x 5in)

*Swainson's work was
ornithologically accurate
as well as being
aesthetically pleasing.
Although he worked
from skins, he generally
managed to invest his
subjects with life, as with
this west African member
of the roller family. This
species lives among mature
savannah woodland,
feeding on insects,
especially grasshoppers,
large beetles, winged ants
and termites. It catches
most of its food on the
ground, but takes some
in mid-air, often after a
rapid, aerobatic chase,
its manoeuvrability aided
by the long tail
streamers, like those
of swallows, terns and
some other birds.*

dramatic paintings, took drawing lessons from him, though eventually
they were to fall out with the American and make veiled criticisms of his
work in print. Because most copies were broken up and the plates sold
for framing, complete copies of Selby's major work are now very rare
and correspondingly valuable.

The man who took the vital first, tentative steps in introducing a new
method of printing illustrations of birds which came to supersede the
engravings and etchings favoured by Selby and others was William
Swainson (1789–1855). A typical nineteenth-century all-round naturalist
and artist, with a special interest in ornithology, he was born in
Liverpool, the son of a customs officer. He became a fine illustrator of
birds, but he also studied and made many drawings of seashells, fishes,
insects and plants.

From an early age, Swainson was fascinated by natural history, and
dreamed of travelling on voyages of discovery. After he had worked in his
home city as a junior customs clerk, his father helped him realise his
ambition at the age of eighteen by arranging for him to join the military
commissariat in the Mediterranean during the campaign against
Napoleon. After a short stay in Malta he was posted to Sicily for eight
years, and he also visited Italy and Greece. He used the opportunity to
build up a collection of animal and bird specimens.

He returned in 1815, and in the autumn of the following year, having
been elected as a fellow of the Linnaean Society, he joined the explorer
Henry Koster on his second expedition to Brazil. The party arrived at the
port of Pernambuco (now known as Recife) in late December 1816.
Shortly after, just as he was preparing to venture into the interior, a
revolution began against Portuguese rule that was to end five years later
in Brazilian independence. As a result, safe travel could not be
guaranteed, and Swainson was unable to penetrate as deep inland as he
had hoped in search of specimens. However, although he had been
deprived of the excitement of exploring uncharted territory, he was
pleased to learn that even the area immediately around Recife had not yet
been explored by naturalists. He was able to collect many new species of
birds, animals and plants; he augmented these with many more when it
became possible, in June 1817, to head inland towards the Rio San
Francisco, and work his way down to the coast in the Rio de Janeiro area.

Swainson returned two years later with an impressive number of

W.S.

219

13

specimens — including more than 750 skins of hummingbirds, toucans and other birds, as well as over 20,000 specimens of insects, 1,200 of plants and 120 of fish preserved in alcohol. He brought back further records in the form of drawings. Examining, describing and drawing this collection was to keep him busy for many years.

Soon after arriving in Liverpool in August 1818, Swainson penned a brief account of his travels in Brazil. This was published in the first volume of the *Edinburgh Philosophical Journal* which appeared in 1819, the brainchild in part of the Scottish philosopher Sir David Brewster. The co-founder and sole editor of this prestigious publication was the influential Professor Robert Jameson of Edinburgh University, who six years later was to become one of those whom Audubon hoped would help publicise *The Birds of America*. In 1820 Swainson was made a fellow of the Royal Society on the recommendation of Sir Joseph Banks.

Although he started out reproducing his drawings by means of the steel, copper and wood engravings that were fashionable at the time, Swainson paved the way for later illustrators by being the first major bird illustrator to adopt the new technique of lithography. The great advantages of this method were that the artist could draw directly onto the stone, rather than relying on an engraver to transfer the design to a metal plate, and that many prints could be 'pulled' from each stone without the loss of definition that occurred with engraving or etching. Swainson was encouraged to try out the new technique for himself by his friend William Elford Leach, assistant keeper of zoology at the British Museum. He then embarked on an intense three-year learning period, during which he described himself as living like a hermit.

Swainson was not at all sure of the new medium with which he had chosen to experiment. As a result, he continued to use straight lines as he was used to with engraving instead of fully exploiting the technique to create a smoother, less angular effect with a softer tone. Frustratingly, it often took him several attempts at drawing on the stone before his printers could obtain good enough impressions on paper. Also, because he worked from dead specimens rather than living birds, his drawings have a certain stiffness. Indeed much of the credit for the attractiveness of Swainson's lithographs lies in their gorgeous hand watercolouring, supervised by Gabriel Bayfield of Walworth, London, who also oversaw or himself painted plates for books by other eminent artists and

PLATE 96.
African Grey Parrot
Psittacus erithacus
Anonymous
Hardwicke/Campbell
Collection
1822. Watercolour.
435mm x 560mm
(19¼in x 22in)

Most of the birds in the Natural History Museum's Hardwicke collection are from India; Major-General Hardwicke, who served there with a regiment of the Bengal Army of the Honourable East India Company, was an accomplished amateur naturalist and one of the pioneers of Indian ornithology. Due to the primitive taxidermic techniques of the time, collectors such as Hardwicke had drawings made of their specimens rather than attempting preservation. This one is, uncharacteristically, of a well-known African species, which may have been taken to India as part of a menagerie, or perhaps as a pet.

naturalists, including Jardine, Gould and Darwin.

Swainson also painted the birds and wrote on their classification for the second volume of *Fauna Boreali-Americana*, a major contribution to the study of the Arctic animals of America north of the 48th parallel. It had the distinction of being the first work on natural history to be subsidised by the British government, who paid the considerable sum of £1,000 towards the production of the plates. This important work was published between 1829 and 1837, the bird volume appearing in 1831 with forty-nine of Swainson's hand-coloured lithographs. It was not until 1834, sixteen years after his visit as a young man, that Swainson finally published seventy-eight lithographs of the birds he had brought back from Brazil.

As well as the use of lithography, another valuable innovation associated with Swainson was his enthusiastic adoption of storing bird skins in drawers rather than as mounted specimens in glass cases. The latter method, still used at the start of the nineteenth century for almost all birds in museums and other collections, had two great disadvantages. The first was that nearly all the cases were sealed, so that the artist could view the specimen whose likeness he was trying to capture only through glass. The second was that the bulky cases took up a huge amount of space. This important advance is a good example of the outstanding practical abilities

of this gifted naturalist, which are all the more impressive because of his lack of scientific training.

Less useful for his acceptance by the scientific community was Swainson's adoption of the bizarre quinary system of classification, which he took up with a missionary zeal. The name 'quinary' refers to the division of birds into five circles representing the main natural groups, or orders, within each of which five more circles represented five tribes, and so on. This contrasts sharply to the linear or tree-like arrangement used in modern taxonomy. Where the circles touched one another, there were affinities between the groups, and analogies could also be drawn through mirror-image reflections on other circles. Swainson's version went even further, since he regarded the circles as three-dimensional.

In 1835 Swainson's wife died, leaving him with five children to care for; two years later he lost half the money his father had left him after the failure of two mines in Mexico in which he had invested. He was forced to take on more and more work to make up the shortfall and spent much of his time writing and editing popular books of others, such as the eleven natural-history volumes of Lardner's *Cabinet Cyclopedia* and some of Jardine's *The Naturalist's Library*.

Swainson was by this time shunned as a scientist because of his tenacious belief in the discredited quinary scheme, and peeved as a result of his failure to obtain the post of assistant keeper of zoology at the British Museum made vacant by the resignation of his friend William Leach owing to ill health. After marrying again, he sought a new life by emigrating to New Zealand. There he virtually gave up painting and writing about birds. He took up farming in difficult conditions, under frequent threat of attack by Maoris who resented the European settlers, and died in 1855.

PLATE 97.
Scarlet Ibis
Eudocimus ruber

John James Audubon

1837. Hand-coloured aquatint.
534mm x 740mm
(21in x 29¼in)

Audubon's inclusion in his book of these Scarlet Ibises (adult on left, immature on right) is interesting, as they are native not to North America, but to mangrove swamps, muddy estuaries and other wetland habitats in northern South America. Here they are a beautiful sight, especially when flying to and from their roosts in glowing red flocks. The few that have been sighted in Florida from 1954 have probably resulted from zoo escapes, while nine 'specimens' were reported from Texas (although this included some from bars and taverns!) Audubon's sight record of one from Louisiana is open to doubt.

PLATE 98.
Savannah Sparrow
Passerculus sandwichensis

**John James
Audubon**
1831. Hand-coloured
aquatint.
496mm x 313mm
(19½in x 12¼in)

*Like all American
sparrows, these birds are
members of the bunting
family rather than true
sparrows, like the
cosmopolitan House
Sparrow. The many races
of the Savannah Sparrow
are found throughout
North America, from
Alaska and northern
Canada, south as far as
Guatemala in South
America. For this plate,
Audubon characteristically
combined meticulous
detail of the birds with a
bold design, in which the
vertical lines of the grass
stems contrast with the
horizontal ones of
the branches.*

PLATE 99.
Barn Swallow
Hirundo rustica

**John James
Audubon**
1833. Hand-coloured
aquatint.
493mm x 310mm
(19½in x 12¼in)

*This is one of Audubon's
most pleasing designs, in
which he uses a plain
background to throw the
combined shape of this
affectionate pair of
nesting birds into sharp
relief. The gracefully
flowing outline, running
unbroken from the tip of
the outstretched wing of
the left-hand bird to the
end of the tail streamers
of its sitting mate,
complements the curves of
the nest cup, and cleverly
recalls the swooping flight
of the birds themselves.*

Barn Swallow
HIRUNDO AMERICANA.
Male, 1 Female 2

Rough-legged Falcon.
BUTEO LAGOPUS.

PLATE 100.
Rough-legged Hawk
Buteo lagopus

John James Audubon

1838. Hand-coloured aquatint.
725mm x 645mm
(28⅝in x 25⅜in)

Characteristically, Audubon has opened the tails and a wing of these two birds to show their distinctive plumage. Known as the Rough-legged Buzzard in Britain, this long-winged bird breeds in the tundra and open uplands of northern Europe, Asia and North America.

PLATE 101.
Hairy Woodpecker & Three-toed Woodpecker
Picoides villosus & Picoides tridactylus

John James Audubon

1838. Hand-coloured aquatint.
770mm x 575mm
(30¼in x 22⅝in)

Although Audubon thought he had illustrated six different species of woodpecker in this busy scene, there are in fact only two species in this unnaturally crowded tree, including adults of both sexes and immature birds.

100.

PL. 101.

PLATE 102.

Trumpeter Swan
Cygnus buccinator

John James Audubon

1838. Hand-coloured aquatint.
656mm x 970mm
(25¼in x 38¼in)

Audubon painted two pictures of this species, the largest of the world's swans, which has a wingspan of over 8 feet (2.5m). One was of a young bird, while this one is based partly on the male he kept in captivity for over two years in Henderson, Kentucky. In his day, this magnificent bird was already being killed in great numbers for its meat, skin and feathers, and its eggs plundered. By 1932 only sixty-nine were known to survive, but since then, with protection, the population has increased to about 16,000 birds.

PL. 103.

PLATE 103.

Gull-billed Tern
Sterna nilotica

John James Audubon

1838. Hand-coloured aquatint.
495mm x 402mm
(19½in x 15½in)

One of several species of the elegant, fork-tailed terns that Audubon painted, this species, which has a stouter, more gull-like bill than most, flies mainly over salt marshes and lagoons rather than over the open sea, and catches mainly insects rather than fish, as accurately shown in this plate. Like the Trumpeter Swan, it suffered badly from egg-collecting and being hunted for its feathers.

PL. 102.

PLATE 104.

Magnificent Frigatebird
Fregata magnificens

John James Audubon
1835. Hand-coloured
aquatint.
970mm x 656mm
(38¼in x 25¼in)

*This unusual composition,
with the aggressively open,
hooked bill, almost bursts
out of the confines of the
page, celebrating a seabird
that is renowned for its
aerial mastery and
piratical habits. It spends
much of its life in the air,
neatly bending its long
bill down to pluck fish
from the surface without
wetting its feathers, which
are not waterproof. Sailing
majestically through the
air with scarcely a
wingbeat, it also steals
food from other seabirds,
seizing a wing or tail to
force the victims to
disgorge their catches.
The detail of the feet
emphasises their weak,
scarcely webbed structure,
useless for swimming.*

PL. 105.

PLATE 105.

American Swallow-
tailed Kite
Elanoides forficatus

**John James
Audubon**
1829. Hand-coloured
aquatint.
524mm x 696mm
(20¾in x 27⅜in)

*One of the birds Audubon
most wanted to find on
his wanderings across
eastern America was this
supremely elegant and
aerobatic bird of prey.
This stunning design,
shows how this kite can
kill and eat a snake on
the wing.*

166

PLATE 106.
Leach's Storm-Petrel
Oceanodroma leucorhoa

John James Audubon
1835. Hand-coloured
aquatint.
313mm x 492mm
(12¼in x 19¾in)

*As with many of
Audubon's other designs,
this dramatic image of a
couple of these little
seabirds riding the wind
just inches above a gale-
lashed sea, uses curves and
angles to superb effect —
and in this case, too, a
symmetry between the two
birds as they face one
another. Only the size of a
Starling and half its
weight, Leach's Storm-
Petrels, like other members
of their family, spend most
of their lives far out to
sea. They fly strongly with
abrupt erratic turns,
bounds and changes of
speed, sometimes pattering
across the wave-tops with
their feet, and feed on
plankton and floating
scraps of offal. They breed
on a few remote islands
in the North Atlantic,
visiting their nest
burrows only at night
to avoid predators.*

PLATE 107.
Northern Gannet
(immature)
Morus bassanus

**William
MacGillivray**
1831. Watercolour.
810mm x 550mm
(32in x 21¼in)

*Here, MacGillivray has
chosen to illustrate an
immature Gannet,
probably a bird in its
third year. These great
dagger-billed seabirds take
over four years to attain
full adult plumage,
starting off entirely grey-
brown with fine white
speckles and gradually
acquiring more and
more white.*

PLATE 108.
Common Kestrel *(male
and young)*
Falco tinnunculus

**William
MacGillivray**
1835. Watercolour.
760mm x 545mm
(30in x 21½in)

*Perched dramatically on
a cliff edge, a male of this
common bird of prey
stands guard over his
family of three young.*

PL. 108.

PLATE 109.
Egyptian Goose
Alopochen aegyptiacus

**William
MacGillivray**
c.1831–41. Watercolour.
745mm x 550mm
(29⅛in x 21⅝in)

*When MacGillivray
painted this picture, the
Egyptian Goose, native to
Africa, had already begun
to escape from collections
of unpinioned birds
brought to Britain to join
the assorted wildfowl and
other birds kept in the
parks of grand houses.
Such escapes were
regarded with interest by
naturalists and others at
the time, and still provoke
comment today when seen
by those who are not
familiar with the species.
Looking like an odd cross
between a duck and a
goose they are classified
in a sub-group of their
own, the shelduck
and shelgeese.*

PL. 109.

PLATE 110.
Eagle Owl
Bubo bubo

**William
MacGillivray**
c.1831–41. Watercolour.
983mm x 668mm
(38¾in x 26¼in)

*Here, the artist has made
a refreshing change from
the usual depiction owls
from the front. Although
there are many old records
and fossil remains of this
imposing bird, among the
largest of the world's owls,
it is no longer native to
Britain. However, escapes
from captivity have been
recorded on numerous
occasions, and a few pairs
have bred, one pair in
northern England for
several years running.*

PL. 110.

PLATE 111.

Black Grouse *(male)*
Tetrao tetrix

**William
MacGillivray**
1836. Watercolour.
755mm x 546mm
(29⅛in x 21½in)

*The handsome Blackcock
(the male of the species)
standing proudly atop the
rock in this painting was
drawn from 'an individual
procured by Mr. Carfrae.
Edinburgh, April, 1836'.*

PLATE 112.

Osprey
Pandion haliaetus

**William
MacGillivray**
c.1831–41. Watercolour.
563mm x 686mm
(22¼in x 27in)

*MacGillivray left the fish
prey of this dramatic
portrait of an Osprey
unfinished, but the rest of
the painting shows the
typical wealth of lifelike
detail that is a hallmark
of this formidable Scottish
naturalist's work.*

PLATE 113.
Lesser Black-backed
Gull
Larus fuscus

**William
MacGillivray**
1836. Watercolour.
764mm x 550mm
(30in x 21¼in)

*This is one of the seabirds
that MacGillivray would
have seen regularly in
Scotland, at least during
the times he spent from
childhood with his uncle
on the island of Harris
in the Outer Hebrides.
Indeed, the west coast of
Scotland was the breeding
stronghold of this gull
during the nineteenth
century. By contrast, it
would have been scarce
or absent from Edinburgh
and Aberdeen, where
the artist spent most of
his adult life, as it was
heavily persecuted
by shepherds
and gamekeepers.*

PL. 113.

PLATE 114.
Great Auk
Pinguinus impennis

**William
MacGillivray**
1839. Watercolour.
770mm x 557mm
(30¼in x 23in)

*MacGillivray painted this
picture only five years*

*before the last two living
Great Auks were seen, on
the island of Elday, off
the southwestcoast of
Iceland in 1844, before
being strangled by
fishermen. He never saw
the species alive, but did
study two preserved
specimens, one of which
belonged to Audubon.*

Black Woodpecker
(female, left, males)
Dryocopus martius

**William
MacGillivray**
1839. Watercolour.
760mm x 542mm
(30in x 21¼in)

*Although MacGillivray
intended this painting of
a group of Europe's largest
woodpeckers to be used for
his* A History of British
Birds, *the species has in
fact never been recorded
with certainty in the
British Isles. This is
surprising, since this crow-
sized bird breeds as near
as northern France.
MacGillivray recorded
that he bought two
specimens, allegedly shot
near Nottingham —
however, the location,
makes it unlikely that
they were obtained in
Britain as claimed.*

PLATE 116.
Hooded Crow
Corvus cornix

**William
MacGillivray**
c.1831–41. Watercolour.
755mm x 550mm
(29¾in x 21⅝in)

*This study of two Hooded
Crows shows the crow
species that would have
been familiar to
MacGillivray in the far
north-east of Scotland.
Further east and south,
it is replaced by the
all-black Carrion Crow.
The two interbreed along
a narrow zone of
hybridisation, and were
until recently regarded
as distinctive races of
the same species.
However, subsequent
research indicated that
the two merit separate
species status.*

PL. 116.

花
星
石

PLATES 117 & 118.

Domestic Pigeon
Columba livia

Anonymous

c.1850. Watercolour.
263mm x 360mm
(10¼in x 14¼in)

*In Japan, as in many other
parts of the world, careful
selection of different stock
and cross-breeding
produced a great variety
of breeds of domestic
pigeon. The paintings of
these birds are just two of
the hundreds of pigeons
illustrated in five volumes
bought from an unknown
source by the Natural
History Museum. The
quality of work suggests
that they were probably
commissioned for the
library of a prominent
Japanese nobleman.*

PL.

PLATE 119.
Sarus Crane, eggs
Grus antigone

Anonymous
Jardine Collection
c.1830–40. Gouache.
191mm x 162mm
(7½in x 6⅜in)

PLATE 120
Egg & chick of Painted
Snipe
Rostratula benghalensis

Anonymous
Jardine Collection
c.1830–40. Gouache.
105mm x 143mm
(4⅛in x 5⅝in)

Grus antigone

*Unimpregnated eggs laid
by a tame bird.*

PL. 119.

PL. 120.

Rhynchea bengalensis.
S. Bengal.

1. Cuculus varius. Taken from the oviduct of a bird in immature plumage! A closely resembles the egg of Oxylophus melanoleucos.

2. Rhynchea bengalensis. Laid in confinement by a bird fresh captured.

PL. 121.

PLATE 121
Eggs of Common
Hawk Cuckoo *(left)* &
Painted Snipe *(right)*
*Cuculus varius & Rostratula
benghalensis*

Anonymous
Jardine Collection
c.1830–40. Gouache.
94mm x 145mm
(3¾in x 5¾in)

*Eggs have been the
subjects of relatively few
ornithological artists.
Painting the subtly glossy
or chalky surfaces, in
many cases with the
ground colour overlaid
with intricate patterns of
spots, blotches or scribbles,
or mixtures of all these,
requires a particular kind
of patience. Many of the
the artworks in these
pages from a scrapbook
that belonged to Jardine
were obtained from the
nineeenth-century
zoologist Edward
Blyth (1810–60), one
of the greatest names
in the history of
Indian ornithology.*

PLATE 123.
Great Blue Kingfisher
Alcedo hercules

Anonymous
Jardine Collection
c.1830–40. Gouache.
179mm x 175mm
(7in x 7in)

This is the largest of the Alcedo kingfishers, larger by a third than the common Eurasian Kingfisher shown opposite. Its alternative common name, Blyth's Kingfisher, commemorates the renowned English ornithologist Edward Blyth, curator of the Asiatic Society of Bengal's museum in Calcutta from 1841–62. He augmented its bird collections to make it the world's biggest outside of Europe and North America.

PLATE 122.
Eurasian Kingfisher (upper) & Blue-eared Kingfisher *(lower)*
Alcedo atthis & Alcedo meninting

Anonymous
Jardine Collection
c.1830–40. Gouache.
390mm x 320mm
(15⅓in x 12⅓in)

A study from the Jardine collection of two species of kingfisher collected in India. The race of the Eurasian Kingfisher shown, bengalensis, is common in the north of the Indian subcontinent. The Blue-eared Kingfisher's odd specific name, meninting, comes from the Javanese Malay name for this species.

PL.

Alcedo grandis, Blyth
from Darjeeling —
J. Gd. XIV, 190

Common Crossbill
(male)
Loxia curvirostra

James Hope Stewart
c.1825–35. Gouache.
170mm x 150mm
(6¾in x 6in)

*This is a fine illustration
shows one of the most
unusual of the European
birds. Far from being a
liability, the oddly shaped
crossed bill enables
crossbills to exploit the
rich crops of conifer seeds,
by inserting the bill into a
cone and twisting out the
seeds within.*

Bat Hawk
Macheiramphus alcinus

Joseph Wolf
c.1860. Hand-coloured
lithograph.
303mm x 245mm
(12in x 9¾in)

*This uncommon bird of
Africa, south-east Asia
and New Guinea is
unusual among birds of
prey in that it hunts at
dusk and even into the
night. It feeds mainly on
small bats, following every
twist and turn of its prey
until it can seize them in
its sharp talons.*

Stewart del. — Cross Bill —

nat. size.

Sibia gracilis, (H. Cibbare).

Khasya hills.

PLATE 126.
Grey Sibia
Heterophasia gracilis

Khuleelooddeen
c.1830–40. Gouache.
137mm x 211mm
(5⅜in x 8¼in)

The painter of this mountain-forest-dwelling babbler was among the few native Asian artists employed by colonists to produce illustrations of animals and plants whose name is known today. His signature, appears on the paintings he made for Edward Blyth, curator of the Asiatic Society of Bengal's museum in Calcutta. Blyth sent over a hundred of the artist's drawings to Sir William Jardine in Scotland.

PLATE 127.

Himalayan Treecreeper
Certhia himalayana

Khuleelooddeen
c.1830–40. Gouache.
138mm x 118mm
(5⅜in x 4⅝in)

*This is the Himalayan
representative of a small
Old World family of very
similar species of little
birds that search for
insects on tree bark by
shuffling with rapid,
mouse-like spurts in a
spiral up a trunk, flying
down to the next tree and
starting all over again.*

PLATE 128.

Nest and eggs of Dark-collared Cuckoo-Shrike
Coracina melaschistos

Khuleelooddeen
c.1830–40. Gouache.
131mm x 200mm
(5¼in x 7⅞in)

The scientific name that can be seen by the nest in the handwritten notes on this illustration is Campephaga *silens, which is an old name for this Himalayan bird. The name label accompanying the eggs lists a more modern name,* melaschistos, *although the bird is now placed in a different genus.*

Leucocirca fuscoventris (?)

PLATE 129.
Nest and eggs of
White-throated Fantail
Rhipidura albicollis

Khuleelooddeen
c.1830–40. Gouache.
220mm x 137mm
(8¾in x 5½in)

*This is another example
of the impressive work of
the native Indian artist
Khuleelooddeen in which
both the generic and
specific names of the bird
have changed completely,
the label describing it as
Leucocirca fuscoventris. The
beautifully fashioned
grass nest, bound tightly
with cobwebs, is typical of
the fantails, with its
tapering base from which
hang trailing strips of
material.*

PLATE 130.
Golden Oriole *(male)*
Oriolus oriolus

**James Hope
Stewart**
c.1825–35. Watercolour.
171mm x 106mm
(6¾in x 4¼in)

*A beautiful picture of a
beautiful bird, this is also
an accurate portrayal of
the strikingly plumaged
though elusive male
Golden Oriole, in a
typical setting high in a
tree. Here, in life, it blends
in surprisingly well with
the sun-dappled foliage.
As well as painting many
illustrations such as this
one for Sir William
Jardine, for which he was
paid one guinea each,
Stewart also earned extra
money by putting the
finishing touches to
the watercolours of
other artists and filling
in backgrounds.*

PLATE 131.
Goldfinch
Carduelis carduelis

**James Hope
Stewart**
c.1825–35. Watercolour.
172mm x 106mm
(6¾in x 4¼in)

*One of the most attractive
members of the finch
family, the multicoloured
Eurasian Goldfinch has
a finer bill than many
of its relatives. Its agile
tweezer-like tips are
perfectly suited for
tweaking out the fine
downy seeds from the
fruiting heads of thistles,
a natural adaptation
reflected in James
Stewart's portrait.*

PL. 130.

PLATE 132.
Little Egret
Egretta garzetta

James Hope Stewart
c.1825–35. Watercolour.
108mm x 171mm
(4¼in x 6¾in)

*One of the most graceful
members of the heron
family, the Little Egret is
among the most
widespread of all Old-
World birds, its range
spanning four continents
from Europe to Australia.
Moreover, it is currently
undergoing a northward
expansion at the edge of
its European range, now
breeding in small but
increasing numbers in
Britain and Ireland. The
rather exaggerated, almost
Audubonesque, pose of
Stewart's painting shows
off the subject, and in
particular its decorative,
wispy breeding plumes, to
best advantage against the
dark background of the
river bank. These delicate
feathers nearly proved its
downfall, as with its close
relatives in North
America, it was
slaughtered in huge
numbers during the
nineteenth century for
the millinery trade.*

PLATE 133.
Short-toed Eagle
Circaetus gallicus

Anonymous
Lord Ashton Collection
c.1840. Watercolour.
642mm x 490mm
(25¼in x 19¼in)

*This is a member of a
group of birds of prey
known as the snake-eagles
that live up to their name
by feeding mainly on
snakes. Its legs and feet
bear thick, rough scales
that protect their owner
against the bites of
venomous snakes.*

PLATE 134.
Dusky Eagle Owl
Bubo coromandus

Anonymous
Lord Ashton Collection
c.1840. Watercolour.
560mm x 433mm
(22in x 17in)

*This scarce owl is found
from Pakistan and India
east to Thailand and
perhaps China. It prefers
to live among trees in
waterside forests, dense
groves or along roadsides,
where it hunts crows,
waterbirds and other prey,
including mammals, frogs
and fish.*

PL. 135.

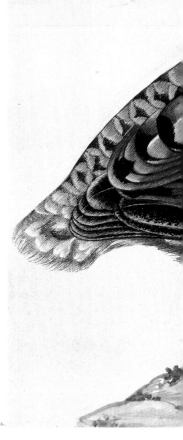

PLATE 135.
Kalij Pheasant *(male)*
Lophura leucomelana

**Lady Mary
Bentinck**
c.1833. Watercolour.
210mm x 307mm
(8¼in x 12in)

*Lady Bentinck was
married in 1803 to an
army officer, who fourteen
years later became
governor general of India.
While in India, she made
paintings of a collection
of fifty-seven birds from
the Himalayas, which were
never engraved or printed,
but were acquired by the
Natural History Museum.
Her use of colour is
skilful, and the birds'
feathers painted with
great detail – as with this
male Kalij Pheasant – but
her subjects appear
wooden and unlifelike.*

PLATE 136.
Common Hill-
Partridge *(male)*
Arborophila torqueola

**Lady Mary
Bentinck**
c.1833. Watercolour.
127mm x 207mm
(5in x 8¼in)

*This small, plump game
bird is an inhabitant of
dense undergrowth in the
evergreen jungle clothing
the mountains of northern
and eastern India and
southern China. Here it
lives in pairs or small
flocks, mainly at altitudes
of 5–9,000 feet
(1,500–2,700m). The
distinctive throat pattern
of the male shown in Lady
Bentinck's painting is
much less prominent in
the female.*

PL. 136.

PL. 137.

PLATE 138.
Wallcreeper
Tichodroma muraria

**Lady Mary
Bentinck**
c.1833. Watercolour.
113mm x 120mm
(4⅜in x 4¾in)

*As with all Lady
Bentinck's illustrations in
the Natural History
Museum's collection, this
one shows the bird
perched rather woodenly
on a rocky mound, in the
stereotyped manner
typical of the bird
illustrations of a much
earlier age. Subtly
beautiful and hard to
find, the Wallcreeper is
one of the most sought-
after of all Old-World
birds. A denizen of high
mountains, from Spain to
the Himalayas, it is at
home on the sheerest
cliffs, using its wings to
help it climb.*

PLATE 137.
Indian Roller
Coracias benghalensis

**Lady Mary
Bentinck**
c.1833. Watercolour.
175mm x 261mm
(7in x 10¼in)

*The name 'roller' refers to
the habit of this and other
roller species of rolling
from side to side in mid-
air during its spectacular
courtship flight, when it
also performs steep dives,
somersaults and loop-
the-loops, to the
accompaniment of raucous
screams, as the dark and
light blue panels (not
visible in this painting)
on its wings flash in
the sun.*

PLATE 139.
Temminck's Tragopan
(male)
Tragopan temminckii

Anonymous
Reeves Collection,
c.1822–29.
Watercolour with
bodycolour.
420mm x 495mm
(16½in x 19½in)

*The Asian high-mountain
pheasants, called
tragopans, are among the
world's most charismatic
birds, sought out with
fanatical zeal by
ornithologists. Temminck's
Tragopan occurs in the
eastern Himalayas and
east to central China. The
name 'tragopan' can be
loosely translated as
'horned wood-god'. The
male's horns are the
erectile fleshy blue
projections of bare skin
that normally lie flat
within the plumage. They
are erected dramatically
during the male's
courtship display, along
with a similarly concealed
area of blue and red skin
that expands down the
breast into a huge flap.*

PLATE 140.
Rock Eagle-Owl
Bubo bengalensis

Anonymous
Reeves Collection,
c.1822–29.
Watercolour with
bodycolour.
494mm x 387mm
(19½in x 15¼in)

*The fine brushwork of the
artist who painted this
large owl for Reeves does
justice to the subtle
beauty and imposing
appearance of a splendid
bird. This owl can be
distinguished from the
superficially similar
Brown Fish-Owl, which
shares its range, by its
fully feathered feet (see
page 111).*

PLATE 141.
Rufous Treepie
Dendrocitta vagabunda

Anonymous
Hardwicke/Campbell
collection
1822. Watercolour.
251mm x 382mm
(10in x 15in)

This is one of the most familiar of all Indian birds, often seen feeding and nesting in trees in city parks, large gardens and villages as well as in wilder areas. Its loud, harsh calls and penetrating, more flute-like, three-note 'song' are one of the quintessential sounds of the Indian countryside. The first syllable of the name 'treepie' refers to the tree-dwelling habits of this bird and its close relatives; the second is pronounced 'pye' rather than 'pee', as with the other long-tailed members of the crow family, the magpies.

PL. 142.

PLATE 143.
Blue Magpie
Urocissa erythrorhyncha

Anonymous
Reeves Collection
c.1822–29. Watercolour.
380mm x 492mm
(15in x 19⅜in)

A close relative of the Rufous Treepie illustrated on the previous two pages, this is a bird of evergreen forests, clearings and small patches of cultivation in China, as well as in other parts of southern Asia. Its lovely colouration and graceful shape, with the long tail echoing the curve of the branch, are incorporated in the overall design with the sensitivity typical of Chinese art.

PLATE 142.
Hanging-Parrots
Loriculus sp.

Anonymous
Reeves collection
c.1822–29. Watercolour.
414mm x 496mm
(16¼in x 19½in)

These charming little sparrow-sized parrots belong to a small group of thirteen species found across southern Asia, from India to southern China and Indonesia, with one species occurring in New Guinea and another on the Bismarck Archipelago. They take their common name (and an alternative one of bat parrots) from their curious habit of resting, preening and roosting by hanging upside down by one or both feet from a leafy branch.

Glandarius Germanicus, Brehon. Mas.

Pl. 144.

PLATE 144.
Eurasian Jay
Garrulus glandarius

**Christian Ludwig
Landbeck**
c.1833–4. Watercolour.
475mm x 294mm
(18¾in x 11½in)

*Christian Landbeck
(1807–90) was a
German ornithologist,
hunter and bird collector
who was also an
accomplished artist. This
rather old-fashioned,
formal portrait of a
Eurasian Jay is typical of
the work he produced in
his native Bavaria, the
bird aptly shown on a
fruiting oak tree with an
acorn in its beak. The old
scientific name beneath in
its flourishing copperplate
reflects the time when
many ornithologists
elevated local populations
of species to the ranks
of subspecies or, as here,
full species.*

PLATES 145 & 146.
Red Avadavat *(male)*
Amandava amandava

Frederick Ditmas
c.1840. Watercolour.
230mm x 186mm
(9in x 7¼in)

*These simple paintings of
one of India's most
familiar and widespread
birds are by a major in the
English army, who served
in the Royal (Madras)
Engineers. They show a
male Red Avadavat (or
Red Munia) in its
dramatic red breeding
colours (Plate 145) and
the very different non-
breeding plumage (Plate
146). One of the large
family of estrildid finches
(waxbills), this attractive
little bird is native to
other parts of south Asia
as far east as south-west
China, and has been
introduced to various
parts of the world, from
Egypt, Israel, Singapore
and Japan to Puerto Rico,
as well as being a popular
cage bird.*

PL. 145.

PL. 146.

PLATE 147.
Small Minivet *(male)*
Pericrocotus cinnamomeus

Frederick Ditmas
c.1840. Watercolour.
230mm x 186mm
(9in x 7¼in)

*As well as birds, Ditmas
painted watercolours of
reptiles and insects. This
one is recognisable as one
of the common Indian
birds that Ditmas would
have encountered while on
army service in India.*

PLATE 148.
Drongo
Dicurus sp.

Frederick Ditmas
c.1840. Watercolour.
230mm x 186mm
(9in x 7¼in)

*In this case, the bird in
Ditmas's painting,
originally titled 'Green
Bird', cannot be reliably
identified. It is probably a
species of drongo
(*Dicrurus sp.*), but could
possibly be one of the
glossy starlings (*Aplonis
sp.*). The artist has
attempted to show a
glossy, iridescent plumage
which is a characteristic of
both groups, but other
anomalies make a definite
identification impossible.*

Green Bird

Chapter Three { 1850—1890

PLATE 149.
Scarlet Macaw
Ara macao

Edward Lear
1832. Hand-coloured
lithograph.
554mm x 365mm
(21⅔in x 14⅖in)

*Lear's brilliant collection
of autolithographed plates
for his Illustrations of the
Family of Psittacidae, or
Parrots, which he produced
with a feverish intensity
between the age of
eighteen and twenty, were
an astonishing
achievement for so young
an artist. This splendid
and imposing macaw is a
typical example, painted,
as with many of his bird
portraits, from life. The
mastery of design, the skill
of the lithography, and the
individual character he
gave to his bird subjects
without sacrificing
scientific accuracy set a
very high standard for the
works of others during
the second half of the
nineteenth century.*

ONE OF THE MOST IMPORTANT OF ALL nineteenth-century natural-history artists working with the new printing technique of lithography was Edward Lear (1812–88). He is famous today for his limericks and other comic verse and nonsense drawings, but he was also one of the finest of all illustrators of birds.

Lear was born in 1812 in Highgate, London, then just a village to the north of the city, the last but one of a huge family of twenty-one children. He was a sickly, nervous child, and for the whole of his life was frequently plagued by ill health, including asthma, bronchitis and attacks of epilepsy that were usually followed by bouts of depression. Extremely short-sighted, he wore spectacles from childhood.

The Lears were originally quite wealthy, but when Edward was a young child his stockbroker father, Jeremiah, lost much of his money, and the family were forced to disperse. His mother, Ann, presumably weary of caring for so many offspring, left Lear in the care of one of his older sisters, also named Ann, who was twenty-two years his senior. A small annuity from her grandmother enabled her to move into lodgings of her own, in Upper North Street, off Gray's Inn Road, and she took Edward with her.

Lear was almost entirely self-educated. He was encouraged to study poetry, the classics and the Bible by Ann and another older sister, Sarah. Both keen artists, they also encouraged him to draw and paint from an early age. At first he gained much useful experience copying hundreds of illustrations of birds and other animals from encyclopaedias. By his mid-teens he brought in modest amounts of money as a jobbing artist from whatever work he could find – hack sketches, painting fans and screens, colouring prints and making disease drawings for doctors and hospitals.

From the age of eleven, Lear often left London to stay with Sarah, who had married and moved near to Arundel, in Sussex. It was on these visits that he was fortunate in being befriended by members of the local gentry who were patrons of the famous painter J. M. W. Turner. These influential art lovers encouraged Lear in his budding interest in becoming a professional artist. As well as giving him the opportunity of extending his

MACROCERCUS ARACANGA.

Red and Yellow Macaw.

appreciation of fine art, they helped serve as an introduction to upper-class society and the kind of people who supported artists both with encouragement and money. The Fawkes family were particularly kind and helpful; Walter Fawkes had an interest in natural history and was a friend of Prideaux John Selby. His daughter, Mrs Wentworth, was probably the person who recommended young Edward to the Zoological Society of London, and to Selby.

From about 1828 onwards, Lear realised his dream of becoming a professional artist, illustrating two volumes of Selby and Jardine's *Illustrations of Ornithology*. In 1830 he embarked on his first major work, a book of plates entitled *Illustrations of the Family of Psittacidae, or Parrots* (1830–32). Lear was the first British bird artist to select the imperial folio (22 x 15 inches) to portray the birds at life size – or nearly so – and his work had a huge influence on subsequent work by bird artists, although Audubon had already published the first volume of his great *Birds of America*, with illustrations reproduced at the even larger double elephant folio size, and Lear could not illustrate the largest parrots, such as the macaws, at life size.

Lear's choice of the parrot family for his first ambitious foray into the world of art publishing was a wise one. He clearly loved these birds, and their exotic nature, colourful plumage and intelligence made them popular with the public, including the wealthy subscribers he needed to attract in order to fund the considerable cost of the book's production. Tame parrots, with their longevity and their ability to form close bonds with their owners and mimic human speech, had long been prized as fashionable pets. As a stream of explorers and collectors constantly returned from the tropics with new species, they provided a great attraction to the public when they were put on display – visiting the parrot house at London Zoo was one of the most popular outings of the day.

Lear was also among the very first bird artists to paint primarily from the living bird whenever possible, and it shows in the liveliness of his representations. Much of his time was spent surrounded by screeching, squawking parrots in the aviaries of London Zoo. A rapid worker, he sketched swiftly in pencil with fluent, expressive lines as the object of his study moved about into different postures or flapped its wings. He was brilliantly gifted at conveying the personality of an individual bird, and had the rare ability of being able to combine scrupulous scientific accuracy with an innate feeling for the bird's character. As he watched, he made careful notes in the margins about the exact colours of different parts of the bird's plumage. Then, with equal skill, he translated these confident sketches into paintings, first tracing the pencilled outlines and inking them in, then applying washes of watercolour. Usually he coloured only the bird itself, though sometimes parts of the perch nearest the bird were picked out in muted colour.

Lear's decision to use lithography to translate his works into printed pictures was doubtless partly due to the fact that he could not afford the expense of paying a skilled craftsman to reproduce them by engraving or etching, difficult techniques in which he had no training. In 1831, he and Ann had moved from Upper North Street to rooms in Albany Street, a location much more convenient for his visits to the zoo, just a short walk across Regents Park. He could hardly move for the piles of prints that were accumulating. Lear transferred his drawings onto the lithographic stones himself. He then carried these heavy objects, together with trial watercolour studies bearing copious notes, to the workshop of the printer Charles Hullmandel in Great Marlborough Street over a mile (1.6km) away.

Lear had made a wise choice, for Hullmandel was England's first really successful lithographer; he made prints for most of the finest illustrated bird books published during the first half of the nineteenth century. In the hands of skilled workers like him, lithography had improved greatly since Swainson's early attempts. Hullmandel or one of his assistants would make trial prints to which Lear – who had high standards – could then make any adjustments necessary to improve them. Sometimes he would ask for several 'pulls' from the stone before he was satisfied, and these trial runs might include prints of the bird's head alone.

But the undoubted quality of Lear's parrot plates was not enough on its own to bring him success. Lear was no businessman. Although he managed to find 175 subscribers for the parrot monograph (including eminent naturalists and fellow artists such as John Edward Gray of the British Museum, Swainson and Selby, as well as seven members of Mrs Wentworth's family), he was unable to ensure that they all paid him quickly enough, and was often unable even to cover the costs of production. Faced with mounting debts to colourists and printers, and sometimes complaining that he could not even afford to eat, he reluctantly decided to curtail his bold attempt to portray all the parrot species known to science at the time, and only twelve of the planned fourteen parts materialized.

However, even though incomplete, *Illustrations of the Family of Psittacidae, or Parrots* was a *tour de force*. It was an incredibly ambitious task for a young man who was just eighteen years old when he started it and had no formal art training or real connections in high places. And despite its financial failure, it made Lear famous, garnering high praise from many quarters. As a result, he obtained more of the paid work he needed, illustrating birds and mammals for various books and journals, including *The Transactions of the Zoological Society of London*, as well as a monograph on tortoises, terrapins and turtles, and volumes relating discoveries made by explorer-naturalists in the Pacific and the Bering Strait.

The happiest period of Lear's life seems to have been the time he spent living at Knowsley Hall, near Liverpool, the family seat of Lord Stanley (1775–1851). The two men – so different in social station and temperament, but sharing a passion for birds – first met when Lear borrowed a parrot from Lord Stanley to use as a model for one of the plates in his monograph, to which the Lord was one of the subscribers. Lord Stanley devoted much of his time to the study of natural history; after the death of his father in 1834, when he became the 13th Earl of Derby, he built up his collection of birds and other animals to create the largest private menagerie in the country, and invited Lear to paint its inhabitants.

Apart from brief visits to attend to work in London, Lear spent five years at Knowsley, from 1832 until 1837, where he had free access to Lord Stanley's fine library and art collection. Here he produced hundreds of drawings of birds, mammals and reptiles in the earl's great menagerie, seventeen plates of which appeared in the *Gleanings from the Menagerie and Aviary at Knowsley Hall*, the illustrated record of the collection that Lord Stanley had asked John Edward Gray, Keeper of Zoology at the British Museum, to write. At first, he felt out of place among the grand family, remarking on one occasion that 'lofty society irks me dreadfully, nothing I long for half so much as to giggle heartily and hop on one leg down the long hall – but I dare not'. But increasingly he spent time with the family, particularly with the children, who gave him their rapt attention as he

E. Lear

189   14

drew strange imaginary birds and created nonsense rhymes.

Although he sometimes painted smaller species, Lear was best at depicting bigger birds that we often regard as comical or ungainly, such as large parrots, toucans, storks and pelicans. He invested them with a certain anthropomorphism, as if he was expressing his feelings about his own oddness and awkwardness. In later life Lear put on a great deal of weight, and his appearance became owl-like, with his round spectacles and portly body. With his endearingly self-deprecating humour, he often caricatured himself in the shape of an owl.

By the time he was in his last year at Knowsley, Lear's eyesight was under strain after years of painting intricate details of plumage. In October 1836 he remarked in a letter that 'my eyes are so sadly worse, that no bird under an ostrich shall I soon be able to do.' The following year he gave up drawing birds and other animals and, deciding that a kindlier climate than that of Britain would be beneficial to his poor health, spent most of his remaining years abroad, painting landscapes. His first trip, through Europe to Rome, was sponsored by Lord Derby, and from then on he was often on the move, his travels taking him to Italy, Sicily, Malta, Greece, Crete, Albania, Egypt, the Middle East and India. He returned to England infrequently to deal with galleries and other business, and to assuage his homesickness.

Despite his health problems, Lear was a resourceful traveller who put up with many hardships and apparently coped with danger with equanimity. At Petra in Jordan he nonchalantly went on sketching despite the noise of a group of hostile Arab tribesmen who were preparing to attack his party. One of his biographers, Susan Hyman, describes how on another occasion while in Greece 'he is entertained by the kicking and shrieking of several storks and an egret who have fallen through the roof', as well as four soaking-wet Jackdaws that came down the chimney and hopped over him until dawn.

Although they may seem a world away from his meticulously drawn early portraits of birds, Lear's much-loved nonsense drawings, including the series of 'nonsense birds' which he drew and coloured to teach children, are superb caricatures, their apparent simplicity disguising the great knowledge of the real thing that made it possible for him to invest them with such life.

His 'bird-people' are hybrids of birds and people with sharp, beak-like

PLATE 152.
Green Turaco
Turaco persa

Edward Lear
c.1835. Watercolour.
231mm x 142mm
(9¼in x 5½in)

The subtle but effective portrayal of the foliage on the bird's perch in this painting is typical of Lear's style. Turacos are a family of fruit-eating woodland and forest birds that are probably most closely related to cuckoos. They are the among the few bird families that are found only in Africa. They are unique in having two copper-based pigments colouring their plumage: turacoverdin, which produces the green body feathers, which is the only green pigment found in bird feathers (the green plumage of all other birds is a result of light refraction); and turacin, producing the red wing flashes and the crest colour of some species.

PLATE 153.
Marvellous Spatuletail
(male)
Loddigesia mirabilis
John Gould
c.1849–61. Lithograph.
545mm x 365mm
(21⅛in x 14⅜in)

*One of the most
spectacular and popular of
Gould's great bird books
was his five-volume work
on hummingbirds, which
he began in 1849. Its
tiny, restlessly darting and
hovering, jewel-like
subjects bore names such
as Woodnymph and
Sunangel that befitted
their splendour, and none
more than the rare
Marvellous Spatuletail.
The male's tail is indeed a
marvel, with its pair of
amazingly long, bare,
wire-like outer feathers
that cross one another,
each ending in a racquet-
shaped vane. Used in
courtship displays, these
are three times the length
of the minute head and
body, which is only just
over an inch long.*

noses, and their arms or the tails of their frock coats thrust out behind them like wings. It is hard to tell whether they represent a human with the features of a bird or vice versa. Often the face is that of Lear himself, and some of these brilliantly drawn, whimsical sketches show him sailing through the air on wings just like the birds he so admired, his hair on end and his glasses falling off his nose.

As with many others who have the gift of humour, Lear's life continued to be marred by the deep depressions that he called 'the morbids', which cannot have been helped by his increasing blindness. During one such bout he wrote, 'On the whole I do not know if I am living or dead at times'. And as his sight grew worse, he was reduced to painting impressionistic images – such as gloomy scenes of ruined buildings, or gale-lashed boats under darkening skies – that mirrored his darkly melancholic mood. These were as far removed as it is possible from the finely detailed, beautifully coloured bird paintings of his youth.

Lear spent his last years at his villa in San Remo in north-west Italy, close to the French border. Here he was cared for by Giorgio Kokali, his devoted manservant of almost fifty years, until Kokali died in 1883. The elderly artist still had for company his much-loved tabby cat Foss, immortalised in many of his drawings, but eventually he too was gone, dying at the age of seventeen. The following year, on 29 January 1888, Lear himself passed away peacefully, and was buried in San Remo.

Apart from Audubon, the greatest name connected with illustrated bird books in the nineteenth century was John Gould. In contrast to the American's bold, melodramatic style of depicting his birds, Gould favoured a far more restrained and delicate approach. While they may lack the impact of Audubon's plates, Gould's illustrations have a subtle beauty all of their own. And, unlike Audubon's exclusively American focus, Gould's great, lavishly illustrated ornithological works dealt with the birds of every continent except Africa and Antarctica.

Gould was born in 1804 at Lyme Regis on the coast of Dorset in south-west England. Soon afterwards his father, a gardener, moved with his work to Stoke Hill near Guildford, Surrey, thirty miles (48km) south-west of London. When John was fourteen the family moved again, this time to Windsor where his father had secured a better position in the splendid gardens of the royal castle. Here Gould taught himself taxidermy and egg-blowing, crafts in which he soon became highly

Drawn by Mrs Gould from Specimen in coll. of Zool. Soc.   Rhynchæa

skilled. He showed his later flair for business by selling his expertly stuffed birds and blown eggs to the students at Eton College nearby.

In 1823, four days after his nineteenth birthday, John Gould moved again, this time to take up a position as gardener at Ripley Castle in Yorkshire; but he left after only eighteen months to follow his real passion. He started in business as a taxidermist in London, preparing mounts of many different birds and other animals for clients who included George IV. By 1827 he had won a competition organised by the Zoological Society of London, founded the year before, to choose a taxidermist. He soon took up his position in the society's museum at 33 Bruton Street, with the impressive title of Curator and Preserver to the Museum. It may well have been at this museum that he met the person who would soon become of great importance to his future achievements. That person was Elizabeth Coxen, who was working as a governess near Buckingham Palace, and the two were married in January 1829. In October of that year, Gould received his most unusual commission: to preserve a giraffe that had been given to George IV by Mehemet Ali, Viceroy of Egypt. A favourite of the king's, the unfortunate creature died in 1829, only two years after its arrival at Windsor Great Park.

But even this mammoth task was dwarfed by Gould's ambitious plans of producing illustrated bird books of his own to rival – or better – those of Swainson, Selby, Audubon and others. He was impressed by the results Lear had obtained by lithography, and realised that it was the way forward. Although he was able to make rough sketches of the birds that showed exactly what he wanted to achieve in his designs, he lacked the artistic skill needed to transform them into beautiful plates. The person he turned to was his wife Elizabeth. Already a competent amateur artist, she improved her technique with practice and was soon able to draw accurately on the lithographic stones.

The first book the Goulds produced was *A Century of Birds hitherto unfigured from the Himalaya Mountains* (1830–33), with its eighty plates showing a hundred birds. The illustrations were made from a collection of skins that Gould had prepared and mounted. It was a great success, Gould having managed to find almost 300 subscribers.

Another attempt at producing a book with illustrations of birds from this region was made by Brian Hodgson (1800–94). He was one of the most remarkable and unusual of all those who manned faraway outposts

PLATE 154.
South American
Painted Snipe
Nycticryphes semicollaris

Elizabeth Gould
c.1835. Watercolour and pencil.
161mm x 227mm
(6¼in x 9in)

The legend in John Gould's hand at the foot of this beautiful illustration reads 'drawn by Mrs Gould from specimen in coll. of Zool. Soc.', referring to the collection of the Zoological Society of London, for whom Gould worked for ten years as curator and preserver. This proved to his great advantage, as he gained access to many specimens which he could use as models for his superlative colour plates. The painted snipe family consists of just two intricately patterned species of tropical wetlands, with an odd distribution. The one shown here lives in southern South America, and the other from Africa to Asia and Australia.

*One of the pioneers of
Indian ornithology, Brian
Hodgson was an
extraordinarily
accomplished man in
many spheres, not least in
the energy and care with
which he organised the
drawing and collection of
Himalayan birds by his
Nepalese assistants and
studied their appear-ance
and behaviour. This
typically lively drawing
shows a male (right),
female (left) and
immature (below) of just
one of fifty-three thrush
species that Hodgson
obtained, for eight of
which he made the first
scientific descriptions.
Cochoas are atypical
thrushes of south Asian
mountain forests, with
intense deep green, blue or
violet-purple plumage in
the males, and wide bills
for eating fruits.*

of the British Empire. A gifted and assiduous scholar, he was an impressive polymath who made major advances in ethnography, the study of Buddhism, linguistics and the history and geography of his adopted country Nepal; all this was carried out as an amateur, in addition to the often difficult tasks he handled with great skill as a colonial administrator. He had an extremely enlightened attitude to the Nepalese. He lived in Nepal for twenty-three years as British representative of the East India Company, and he came to love the country and its people, as well as developing a passionate interest in its wildlife.

Hodgson made extensive collections of birds in Nepal. He amassed over 9,500 bird specimens, comprising some 670 species, of which more than 120 were previously unknown to science – although he was credited with the discovery of only 80 of the latter. His careful observations, notes, scientific descriptions and drawings laid the foundations for modern knowledge of Nepalese wildlife. He wrote over 140 scientific papers on natural history alone, 64 of them on birds. Including his scholarly writings on other subjects, he produced his papers at the phenomenal average rate of one every seven weeks for thirty years.

Hodgson also built up a collection of beautiful and accurate illustrations of birds and mammals, many of them exquisitely coloured. These were made by Rajman Singh and other native Indian artists. Unlike the plates in Gould's *Century*, the illustrations Hodgson commissioned were made from direct observation in the field. They were more lifelike and accurate as a result, with the correct colours of bills, eyes, legs and plumage compared with the often faded versions shown by Elizabeth Gould, who was working from skins.

His contact with Gould was brief and unfortunate, ending on a sour note from Hodgson's point of view. Perhaps inspired partly by Gould's work, Hodgson wished to produce a book of his own on Himalayan birds and mammals. Back in England, his father approached Gould to try to enlist his help. Ever the hard-nosed businessman, Gould said he would consider the book proposal only on his terms. It must deal solely with birds, and Gould and his wife were to draw the illustrations anew since, with the prejudice typical of the time (but not of Hodgson) Gould felt that 'no work executed from the drawings of Indian artists will sell'. And that was not all. Hodgson was to write only part of the text, and the book was to be presented as an extension of Gould's *Century*. The last straw, as

far as Hodgson, and his father back in England, negotiating with Gould on his behalf, were concerned, was that Gould should be sent Hodgson's paintings and specimens for his use without any commitment to start the work for eighteen months. Not surprisingly, Hodgson rejected the proposal. On the other hand, Gould would have been very unwise to have abandoned or delayed his own work, which was proving so successful, to accommodate the wishes of a man whom he had probably never met and to whom he owed nothing.

Despite his lasting conviction that his projected book had great potential, Hodgson, who lived to the great age of ninety-four after returning to England, never saw his hopes realised, and to this day the paintings, like the man himself, are little known outside the libraries of the Zoological Society of London and the Natural History Museum where they are kept.

Another man of genius with whom Gould was associated but to whom he did not always endear himself was Edward Lear. This gifted artist did many of the best illustrations in Gould's *The Birds of Europe* (1832–7) and *A Monograph of the Ramphastidae, or Toucans* (1833–5), and also helped with *A Monograph of the Trogonidae, or Trogons* (1835–8). Gould immediately recognised Lear's talent and learned a great deal from him, incorporating much of the artist's innovative approach in the plates for his own books. He may have engaged Lear to work for him at least in part because he was concerned that if he didn't Lear might achieve greater success on his own and become a serious rival.

Thanks to his dogged businessman's persistence and his gift for self-advertisement, and aided by the efforts of his efficient and assiduous secretary Edwin Prince in ensuring his subscribers kept up their payments, Gould's *Century* was a success, unlike poor Lear's parrot monograph. Indeed, with the first part published only weeks after the first two of Lear's work, the Gould production completely overshadowed it, and it was Gould rather than Lear who received the accolades for setting new standards of excellence in illustrated bird books. The Royal Society observed that Gould's work was 'by far the most accurately illustrated work on foreign ornithology' that had been issued up to that period.

On the whole, Lear didn't get on with Gould. They were totally different in personality: Lear was sensitive, emotional, self-critical and wary, but generous to his numerous friends, and very unworldly in many ways; Gould was extremely practical and unsentimental, the epitome of the successful, impatient, hard-bargaining, self-made businessman. This is brought out dramatically in the exchange of correspondence between the two. After leaving England Lear, driven no doubt partly by loneliness and his fear of rejection, kept in touch with his many friends with frequent, affectionate, humorous and often long letters, while Gould's replies were evidently infrequent, characteristically terse and unemotional. This led Lear to complain 'when I do write, you answer me by a short scrawl'. It was doubtless an exaggeration when many years later, after Gould's death in 1881, Lear wrote of his former employer, 'He was one I never liked really, for in spite of a certain jollity, and bonhomie, he was a harsh and violent man'. One has to remember that, as well as having the delightful attractive side to his character that endeared him to friends both young and old, Lear could be difficult, complaining and prone to feelings of martyrdom and even paranoia. And, as Ann Datta of the Natural History Museum points out in her book *John Gould in Australia*, 'Perhaps behind Lear's bitterness also lies the fact that Gould's publications were a financial and scientific success, while his own had not been'.

Gould has often been criticised for his supposed brusqueness and meanness in acknowledging others, including his own wife Elizabeth as well as Lear. But for every biographer or art historian critical of Gould in this respect, one can find another ready to spring to his defence. Some of Gould's biographers have argued with a considerable amount of justification that his attitude to those who were after all his employees was no different from that of many other businessmen. He was not obliged to treat them as close friends, and he invariably made sure he paid them fairly and on time for their work. And despite his often apparently cold, work-obsessed manner, he was capable of acts of great kindness. At the age of sixty-seven, although very unwell himself, he drove out daily to comfort his utterly loyal secretary Edwin Prince during a serious illness near the end of his life. He left Prince's family £100 (a generous sum in those days), as well as bequeathing £100 to one of his artists, Henry Richter, and double that sum to another, William Hart, because he had a large family to support.

PLATE 157.
Pink-footed Goose
Anser brachyrhynchus

John Gould
c.1865. Watercolour and ink.
180mm x 133mm (7in x 5¼in)

Another example of a couple of Gould's confident and accurate preliminary pencil and watercolour sketches shows his skill at capturing the essential features of the bird. His handwritten notes are detailed instructions about colour and form to the artist that would ensure that the bird is represented accurately. He kept a very close eye on the progress of each plate from the moment he handed over his design to the final corrected lithograph.

Criticisms of Gould by some ornithologists centre round the fact that he was not an innovator and made no major scientific discoveries himself, and was not always careful when recording information about specimens. Set against this, however, he was a highly skilled taxidermist and for someone of his background with no serious education, let alone scientific training, it was a great achievement for him that he became renowned as the most famous British ornithologist of his day. No one named more new species than Gould, to whom a remarkable 377 names are attributed. (Although some were later found to be merely hybrids or races, an over-enthusiasm for finding new forms was by no means restricted to Gould.) But his crowning achievement was his ability to work so tirelessly and efficiently as an impresario, businessman, taxidermist, author, illustrator and publisher to get the best out of his team of collectors, illustrators, lithographers and others in producing an unrivalled number of fine bird books.

A good example of Gould's scientific ability was in the help he gave to Charles Darwin in correctly identifying some of the unique birds the young naturalist had collected during his famous voyage aboard HMS *Beagle*. Gould realised that the assortment of little birds with dramatically differently sized and shaped bills that Darwin had collected on the Galapagos Islands and given him to examine were all closely related species of finch (Darwin had identified some as finches, but thought that the others, which had very unfinchlike bills, were warblers, wrens and American blackbirds). Equally importantly, Gould established very quickly that they were not merely varieties, as Darwin had supposed, but distinct species. Neither Darwin nor Gould realised the full significance of this revelation – that after arrival on the islands, the original finch ancestors could, in isolation, evolve into different species, their differently sized and shaped beaks becoming adapted by a process of natural selection to feed on different foods. Although Darwin, in his bestselling revised edition of his *Journal of a Voyage in HMS Beagle*, mused 'Seeing this gradation and diversity of structure in one small, intimately related group of birds, one might really fancy that from an original paucity of birds in this archipelago, one species had been taken and modified for different ends', he did not use the finches in his formulation of his evolutionary theory. They do not appear anywhere in *The Origin of Species*. Darwin's real avian stars that he chose as examples to support his

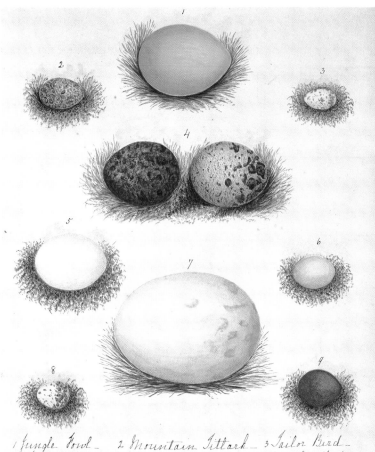

1 Jungle Fowl —   2 Mountain Tittark —   3 Tailor Bird —
4 Kestrel —   5 Neilgherry Wood Pigeon —   6 Smaller Hoopoe —
7 Hawk Eagle —   8 Velvet fronted Nuthatch —   9 Cuckoo —

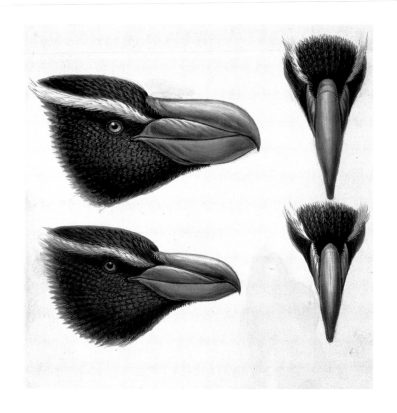

theory were domesticated birds – pigeons, chickens and ducks. It was left to later researchers, notably the British ornithologists David Lack (in the late 1930s and 1940s) and Peter Grant (since 1973), to make the finches famous. Indeed, the name 'Darwin's finches' for the group was coined by David Lack, who used it as the title of his classic study of the birds, published in 1947.

Darwin also had cause to be grateful to Gould for his skilful reconstruction of the carcass of a rhea (a South American ostrich-like flightless bird) that he brought back from HMS *Beagle* voyage. This was all that remained of the huge bird after Darwin and his shipmates had eaten it for their Christmas dinner. Darwin had belatedly realised that this was a new, somewhat smaller and fluffier species, distinct from the Great or Common Rhea that he had heard about earlier from Patagonian Indians. In addition to the literal sustenance he had obtained from the bird, Gould's identification may have helped Darwin gain metaphorical food for thought during the long gestation period of his theory of evolution by natural selection. Also, Gould, in his formal scientific description of the bird, gave this smaller bird the scientific name *Rhea darwinii* in his honour. Darwin's name has not been perpetuated in this way, as today the bird he ate is regarded merely as one of two or three subspecies of the species called the Lesser Rhea, *Rhea pennata*. However, the common name Darwin's Rhea is sometimes used to distinguish this subspecies of Lesser Rhea from the other(s), known as the Puna Rhea.

With regard to Darwin's revolutionary theory, Gould himself sat firmly on the fence. He never wrote or committed himself in any way on the radical subjects of natural selection and evolution, being anxious to avoid offending the delicate religious sensibilities of some of the wealthy subscribers to his works.

With his privileged position as curator at the Zoological Society of London, Gould had access to skins of Australian birds; he was also sent many descriptions and specimens by his brothers-in-law who had emigrated to New South Wales. Thrilled by the uniqueness and beauty of many of the birds being discovered in increasing numbers as that part of the world continued to be opened up to explorers, he decided that this would form the subject of his next great work. After producing a synopsis and two parts of *The Birds of Australia and the adjacent islands* in London, from 1837 to 1838, he realised that he could not create the authoritative

PLATE 159.
Snares Penguin
&Fiordland Penguin
Eudyptes robustus & Eudyptes pachyrhynchus

**John Gerrard
Keulemans**
c.1887–1905.
Watercolour.
181mm x 176mm
(7¼in x 7in)

Keulemans was a most industrious and versatile artist, who produced a vast number of illustrations for scientific journals, catalogues, monographs and other books, ranging from complex scenes with numerous birds and detailed backgrounds to studies of detailed parts of birds, like this one of two similar species of penguin.

PLATE 160.
Buller's Albatross
(upper) & Salvin's
Albatross *(lower)*
Thalassarche bulleri &
Thalassarche salvini

**John Gerrard
Keulemans**
c.1887–1905.
Watercolour.
292mm x 232mm
(11⅞in x 9¼in)

*These subtly coloured and
detailed drawings show
the salient features of
the heads of two similar
albatross species that
breed on islands off New
Zealand. The bill of
Buller's Albatross above
has a broader, more
conspicuous, orange-tinged
top plate to the upper
mandible, contrasting with
a black lower plate, while
the lower mandible has
a distinct yellow stripe.
Keulemans' careful
drawing shows how this
differs from the plainer,
paler bill of
Salvin's Albatross.*

book he envisaged unless he made the long journey to Australia to see the birds for himself. For this reason, he cancelled the first two parts. He did not produce any parts of the 'official' version, retitled *The Birds of Australia*, until after he had returned to England.

In May 1838 he left his business in the capable hands of Edwin Prince and, accompanied by Elizabeth and their eldest son, seven-year-old Henry, together with a nephew, two servants and John Gilbert, one of his collectors, he set off for Australia. After a four-month sea passage they arrived in Hobart, the capital of Tasmania, then known as Van Diemens Land. Here Gould left Elizabeth, who was pregnant with their seventh child, while he made expeditions to the north of the island and to various parts of the mainland, including New South Wales and the mallee scrubland near Adelaide. Gilbert was sent to collect in Perth far away in the west. After Gould returned to Van Diemens Land, the family went with him to Sydney, where he continued to search for new birds while Elizabeth went on with sketching them.

John Gilbert, Gould's main provider of birds in Australia and a brilliant collector, museum curator and field naturalist, was asked by Gould to stay behind to find more birds. Thanks to research carried out by Dr Clemency Fisher, Curator of Birds and Mammals at the Liverpool Museum in England, we know that the scientific value of Gould's great Australian project depended hugely on the skill of this young man, who was tragically killed at the age of just thirty-three during an attack by hostile Aborigines during an expedition he had joined.

On a happier note, Gould has the distinction of having introduced the budgerigar to Britain. He was frequently amazed and delighted by the brilliant plumages and lively behaviour of many of the new birds he encountered in Australia, and was taken with the sight of huge flocks of the attractive little parrots known to the Aborigines as 'gijirrigaa' or 'betcherrygah' – a word possibly meaning 'good-to-eat (parrot)'. Gould obtained live Budgerigars from his brother-in-law, Charles Coxen, in Queensland and, on his return to England, showed them off at high-society parties and scientific meetings alike, and also presented some to Lord Derby. The 13th Earl has been credited with being the first person to breed the species in Britain, in 1848. The 'budgie' is now the world's most popular cage bird, its numbers in captivity vastly exceeding the wild populations that roam the Australian bush.

After having spent more than two years in Australia, the Goulds sailed for home, returning in August 1840 with a wealth of information, specimens and drawings for the great book. In summer 1841 they settled happily in a cottage at Egham in Surrey, not far from Windsor where John Gould had lived as a youth. But their happiness was short-lived, for within a few months Elizabeth died, stricken by puerperal fever after the birth of her eighth child. She was just thirty-seven years old, and they had been married for just over eleven and a half years.

With his hard-working wife gone, Gould was without a skilled interpreter to work up his rough sketches in readiness for printing. He had already employed the English artist and lithographer Henry Constantine Richter (1821–1902) to paint kangaroos for him, and now he turned to the young man to fill in this major gap in his team.

Richter's family background was steeped in art: his German grandfather was an artist and

1. *Diomedea bulleri*
2. *Diomedea salvini*

engraver, his father, Henry James Richter (1772–1857), was a painter and engraver of historical scenes and president of the Associated Artists in Water-Colours for the year 1811–12, and his sister Henrietta had her miniature portraits exhibited at the Royal Academy from 1842 until 1849. Richter was one of Gould's most faithful and long-serving assistants, producing some 1,600 lithographic plates and watercolour paintings for him. As well as those for *The Birds of Australia*, he worked on many other Gould titles, including those on birds as different as the American partridges and hummingbirds, as well as *The Birds of Asia*. His ability to paint beautiful backgrounds for the birds with such skill was a major factor in ensuring the appeal of Gould's books to the public.

The eight magnificent volumes of *The Birds of Australia and the adjacent islands* (seven volumes of which appeared between 1840 and 1848, with the eighth, the supplement, from 1851 to 1869) are among the world's finest illustrated books, and a landmark in the ornithology of Australia.

PLATE 161.
Rufous-necked
Hornbill *(female)*
Aceros nipalensis

Anonymous
Hardwick Collection
c.1800–30. Watercolour
and pencil.
372mm x 271mm
(14¾in x 10¾in)

This preparatory drawing
and colour sketch shows a
female of one of the
largest of all hornbills.
The male differs in having
a bright chestnut-coloured
head, neck and
underparts. Like so many
members of this
fascinating family of
birds, this species, found
from north-eastern India
to southern China and
north-western Vietnam,
has declined or
disappeared from much of
its range since the time
these drawings were made,
chiefly as a result of
deforestation and hunting.

They represented the pinnacle of Gould's scientific achievement, being the first comprehensive account of the birds of this most recently settled continent. They were also a huge success financially for Gould, who claimed among his subscribers twelve monarchs, eleven royal highnesses, sixteen dukes, thirty earls and a bishop. As always, the books represented a cooperative effort between Gould the impresario and his faithful and hard-working team of collectors, artists and lithographers. The work contains 681 superbly hand-coloured lithographs in total. By far the majority, 595 in all, were done by Richter, the rest being the work of Elizabeth Gould, who was responsible for 84 plates, Edward Lear, whose two plates were of a Cockatiel (copied from his *Psittacidae*) and a Spotted Cormorant, and Benjamin Waterhouse Hawkins, who did just one plate, of an Emu with chicks.

Hawkins (1807–89) was another of Gould's team of illustrators who replaced Elizabeth after her death. He was a man of many talents, having studied palaeontology, physiology and natural history as well as being a painter of portraits and animals, a lithographer and etcher, and a sculptor. Hawkins was the designer of the spectacular life-sized cement models of dinosaurs in Crystal Palace gardens at Sydenham Park, south-east London. He was a competent and hard-working artist who had already proved his worth in drawing and lithographing the plates for *Illustrations of Indian Zoology*, with text by Dr John Edward Gray, keeper of zoology at the British Museum. Published between 1830 and 1834, this important work was based on the large collection of drawings by English and native Indian artists, including 1,735 of birds. This collection was accumulated in the late eighteenth century by Major General Thomas Hardwicke, one of the most renowned pioneers of the study of Indian ornithology, who bequeathed it to the museum.

As with Richter, Gould used Hawkins to help him after his wife's death, but his contribution was far smaller. As well as the Emu and chicks he painted for *The Birds of Australia*, Hawkins also lithographed for Gould sixteen plates of specimens collected during explorations of the western coasts of the Americas and various Pacific islands, which were reproduced in the two-volume work *The Zoology of the Voyage of HMS Sulphur*, by Richard Hinds (surgeon and naturalist on the voyage). This was published between 1843 and 1844, and of the sixteen plates, six are attributed to Gould himself, who also wrote the eleven pages of text on birds.

Of all the huge variety of bird skins that passed through Gould's hands, those of the hummingbirds were special favourites. He amassed a huge collection of these brilliant little New World birds, sent to him from many parts of the Americas by collectors. Through the generosity of another hummingbird fanatic, George Loddiges, he was able to examine those species he did not have himself, and use them as models for the plates in one of his most sumptuous works, the *Monograph of the Trochilidae, or Family of Hummingbirds* (five volumes, 1849–61, plus Volume 6, a five-part supplement, 1880–87, the final three parts completed after his death by Richard Bowdler Sharp).

Gould soon realised that his illustrator at the time, William Hart, faced a considerable challenge in representing on paper the glorious iridescence of the feathers of the male humming-birds. In fact the problem had already been tackled by others, including the Frenchman Jean Baptiste Audebert who, together with the French ornithologist Louis Vieillot, produced a two volume work on hummingbirds, *Oiseaux dorés, ou à reflets métalliques*, published as early as 1802 with gold highlights on the birds' plumage. The most recent attempt was by the young naturalist and artist William Lloyd Baily (1828–61) in Philadelphia, USA, who had used his method of applying gold leaf in a series of fifty-eight paintings for a planned monograph that was never published.

Baily wrote with valuable advice on his technique to Gould, who pursued the matter in subsequent correspondence, and when he met Baily in Philadelphia in 1857. Gould then adopted it with modification – Henry Richter, his artist for most of the hummingbird plates, painted over with transparent oil paints and varnish rather than the watercolours Baily used – but claimed it exclusively for his own by means of a patent, and never acknowledged Baily's contribution. Be that as it may, Gould's new work was published to lavish acclaim and the privileged subscribers (proudly described by Gould as including 'nearly all the crowned heads of Europe') must have gasped as the images of so many different species of tiny hummingbirds glittered under the gaslight as they turned each page to reveal more wonders.

It was characteristic that Gould based his great hummingbird monograph on skins, not living birds. Indeed, he had never seen a live hummingbird until the work was well advanced, when he crossed the Atlantic in 1857 expressly to rectify this omission. He was far from disappointed when Baily showed him a Ruby-throated Hummingbird in a Philadelphia botanical garden. Fascinated by these avian jewels – and ever mindful of the opportunities for publicising himself and his latest work – Gould was eager to succeed in his attempt to bring back two live hummingbirds to Britain, transporting them on the long sea voyage in a little cage and feeding them on a sugar and honey solution laced with egg yolk. Unsurprisingly, the tiny birds survived for only forty-eight hours back in London.

In 1851, the year of London's Great Exhibition, Gould exhibited a total of 1,500 mounted specimens of over 300 species of hummingbirds to the public within a pavilion he had persuaded London Zoo to have built at his expense – an expense he more than recouped by charging sixpence admission per person. The birds were displayed in twenty-four mainly octagonal glass cases with canopies above each one to diffuse the light, specially designed so that the bird's iridescent colours could be viewed from various angles. The exhibition was a huge success, helping Gould to establish himself as one of the world's most famous bird collectors: in its first year it attracted over 80,000 visitors, including Queen Victoria and Prince Albert, as well as Charles Dickens, and it was extended for a second year. In a sense, the exhibition lives on today, on the back of many of Gould's specimen labels which he cut up from admission tickets; also a few cases of mounted hummingbirds still exist at the Natural History Museum in South Kensington and Tring.

Many of the 335 species of hummingbirds recognised today were described and named by Gould. In gratitude for granting him free access to his collection, Loddiges was rewarded in the manner often employed by ornithologists when Gould named the most spectacular of all the species Loddiges' Spatuletail (*Loddigesia mirabilis*); like Hodgson, his friend had joined the select few whose names were commemorated in an entire genus. Although the scientific name still stands, the common name usually used today – the Marvellous Spatuletail – is more apt for such a uniquely stunning bird. In his turn, Loddiges repaid the compliment by naming one of the new species he described *Lesbia gouldii*.

After Gould's death, his collection of 5,378 hummingbird specimens, along with 7,017 skins of other birds, including trogons, toucans and birds of paradise, and over 1,700 eggs, was sold to the British Museum (Natural History), now the Natural History Museum, for £3,000.

THAUMALEA AMHERSTIÆ.

Gould's total output was truly prodigious, reflecting the uncompromising work ethos of the man. In the fifty years between 1830 and 1880, he was responsible for the production of eighteen folio works, some numbering as many as seven volumes each. These contained no fewer than 2,999 huge folio-sized, hand-coloured lithographs, some of which were reproduced and painstakingly coloured by hand hundreds of times in his most popular works – a tribute to the industry and loyalty of the teams of assistants he controlled with his characteristic businesslike efficiency. In addition, Gould wrote over 300 smaller works, scientific papers, notes and memoirs.

The limited market for such sumptuous but costly productions can be appreciated when one learns that there were only 1,000 or so subscriptions to his works at the height of his fame, and a good many of these were from libraries and other institutions. Nevertheless, the Bird Man, as he loved to be known, made a great deal of money from his work, and became renowned as the most prolific publisher and author of fine illustrated bird books in the world – as well as the most famous British ornithologist of his day.

Of all the artists who helped Gould achieve his ambition, one of the most talented was Joseph Wolf (1820–99). Although German, he spent most of his life – over fifty years – in Britain. Born Mathias Josef Wolf in the village of Mörz near the city of Koblenz in western Germany (then Prussia), he was a farmer's son. Koblenz is at the meeting of the Rhine and Mosel rivers, and the surrounding countryside was home to a wide range of birds and other animals. Wolf endured the censure of his family and neighbours for his frequent escapes from farming duties to watch and trap birds, many of which he kept in captivity to serve as 'models' from which to make drawings and watercolour paintings. He also visited Prince Maximilian's private collection of South American birds in Neuwied, walking twenty miles to get there.

In 1836, when he was sixteen, Wolf left the family farm and became apprenticed to a firm of lithographers, the Becker brothers in Koblenz. The skills he acquired there, together with his natural talent for drawing, soon helped to bring him to the attention of leading German ornithologists such as Eduard Rüppell, who commissioned him to make plates for the book he was writing on the birds of north-east Africa. But his most important commission at the time was from Professor Hermann

PLATE 162.
Lady Amherst's
Pheasant *(male)*
Chrysolophus amherstiae

Joseph Wolf
1872. Lithograph.
450mm x 592mm
(17¼in x 23¼in)

This superb painting of one of the most gorgeous of all pheasant is by one of the greatest of all bird illustrators. This was one of the eighty-one plates by Wolf in one of the finest lithographed bird books, A Monograph of the Phasianidae. *It was written by Daniel Giraud Elliot (1835–1915), Curator of Zoology at the Field Museum in Chicago and co-founder of the American Ornithologists' Union, and published in London in 1873. Elliot's independent wealth made it possible for him to produce a series of superb bird monographs like this one, illustrated by the finest bird artists, long after most publishers found it uneconomic to do so.*

Schlegel (1804–84), the curator of the famous natural-history museum in the city of Leyden (now Leiden) in the western Netherlands. Schlegel was a good bird artist himself, and also an enthusiastic early advocate of lithography. He was so impressed with Wolf's skill that he asked him to come to Leyden in 1840 and paint plates for a book on the history and technique of falconry that he was preparing with A. H. Verster de Wulverhorst. Published in Leyden between 1844 and 1853, *Trait de Fauconnerie* was a sumptuous work which was made possible by the resurgence of interest in the ancient art of falconry in Holland, due to the establishment of a royal falconry club there.

Wolf also painted the first twenty plates for 'Birds of Japan', part of Philipp von Siebold's *Fauna Japonica* (1844–50). Containing the first scientific descriptions of birds from Japan, this important work was edited by Schlegel and his mentor and predecessor at the Leyden museum, the great Dutch ornithologist Coenraad Temminck (1770––1858), by then an old man.

In 1848, after Wolf had spent a brief period studying oil painting at Darmstadt and later in Antwerp, an eruption of revolutionary fervour spread across much of Europe. Faced with the threat of being called up to serve in the army, the up-and-coming artist was glad to accept an invitation from David William Mitchell, animal illustrator and secretary of the Zoological Society of London, to work there, well away from the turmoil on the continent. London was the place to be for a young, ambitious naturalist and animal painter, and Wolf had Gould to thank for recommending him to Mitchell. His first task was to collaborate on plates for the *List of the Genera of Birds* with George Robert Gray, brother of John Edward Gray and his long-serving senior assistant at the Natural History Department of the British Museum. Gray's influence in the museum and at the Zoological Society of London was of great help to Wolf in establishing him as a serious naturalist and artist.

Wolf took to his adopted home with enthusiasm, anglicising his Christian name to Joseph; although he never became naturalised, he remained in London for the rest of his life, apart from field trips and holidays (which included almost annual visits to his family in Germany).

He was very much his own man, and avoided becoming tied to a single author or publisher. He worked with a wide range of different techniques, from lithography and wood engravings to oils and watercolours. When his designs were lithographed by others, the results sometimes did not do full justice to his great skill. Less well known than his book illustrations, but even finer, were his bold and dramatic watercolour and oil paintings of game birds and birds of prey. In 1849, John Gould commissioned Wolf to paint a picture entitled *Woodcocks seeking shelter*, which was exhibited at the Royal Academy summer show. Edwin Landseer, the most revered British animal artist of his day, was impressed by Wolf's painting, and made sure it was given the best chance of being noticed by having it hung 'on the line' (at eye level). Landseer became a great admirer of the German painter's work, which was close to his in spirit. He was full of praise for Wolf's ability to capture the very essence of the living bird, observing that 'he must have been a bird before he became a man'.

Wolf did very well out of his portrait of the Woodcock, going on to produce a number of other studies of the species which became very popular as prints with the public. A portly, pigeon-sized wader with a long bill, the Woodcock is unusual among this group of birds in breeding in woodland rather than in open country. The success of Wolf's portrait results partly from its subject being a highly sought-after game bird, and partly because of the beauty of the bird itself. It presented a major challenge to the shooter, with its feathers intricately barred and mottled in many shades of brown, grey and black in a dead-leaf pattern that rendered the bird invisible as it rested on the forest floor by day, and its fast, zigzagging flight that enabled it to dodge between the tree trunks when disturbed.

In 1851 Wolf was appointed official artist to the Zoological Society of London, and many of the lively portraits of animals he made there were published between 1856 and 1861 in his *Zoological Sketches*. As well as his paintings of birds, Wolf illustrated works for many explorers and naturalists, including Dr David Livingstone's memoir of South Africa, *The Malay Archipelago* by Alfred Russel Wallace, the explorer-naturalist who was the co-founder of Darwin's theory of evolution, and *The Expression of Emotions in Man and Animals* by Darwin himself.

Wolf had the enviable ability for a wildlife artist of being able to transform what lay before him as a lifeless skin into an image that almost flies off the page. He was a master at rendering fine details of plumage, and claimed to be the first to introduce to English bird art a systematic study of the way in which the feathers are arranged on the bird. Engagingly, his feathers are not always attached to the bird: stray down feathers float from a nest, or rest lightly on the ground. He loved drama in nature, and if any criticism is justified, it is that sometimes he allowed this to become too exaggerated; but it appealed greatly to Victorian taste and temperament especially when, as often, it dealt with the grand themes of life and death, as represented by the hunting eagle or other raptors and their prey.

One of the reasons that Wolf's paintings were so true to life – if not larger than life – was that he was a great field naturalist, spending much of his time observing and sketching the birds and other animals of the British countryside. He was particularly fond of going on trips to the Scottish Highlands, where he could paint his favourite subjects – game birds and birds of prey – among the moors and mountains. Another habit of his that helped in this connection was that of paying frequent visits to the gardens of the Zoological Society of London to study and draw the animal inhabitants; and despite living in the city, Wolf shared his rooms with tame Bullfinches, Nightingales and other songbirds, just as he had as a boy in the country.

His motto as a wildlife painter was 'Life! Life! That is the great thing!' By contrast, he commented disparagingly on museum ornithologists: 'These fellows know very little. To put a bird right, they smooth it down with their hands, and tie paper round it very tightly, but this gives a totally false impression. The feathers are naturally full of spring, and lie lightly'. This is true, as anyone will know who has handled a live – or recently dead – bird. He also remarked that museum men were often unaware of the true colours of birds' eyes, since they looked only at skins of dead birds.

In his youth Wolf had enjoyed shooting birds, but as he grew older and more knowledgeable about the threats to wildlife, he decided to put down the gun and became a passionate opponent of the wholesale slaughter of birds for the plume trade, averring that man was 'the most destructive and carnivorous animal in the world'. He even went as far as scooping up in a butterfly net the Blackbird fledglings he found in his London garden on summer evenings and keeping them indoors overnight, safe from marauding cats.

When he was in his early fifties, Wolf started to suffer badly from rheumatism, which was to afflict him for the rest of his life. The pain in his arm slowed down his work, although he continued to paint birds and mammals until his death.

William Hart (1830–1908) was one of the hardest-working of all painters, lithographers and hand colourists specialising in birds. The son of a watercolour artist of the same name, he was born in Limerick in western Ireland, but moved to London and married by the time he was twenty-one. In all, Hart produced some 2,000 plates of birds. His work involved various stages of responsibility: colouring or overseeing other colourists from 1851 onwards, when he started working for John Gould; making the lithographic plates from 1871; and painting the original watercolours from 1881, the year of Gould's death, by which time he was working for Dr Richard Bowdler Sharpe, Head of the Bird Room at the British Museum (Natural History).

Hart exceeded even Richter in the length of his association with Gould, working on many of his employer's great book projects for nearly fifty years. On the occasions when he was not busy producing work for Gould or Sharpe, or colouring work for other artists – much of his life was spent colouring prints for other bird books – Hart made some paintings of birds and fish in oils, a medium well suited to the rich colours of tropical birds.

Like Wolf and the other artists who at various times worked for Hermann Schlegel at the Leyden Museum, Joseph Smit (1836–1929) became a very good illustrator of birds, as well as other natural-history subjects. Born in Lisse in the Netherlands, he received his first commission when he was asked to work on the lithographic stones for printing Dr Schlegel's own drawings for a book he was writing on the birds of the Dutch East Indies. This appeared in three large quarto volumes between 1863 and 1866, and contained fifty hand-coloured plates.

In 1866, Smit left Leyden for London. He was invited by Philip Lutley Sclater, who was then secretary of the Zoological Society of London and who later became editor of *Ibis*, the august journal of the British Ornithologists' Union. At the time, Sclater was busy writing his *Exotic Ornithology*, and he asked Smit to make the original watercolour paintings and lithographs for this major work on new and rare bird species from America. It was eventually published between 1866 and 1899, and contained 100 of Smit's hand-coloured plates.

Not long after his arrival, Smit began a close friendship with Joseph Wolf, and for many years they worked as a team on the illustrations for numerous fine books about birds and mammals, Wolf making the initial drawings and Smit producing the lithographs.

Smit's son, Pierre Jacques Smit (1863–1960), was just two years old when he and the rest of the family arrived in London with their father. As a young man he had the enterprising idea of drawing and painting small pictures of birds at London Zoo, which he sold to visitors to the collections to help them identify the unfamiliar birds they saw. Later, along with John Gerrard Keulemans (see below), he helped his father with his mammoth task of illustrating thirteen volumes of the twenty-seven-volume *Catalogue of the Birds in the Collections of the British Museum (Natural History)*, which was edited and partly written by Bowdler Sharpe and published between 1874 and 1898.

By the late nineteenth century, Britain had become the centre of the trade in fine bird books, with their beautiful and scientifically accurate illustrations. Huge numbers of animal specimens, including those of new and rare bird species, flooded in from all corners of the globe – and particularly from the vast and still-expanding British Empire. These kept an increasing army of museum specialists busy describing, naming and studying them; the artists were busy as never before in illustrating them.

One of the most prolific exponents of this 'museum art' was John Gerrard Keulemans (1842–1912), another Dutchman who had gravitated to the Leyden Museum as a protégé of Schlegel before becoming one of the busiest bird illustrators of the late nineteenth century after relocating to London. As a young man, he travelled extensively in Europe and Africa, aided by his ability to speak five

languages. He collected specimens, learned to prepare skins and sketched birds from life. After contracting a fever in West Africa, he returned to Europe. His skill at draughtsmanship and design was first properly demonstrated in the 200 lithographs he made to illustrate his own book *Onze Vogel in Huis en Tuin* ('Our Birds in House and Town'), which was published in the Netherlands in three volumes between 1869 and 1876.

Keulemans was encouraged to come to London in 1869 by Bowdler Sharpe, who asked him to illustrate his kingfisher monograph. The Dutchman's subsequent output was huge, with few serious publications on birds in Britain during the last quarter of the nineteenth century lacking at least some plates by him. He contributed to more than 115 books, and leading journals for which he made illustrations included *Ibis* and both the *Proceedings and Transactions of the Zoological Society of London*. As Barbara and Richard Mearns write in their fascinating book *The Bird Collectors*, 'He had the dubious privilege of painting more birds, now extinct, than any other artist of his generation'. Among the many illustrations he produced for the famous zoologist and collector Lord Lionel Walter Rothschild were a good number for the latter's 1905 book, *Extinct Birds*. Rothschild was a great patron of ornithological artists, owning many of the fine bird books described in this chapter, including works by Gould, Lear and Audubon. Rothschild generously donated his entire museum of zoology specimens and his magnificent library to the British Museum (Natural History).

Keuleman's approach to bird illustration was diligent, methodical, academic and unvarying in style and composition, resulting in technically skilled but often rather lifeless portraits. However, what he lacked in this way was partly compensated for by the fact that he was remarkably versatile in being able to draw with equal accuracy a great range of birds, from tiny, glittering-plumaged, tropical sunbirds to nocturnal, sombre-hued nightjars, and from familiar garden species such as Blue Tits and Robins to exotic birds of paradise. His watercolour paintings, sometimes with the addition of gouache, are freer and more lively than his illustrations for books and journals, portraying such scenes as a colony of Black-headed Gulls or Northern Gannets – although even these lack the charisma of similar subjects by Wolf and others.

Not all the artists painting birds at this time were engaged in producing work for the expensive books of museum men like Gould, Sharpe and the rest, and some did not belong to this mainstream at all. There are no better examples than the contrasting characters of Joseph Crawhall (1861–1913) and Léo Paul Samuel Robert (1851–1923).

Born in Northumberland in 1861, Crawhall came from a family of artists, receiving encouragement from his father and uncle. He studied art in London and then in Paris, where he became strongly influenced by the famous artist James Whistler. Afterwards he went to live in Scotland for a few years where he became one of the Glasgow Boys, a school of painters working in the great Scottish city at the turn of the century. He ended up living in Yorkshire. Although he painted mainly people and horses, he also made some outstanding watercolour and gouache paintings of birds, including ducks, swans, parrots, pigeons and Rooks.

Crawhall had a particular gift of being able to distil the essence of a subject by staring at it intently for up to an hour or more. Back in his studio, he would then paint from memory what he had seen. Although he did not consciously imitate Japanese and Chinese artists, his work was imbued with the deep understanding of the essence of the bird which their paintings so often exhibit.

Léo Paul Samuel Robert was a very different painter, but equally modern in his approach. He is acclaimed by many modern bird artists and art historians, some of whom regard him as the greatest ever portrayer of birds. In all, Robert painted about 500 watercolours of birds. He favoured the small songbirds, and painted them best, the plumage details and animation of their faces giving them an authenticity instantly recognisable to anyone who has studied them in the field. His particular genius was to see birds not only as an integral part of their habitat, but to paint the scene from the bird's viewpoint. Looking at his pictures, we are always at the bird's level, whether the perspective is that of a Hoopoe flying high above a valley, a Cirl Bunting singing from a branch on a slope above terraced fields or a pair of Dunnocks shuffling about mouse-like in search of food among the dead leaves on the ground.

PLATE 165.

Flame Bowerbird
(male & female)
Sericulus aureus

John Gould

c.1875–88. Hand-
coloured lithograph.
548mm x 364mm
(21½in x 14¼in)

This plate shows two
males (immature in
front) of one of the
island's scarcer species.
The male builds a bower
of sticks to attract a
female (rear of picture)
to mate with him, his
brilliant plumage
glowing in the gloom
of the forest.

PLATE 166.

Resplendent Quetzal
(male & female)
Pharomachrus moccino

John & Elizabeth Gould

1838. Hand-coloured
lithograph.
969mm x 347mm
(38¼in x 13¼in)

This lithograph by
Elizabeth Gould of one
of the most beautiful
birds in the world
appears in the first
edition of A Monograph
of the Trogonidae, or
Family of Trogons. *The*
male's tail is so long that
a special folded double
page was needed to
accommodate it.

TROGON RESPLENDENS.
Trogonidae Trogon

he *Pokrass Pheasant (female)*

PLATE 167.
Koklass Pheasant
(female)
Pucrasia macrolopha

Rajman Singh
c.1856–64. Watercolour.
256mm x 367mm
(10in x 14½in)

This illustration, by one of the main Nepalese artists Hodgson employed to record his ever-growing collection of birds, shows one of the more widespread of the pheasants that he recorded. The long spiky crest and lance-head shape of the body feathers makes the male distinctive; these are reduced but still noticeable in the female, shown here.

PLATE 168.
Cheer Pheasant *(male)*
Catreus wallichii

Rajman Singh
c.1856–64. Watercolour.
358mm x 256mm
(14in x 10in)

Hodgson obtained only three species of pheasants from western Nepal, including the two species shown here. Deforestation, coupled with continued hunting, has resulted in the Cheer Pheasant being classified as 'vulnerable', with a total population that may number only a few thousand.

The Cheer Pheasant –

Sketch of Yellow-tipped Penguin.

PLATE 169.

Fiordland Penguin
(immature)
Eudyptes pachyrhynchus

Richard Laishley
c.1863–83. Watercolour &
pencil.
254mm x 178mm
(10in x 7in)

*Richard Laishley
(1816–97) studied
painting in London,
including a spell at the
Royal Academy schools.
He then trained for the
ministry and in 1860
travelled to the other side
of the world for a new life
as a missionary in New
Zealand. The Rev. Laishley
remained passionately
interested in natural
history, and continued to
paint. The Natural
History Museum has a
book of his drawings of
the wildlife of New
Zealand, from which the
carefully painted study of
this penguin is taken.*

PLATE 170.

Brown Kiwi
Apteryx australis

Richard Laishley
c.1863–83. Watercolour.
535mm x 425mm
(21in x 16¾in)

*These delightful little
sketches of a Brown Kiwi
are interesting in that
they show well the bird's
method of feeding:
making a test probe
(upper right) with its
long curved bill to sniff
out prey with the nostrils
at its tip, and finally,
removing a worm
(bottom right).*

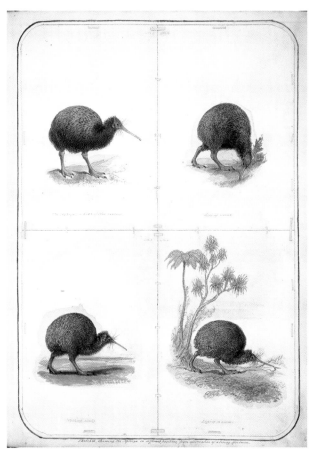

PLATE 171.
Long-billed Pipit
Anthus similis

Margaret Bushby Lascelles Cockburn
1858. Watercolour.
201mm x 254mm
(8in x 10in)

Relatives of the wagtails, the fifty or so species of pipits are found almost worldwide, from Alaska and Siberia to the subantarctic island of South Georgia, and from the British Isles to Japan. Like wagtails, pipits have long tails, which they frequently pump up and down; most have much plainer, streaked brown plumage than wagtails. This species has a very wide range, from Africa through the Middle East to India and Burma, and more than twenty distinct geographical races of the Long-billed Pipit (also known as the Brown Rock Pipit) have been described.

Bird of Paradise Flycatcher male & female
Muscipeta Paradisea 2 & 8 — Jerdon

PLATE 172.
Asian Paradise-
Flycatcher
(male, above, & female)
Terpsiphone paradisi
**Margaret Bushby
Lascelles Cockburn**
1858. Watercolour.
254mm x 201mm
(10in x 8in)

*This beautiful, strikingly
plumaged bird, one of the
most charismatic of all
Asian songbirds, is one of
the more abundant of the
fourteen species of
paradise-flycatcher found
in Africa, Madagascar
and Asia.*

PLATE 173.
Vernal Hanging-Parrot
Loriculus vernalis
**Margaret Bushby
Lascelles Cockburn**
1858. Watercolour.
254mm x 201mm
(10in x 8in)

*The name 'lovebird' is now
restricted to the African
species of small parrots
that are most familiar as
cage birds. The bird shown
here is one of the group of
even smaller parrots
known today as hanging-
parrots, from their habit
of hanging from a perch
to sleep at night.*

Love Bird. or Dwarf Parrot.

Psittaculus bernalis. 153-Jerdon.

(This is female)

Pl. 174

PLATE 174.
Spectacled Cormorant
Phalacrocorax perspicillatus

**John Gerrard
Keulemans**
c.1905. Watercolour.
825mm x 620mm
(32⅛in x 24⅖in)

*Unwary of humans, and
moving with only a
clumsy waddle on land,
this virtually flightless
seabird proved an easy
target for hunters on its
breeding grounds on rocky
islands in the Bering
Strait. The last ones were
probably killed for food by
the mid-1800s.*

PLATE 175.
'Oiseaux Bleu'
('Blue Bird')
Apterornis coerulescens

**John Gerrard
Keulemans**
c.1905. Watercolour.
806mm x 621mm
(31⅞in x 24⅖in)

*This bird, said to have
lived on the Indian Ocean
island of Réunion, is
known only from the
Frenchman 'Le Sieur'
Dubois' journal of his stay
on the island.*

PLATE 176.

Great Bustard, Little
Bustard & Houbara
Bustard *(males)*
*Otis tarda, Tetrax tetrax &
Chlamydotis undulata*

**John Gerrard
Keulemans**
c.1862–1912. Oil on
canvas.
1190mm x 2230mm
(46¾in x 87¾in)

*Simply titled 'Bustards',
this large oil painting
shows both species of
bustard that breed in
Europe, set in a splendidly
romantic landscape.*

PLATE 177.

Black-billed Magpie
Pica pica

**John Gerrard
Keulemans**
c.1896. Watercolour and
gouache.
635mm x 523mm
(25in x 20½in)

*As with the work of many
late nineteenth- and early
twentieth-century wildlife
illustrators, this carefully
observed and wittily titled
painting, 'Suspicion', tells
a story. This is typical of
the freer, more animated
style of Keulemans'
oil paintings.*

PL. 177.

PLATE 178.

Kakapo *(male & female)*
Strigops habroptilus

John Gerrard Keulemans
c.1887–1905.
Watercolour.
295mm x 244mm
(11⅝in x 9⅝in)

This atmospheric and accurate portrait of a pair of these very rare parrots was one of many Keulemans painted for the second edition of Sir Walter Buller's Birds of New Zealand. The Kakapo is unique in being the heaviest of the world's 350 or so species of parrot, as well as being the only flightless one, and the only one to display to females at a communal 'lek'. It is also among the very few species that are nocturnal. An alternative name is Owl Parrot.

PLATE 179.

Réunion Crested Starling
Fregilupus varius

John Gerrard Keulemans
c.1905. Watercolour.
385mm x 278mm
(15¼in x 11in)

This striking and enigmatic extinct bird lived on the island of Réunion in the Indian Ocean until the 1840s and perhaps a little later. It was once known to islanders and naturalists as the huppe (or hoopoe, from its longish downcurved beak, recalling a Hoopoe's). Like so many island birds, it was tame and easily killed by being knocked off its perch with a stick.

Chapter Four { 1890—TODAY

PLATE 180.
Blue Tit, Canary Islands
races
Parus caeruleus

Subspecies (from top to
bottom): *degener, teneriffae,
palmensis, ambriosus.*

Henrik Grönvold
c.1920. Watercolour.
260mm x 185mm
(10¼in x 7¼in)

*Grönvold was kept busy
painting ornithological
plates such as this one he
did for Ibis, the journal of
British Ornithologists'
Union, showing a series of
specimens of Blue Tits
from the Canary Islands,
for museum ornithologists.
Such work requires a
discerning eye and a
meticulous attention to
detail for showing clearly
the subtle distinguishing
features of the birds. The
four races, found on the
different islands, differ
slightly in the colour of
the back, the wing
pattern, and the colour of
their belly, as well as in
small differences in wing,
tail and bill length.*

*T*HE CLOSE OF THE NINETEENTH CENTURY marked the beginning of
the end for the lavish, expensive, hand-coloured lithographed bird
book. The final creator of such lithographs was the last artist of the
quartet of Europeans to move to England to make a name as a bird
illustrator: Henrik Grönvold (1858–1940). Unlike Wolf, Smit and
Keulemans, Grönvold was Danish rather than German or Dutch.

His first work as an artist was as a draughtsman, working for the Danish
artillery and for mill builder. Soon, however, he secured a job that was
more in keeping with the passion for nature and drawing wildlife which
he had shown from childhood: drawing and painting fish at the Danish
Biological Research Station in Copenhagen. The drawback was that there
was little prospect of advancement there, and when he was thirty-four
years old, Grönvold opted to leave Denmark to try his luck in America.

After arriving in London, from where he planned to sail to the United
States, Grönvold learned that there was a vacancy for a job preparing and
mounting bird skeletons at the British Museum (Natural History), which
he secured. He proved adept at this task, and was also proficient at
making skins, a skill he had acquired back in his youth in Denmark when
he shot birds and prepared specimens. After two years, early in 1895, he
resigned from this position, but he stayed on in the museum, working in
an unofficial capacity as an artist. Over the years there, he made use of his
early experience as a draughtsman in preparing many detailed anatomical
drawings of reptiles and fish as well as birds for the museum.

Although some of his finest work was for the last of the great
lithographed bird books, Grönvold's work demonstrates the transition
phase between nineteenth- and twentieth-century techniques of bird
illustration. His paintings were reproduced by a variety of different
methods, from hand-coloured lithography and chromolithography to
photogravure and three-colour letterpress printing. Almost all his work
was in watercolour, a notable exception being the fifteen oil paintings he
made for the great explorer-naturalist Charles William Beebe's *A
Monograph of the Pheasants* (1918–22), which were reproduced by
collotype, a type of lithography using a flat surface of hardened gelatine.

Original by
Henrik
Grönvold

a. Breast feathers of Francolinus nobilis nobilis Reichs.
b.   "   "   Francolinus nobilis chapini Grant & Lord.

Grönvold's paintings of birds' eggs were among the best of their kind. Egg plates are the Cinderellas of bird art, most artists being happy to avoid the difficult task of rendering faithfully the subtle appearance of the matt or glossy shells and their often intricate markings.

By the end of World War I, hardly any illustrations in natural-history books, or indeed any other books, were still being reproduced by chromolithographic printing, let alone the especially expensive hand-coloured lithographic process. Grönvold had the distinction of providing many of the plates for the last of these magnificent books.

Among these was *Birds of Australia* by Gregory Mathews, an Australian who was able to indulge his love of ornithology due to independent means, having made a fortune by investing in mining shares. After marrying an English woman, he moved to England in 1902, choosing a house strategically situated halfway between Lord Rothschild's great zoological museum in Tring and the British Museum (Natural History) in London.

Mathews had accumulated a huge collection of 30,000 skins of Australian birds, together with an impressive library of books and papers on the subject. Furthermore, he amassed a great deal of information on the lives of Australian birds in the wild from the team of collectors who supplied him with his specimens. It was seventy years since the last volume of Gould's great work *The Birds of Australia* had been published, and the lack of recent research on the subject, especially in Britain, meant there was a pressing need for a thorough and comprehensive work on Australian birds. The result was a handsomely illustrated twelve-volume treatise with the same title as Gould's pioneering work, minus the definite article. This mammoth undertaking took the author and Grönvold, whom he had chosen as his principal artist, seventeen years to produce, appearing between 1910 and 1927. One of a dying breed, like the great works of Audubon, Gould and the other nineteenth-century giants, it appeared in parts (no less than seventy-nine of them) and depended on rich subscribers or museum libraries; as a result, it was limited to only 225 copies.

The hand-coloured lithographs were the work of five different artists, although Grönvold produced well over half of them, 360 in total. Others were done by John Gerrard Keulemans, Roland Green and Herbert Goodchild, and George Lodge contributed a single plate.

Mathews went on to write two more works on the region, dealing with the birds of various Australasian islands. *The Birds of Norfolk and Lord Howe Islands and the Australasian South Polar Quadrant* appeared in 1928, with plates by Grönvold and Frederick Frohawk. Eight years later a supplement appeared which contained fifty-seven plates, all but nine of them by Grönvold: it was this that was the very last British bird book to contain hand-coloured lithographs.

Like some of the other museum artists such as Smit and Keulemans, Grönvold usually produced work that was artistically pleasing as well as being accurate ornithologically. A modest man, he was a very good team player, giving credit to other artists and going to great trouble to provide them with exactly what they wanted. He usually managed to invest his subjects with life and charm, even when working solely from skins. Even so, his considerable output (he worked on sixteen major works, as well as contributing to other books, journals and museum illustrations) was variable in quality. He was often unimaginative in his choice of posture, so that there is a sameness, and at times a stiffness, to the pictures; apart from a few distant silhouettes he avoided tackling birds in flight.

Grönvold was at his best painting smaller birds, and was especially skilled at rendering the subtle colour patterns of the difficult-to-identify 'little brown jobs', as birdwatchers often call them, such as the warblers that appear in what is generally regarded as his most pleasing work, that for *The British Warblers* (1907–14). Subtitled *A history, with problems of their lives*, this two-volume work was written by Henry Eliot Howard, a steel manufacturer who was an amateur ornithologist and pioneer in popularising the study of bird behaviour, notably the concept of breeding territory. As well as the thirty-five chromolithographs of twenty-six warbler species and their eggs, Grönvold produced fifty-one drawings for this book which were printed by the photographic process known as photogravure. One criticism of these otherwise fine plates is that, like his other small birds, the warblers tend to look very plump, although this

PLATE 181.
Handsome Francolin
(breast feathers)
A. *Francolinus nobilis nobilis*
B. *Francolinus nobilis chapini*

Henrik Grönvold
c.1934. Watercolour.
139mm x 146mm
(5⅜in x 5¾in)

Grönvold was a skilful painter of eggs, downy chicks and, as shown here, of feathers too, conveying their light and delicate structure with great sensitivity. A good example is this careful study of the breast feathers of the two subspecies thought to exist of this delightfully named and very localised African gamebird. Accompanying paintings of the birds themselves, they were done for plates in a 1935 issue of Ibis, the journal of the British Ornithologists' Union. Today, no subspecies are recognised, since the distinguishing characters used to separate the race chapini, from Uganda's Ruwenzori Mountains, are known to vary within populations.

was a common feature of the work of Scandinavian artists used to seeing birds whose plumage was fluffed out to insulate them from the cold.

After he settled in Britain, Grönvold left his adopted country only twice. On the first occasion, in 1895, just three years after his arrival, he accompanied William Ogilvie-Grant, his friend and colleague at the British Museum (Natural History), on a trip to collect shearwaters, storm petrels and other seabirds on the Salvage Islands, a group of tiny islands lying between Madeira and the Canaries. On the second, in 1910, he journeyed only as far as Berlin to attend an international ornithological congress. He continued to work almost until his death at the age of eighty-one.

As well as the many museum illustrators, such as Grönvold, who flourished at the turn of the century in Britain and other parts of Europe, as well as in America, there were also a number of fine artists who chose to specialise in painting wildlife, including birds. Unquestionably one of the most accomplished of them, and indeed one of the greatest wildlife artists of all time, was the Swede Bruno Liljefors (1860–1939). In his dramatic oil paintings, he was able to convey to the viewer a sense of being in the scene, surrounded by the sights and sounds and smells of nature. Like Wolf before him, he always strove to paint what he saw – his birds and mammals are engaged in the many businesses of their daily lives, not stuck in some fanciful pose to suit the artist. At the same time, his paintings are hugely satisfying as works of art, and have a tremendous emotional impact.

A skilled and devoted hunter all his life, Liljefors was intimately and passionately involved with wildlife and wild places, and as a result his work lacked any hint of sentimentality. He identified strongly with the predators that shared his quarry, and made many paintings of Golden Eagles, White-tailed Eagles, Eurasian Eagle Owls, Red Foxes and even fellow human hunters chasing or catching prey.

After he had been attending the Royal Academy of Fine Arts in Stockholm for three years, he found that his father could no longer support him, and he had to spend time away from lessons drawing caricatures for newspapers to fund his course. When a new director decreed that all students had to attend full time, his fellow student and lifelong best friend Anders Zorn, who had also taken time out to earn money, by teaching art, left the Academy, convinced it had nothing more to teach him, to continue studying and practising art abroad. He advised Liljefors to do the same, and to paint directly from nature.

Zorn, who went on to become Sweden's most famous painter, was of great help to his friend in developing his technique. Liljefors's other main influences were the Impressionists and, especially in his earlier work, Japanese and Chinese painting. In 1882 he left Stockholm and went to Düsseldorf, where he studied for a while under the elderly Professor Carl Deiker, one of Germany's best-known animal painters. After following his friend's advice and painting outdoors in Bavaria and Italy, he exhibited his first Impressionist paintings at the Paris Salon exhibition in the spring of 1883, before returning to Sweden in the winter.

Liljefors matured into a brilliantly proficient painter – as the artist John Busby puts it, 'he handled paint with the mastery that Rubens would have admired'. Despite periods of hardship and desperation, he eventually became a very successful artist, due in no small part to the patronage of a wealthy financier, Ernest Thiel, and he was able to buy a large country property and build up a menagerie of eagles, hawks, falcons and other birds, as well as foxes and other mammals; they served as live models for his paintings. In 1925, at the age of sixty-five, Liljefors was honoured with his country's highest award, the gold Tessin Medal.

Much of Liljefors's success as a wildlife painter depended on his approach to his subjects. In a method reminiscent of that of Audubon, he often used propped-up dead birds to study the dramatic postures and effects of light and shade he wished to capture. Although the models he used were dead and still, the paintings are far from static, being full of action and invested with an amazing sense of life thanks to the artist's keen eye and the intimate experience of his subjects, gained from countless hours of patient stalking and watching as a hunter as well as an artist. A perfect example is his masterful painting of a Northern Goshawk that has singled out a cock Black Grouse from a flock and is striking it with its outstretched talons among the tops of conifers in the mist, creating a flurry of detached feathers in the process.

Liljefors was one of the first to show convincing images of birds in flight in a way that conveys the mastery of the bird over the air, and its lightness and speed. While it is true that at times, as with Audubon before him, his desire to make a dramatic painting sometimes led him to overlook certain details that were not true to life, the overall effect works brilliantly.

PLATE 182.
Brünnich's Guillemot
& Guillemot
Uria lomvia & Uria aalge

Archibald Thorburn
c.1885-97. Watercolour.
247mm x 170mm
(9¾in x 6¾in)

*Thorburn combined
accuracy with atmosphere
in the superb paintings he
made of British birds,
generally acknowledged as
some of the finest ever
done. This example shows
two closely related auk
species in winter plumage,
the Guillemot (known to
North Americans as the
Common Murre) in the
foreground and its more
northerly counterpart,
Brünnich's Guillemot
(called Thick-billed Murre
in North America) behind.*

Instead of the idealised, detailed representations of structure and plumage with every feather detailed – the hallmarks of many bird painters – Liljefors's birds look the way one often actually sees them, whether with their wings blurred in flight, partly hidden by foliage, or silhouetted against the light. He achieved the apparent paradox of creating more exact and truthful representations of nature despite defining less detail.

Above all, Liljefors was among the greatest of all bird painters in showing the bird as an integral part of its environment. He clearly loved the challenge of rendering in paint the infinitely subtle browns, olives, ochres, greens and greys of the Scandinavian wilderness, and the effects of half-light: many of his most atmospheric paintings depict scenes at dusk or dawn.

Instead of showing the bird standing out sharply from its background, he delighted in showing his subjects almost merging into it as they so often do in nature, as in his wonderful paintings of waders portrayed against brownish marshland, Grey Partridges amid a golden cornfield or the great grouse called Capercaillie in the gloom of a coniferous forest. The birds are hard to make out at first, for just as in real life the subtle camouflage of their plumage hides them among the similarly coloured background, and they are dwarfed by their environment rather than being exaggerated in scale and impact. Looking at such a painting creates a powerful feeling of being there, and the fact that the birds are not overwhelmingly apparent only adds to one's pleasure in a way that approaches the joy of finding the real birds in the field.

Another of this unique artist's talents was that instead of making composite representations showing the average appearance of the species, he created paintings that are true portraits of individuals. For all these reasons and more, many regard this remarkable man as the greatest of all bird artists.

Two other outstanding bird painters were born in the same year as Liljefors in Britain. The famous Scottish bird artist Archibald Thorburn (1860–1935) was a great admirer of the paintings of Joseph Wolf, asserting that they had 'an indescribable feeling of life and movement attained by no other wildlife artist'. Thorburn's contemporary, George Edward Lodge (1860–1954), felt similarly. He recalled in his memoirs the time he was 'told by a very eminent ornithologist of [the old] days that

A.Thorburn

the great fault of Wolf's illustrations were that they were too "artistic"; he countered that Wolf was 'the greatest draughtsman of birds who ever lived, and, as I truly think, ever will live'. Both artists certainly owe a great debt to this earlier genius, but also bring qualities quite of their own. Wolf recognised Thorburn's abilities early on in his career, and gave him valued encouragement. The old master's praise was well-deserved, and the many more recent commentators who eulogised his work include the famous artist and conservationist Sir Peter Scott, who wrote that Thorburn 'portrayed the texture of feathers more brilliantly than anyone else before him', and the ornithologist, writer and broadcaster James Fisher who claimed that 'Of the British bird artists of living memory the greatest is certainly the Scot Archibald Thorburn'. Another less welcome mark of his acclaim is that some buyers have been disappointed when their purchases of Thorburn paintings have turned out to be carefully crafted fakes of the real thing.

Born in Lasswade near Edinburgh, Thorburn had a good but hard master in his youth, for his father, Robert, was a famous miniaturist who painted Queen Victoria on no less than three occasions, and was also responsible for her favourite portrait of Prince Albert. Although Archibald was sent to an art school in St John's Wood, London, for a brief period, he said that he learned far more about drawing and painting at his father's hand – which does not appear to have been a light one, since its owner tore up any work which did not come up to his exacting standards. While in St John's Wood, however, Thorburn was near his hero Wolf, and benefited from his advice and interest.

Thorburn's first major commission was to paint the watercolours for 144 chromo-lithographed plates for a popular work, *Familiar wild birds*, written by a Brighton taxidermist and naturalist, Walter Swaysland. This brought him to the attention of Lord Lilford, who employed him to paint many of the plates for his seven-volume *Coloured figures of the birds of the British Islands* (1885–98). The original illustrator of this ambitious and beautiful work was Keulemans, but by 1887, after he had painted 125 plates for the earlier volumes, he had become too ill to continue with the work. Lilford asked Thorburn to complete what amounted to 264 plates out of a total of 421; other artists finished the remainder. This huge task occupied Thorburn for a period of ten years, at an average of one finished watercolour plate, sometimes containing a dozen or more individual birds, per fortnight.

Compared to the very expensive works of Gould and others, the *Coloured figures* reached a wide audience, thanks to Lilford's policy of keeping the price as low as possible, despite the fact that the venture cost him about £15,000 ($26,000). After Thorburn's first plates appeared in 1888, there were three times as many subscribers as for the earlier volumes, which contained Keulemans's accurate but comparatively lifeless illustrations. Thorburn's plates continued to reach an ever-wider public for almost 100 years after their first publication (albeit reproduced less well by more modern printing methods), for they were used to illustrate both Thomas Alfred Coward's *The Birds of the British Isles and their eggs* (which first appeared in two volumes from 1920 until 1925, as a three-volume work from 1926 to 1950, and then in 1969 as a condensed and revised single-volume edition), and from 1937 until the late 1970s the little *Observer's Book of British Birds* (from 1953 as the *Observer's Book of Birds*) by Vere Benson. The latter was one of the first two titles to be published in this very popular series, and sold over three million copies

PLATE 183.
Carrion Crow
Corvus corone

Archibald Thorburn
c.1885–97. Watercolour.
150mm x 227mm
(6in x 9in)

This illustration conveys well the predatory tendencies of this very widespread and abundant member of the crow family, as it holds down a tiny, helpless gamebird chick – although this does serve to show the great size of the Raven, and as a moral overtone typical of much Victorian animal painting, may be intended to show its supposedly cowardly nature. As usual, Thorburn has set his bird in a habitat typical of the species, atop a prominent ridge with a big conifer tree that could hold its bulky stick nest.

in its long lifetime.

Even better than this work of the closing years of the nineteenth century were the plates Thorburn painted to illustrate his four-volume *British Birds*, one of the four books he wrote himself in the early years of the twentieth century. This was first published from 1915 to 1916, with a supplement in 1918. Originally limited to 250 copies, the first edition soon sold out and was reprinted in a number of editions. Each plate depicted several related species, enabling comparisons to be made between them in the way that came to be standard in field guides and monographs of bird identification.

Like Wolf, Thorburn loved the Scottish grouse moors and mountains, and spent much time sketching from nature there. He was particularly fond of illustrating gamebirds and birds of prey and did so with great skill, and of course good paintings of these subjects were very saleable to wealthy sportsmen. However, he was equally able to produce beautiful and accurate studies of smaller birds, with a delicacy and liveliness rarely matched even to this day.

Thorburn was also a great painter of wildfowl. He contributed several plates of ducks for two fine books on wildfowl written by John Guille Millais, himself a good painter of birds and responsible for many of the plates. He was the fourth and youngest son of Sir John Everett Millais, the famous painter and member of the pre-Raphaelite brotherhood. Thorburn's contributions are well-designed and excellent at conveying the atmosphere of the lakes, marshes and estuaries, and the birds themselves are beautifully painted; but his tendency to dramatise his birds is sometimes responsible for some inaccuracies, such as the distinctly overlarge heads of some of the ducks (also a feature of some of his paintings of other bird groups), and a habit of depicting the swimming birds too high in the water.

In contrast to Liljefors's bold approach, Thorburn's style was delicate and did not suit oils, and almost all his work was in watercolour and body colour, sometimes heightened with white gouache. He had a superb watercolour technique, and was gifted at the handling of light and shade: his birds have a solid look about them compared to the flat images of many lesser artists. His backgrounds were accurate evocations of each bird's characteristic habitat, with delicate detail and an excellent sense of design.

36

In addition to the plates he painted for many books, Thorburn was kept busy painting pictures – some of them huge – for galleries or private buyers. He had his paintings exhibited at the Royal Academy in London fifteen times during the last twenty years of the nineteenth century, the first two being accepted in 1880 when he had just turned twenty.

Thorburn enjoyed shooting regularly as a young man, but gave it up after hearing a Brown Hare he had wounded screaming in agony. He was one of the earliest bird artists working in Britain to lend his talents to the cause of the rapidly growing conservation movement, especially the Royal Society for the Protection of Birds (RSPB). He produced designs for nineteen of the society's annual Christmas cards between 1899 and 1935; he painted the last one, depicting Europe's smallest bird, the Goldcrest, with difficulty while bedridden and in pain not long before he died. Although he had become the most famous of all Britain's bird painters, and earned considerable sums from each of his paintings, he charged nothing for those he did for the RSPB, donating all but one of them free of charge to the Society, which was then able to raise much-needed funds by selling them. The exception was his painting of a Chaffinch for the 1933 card, which was presented to King George V, the patron of the RSPB, on the occasion of his silver jubilee.

Although born in the same year as Thorburn, George Lodge outlived him by over eighteen years, and remained alert and active until he died at the age of 93. Together with Thorburn, he had one foot in the Victorian school of British lithographic artists painting sporting pictures for wealthy patrons, and one in the modern era of colour printing for books aimed at ornithologists and the new breed of birdwatchers.

Born into a large and long-lived family in Scrivelsby, Lincolnshire, England, he had a passion for birds from early boyhood. Often accompanied by his elder brother Reginald, he spent much time exploring the local countryside and its bird life, and started shooting birds at the age of twelve to make a collection of skins from which to draw. Reginald went on to become one of the great pioneers of bird photography, and during the 1870s George often accompanied him on field trips, when they pushed a huge, unwieldy plate camera across country on a wheelbarrow.

He was educated mainly at home, but also attended Lincoln College of Art where he won prizes when only fourteen years old. At sixteen, Lodge became apprenticed to a wood engraver and became highly proficient at this craft, producing many fine woodcuts of birds, including illustrations for books by the great ornithologist and specialist on the birds of Siberia, Henry Seebohm.

Unlike his contemporary and friend Thorburn, Lodge remained an avid country sports-man all his life, both on the grouse moors and in the salmon rivers of Scotland. He also shot birds to add to his reference collection, and kept superbly mounted specimens of falcons and other birds in the studio of his home – appropriately named Hawk House – in Camberley, Surrey. A very skilful taxidermist and dissector of birds, Lodge said that it was not possible to paint the outside of a bird properly without knowledge of its insides.

He was also a remarkable bird tamer: his garden at Hawk House was full of small birds that had learned they had nothing to fear from this patient and quiet observer of their lives. House Sparrows, Chaffinches, European Robins and Blue Tits were among the many regular visitors taking crumbs from his fingers.

From an early age, Lodge also had a passion for falconry and could often be seen walking around the streets of London with a falcon on his wrist. He was particularly keen on painting birds of prey, and these were the birds he painted best, without sentimentality. Philip Glasier, who was then one of the last professional falconers in the British Isles, recalls Lodge's skill in this respect in his 1963 book *As The Falcon Her Bells*. He remembers that at Avebury there were fifteen merlins that, to the average eye, looked as alike to each other as sheep do. Lodge's great ability was to distinguish between these seemingly identical birds in the sketches he would make of them as they were bathing and preening. Lodge was equally gifted at capturing the fleeting moments of a kill and – in marked contrast to Thorburn, who admitted his deficiency in this respect – outstanding at accurate and convincing portrayals of birds in flight.

Over the course of his very long life, Lodge produced a huge number of illustrations for almost seventy books on birds, as well as for magazines such as the *Avicultural Magazine*, and also many paintings in oils and watercolours for galleries and private buyers; his earlier work was often hung in the Royal Academy.

As he recorded in the only book he both wrote and illustrated (in his eighty-fifth year), *Memoirs of an Artist Naturalist*, published in 1946, Lodge

PLATE 185.
Green Woodpecker
Picus viridis

Frederick William Frohawk
1920. Pencil and monochrome wash.
228mm x 169mm
(9in x 6¼in)

Although Frohawk enjoyed shooting birds, he used his gun relatively sparingly for specimens he felt it essential to study, and also made many drawings of birds from life, often accompanied by detailed notes of his observations, for he was particularly interested in bird behaviour. This drawing of a Green Woodpecker resting on a trunk in the rain, which he watched through his telescope, is a fine example.

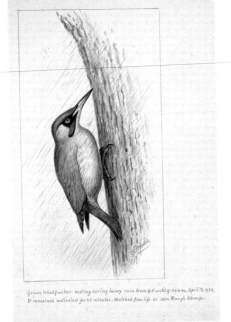

Green Woodpecker resting during heavy rain from 9.5 until 9.30 a.m. April 12.1920.
It remained motionless for 25 minutes. Sketched from life as seen through telescope.

visited and painted in many parts of the world, 'from the Tropics to the Arctic regions'. In the latter, he 'never hesitated to take out easel, canvas and painting gear in midwinter … I would work all day with snow deep on the ground, or skate out on to the ice and paint away until I was too cold to work, and so had to stop and take a cruise around on my skates until circulation was good enough to allow me to continue work.' Lodge devoted the last chapter of this book to making 'some observations on painting birds', and it is a mark of the man's prowess and understanding that much of what he says in it can be read with profit by the aspiring bird artist today.

One of the hallmarks of book illustrations and paintings by Lodge is the scrupulous attention he showed to the birds' background. He spent much time when invited to join shooting parties sketching details of the habitat as well as the birds themselves. And in his memoirs, the artist relates that when he lived in London for thirty-nine years of his life before moving to Camberley, he found some advantage in being near the zoo and the British Museum (Natural History), which later moved to South Kensington, London, and became the Natural History Museum, where he could make studies of birds that he would not have been able to do elsewhere, but faced problems when he wanted to paint authentic backgrounds of rocks against which to set a Peregrine Falcon, or a stubble field for his Grey Partridges. He was in the habit of creeping into city parks at night and surreptitiously 'lifting' twigs and foliage for drawing perches for songbirds, but for other material he had to write to family or friends in the countryside and ask them 'for some rubbish or other to be sent … by post'.

Finding that rocks, with their great variation in shape, colour, smoothness and also the particular kinds of lichens or mosses that grow on them in different habitats, were particularly difficult to draw convincingly from imagination or memory, he filled many sketchbooks with beautiful, detailed studies in pencil or oils. Lodge was a very good observer of birds and their behaviour, noting, for instance, that the loud 'drumming' sounds made by woodpeckers in proclaiming their territories and attracting mates were made mechanically, by the lightning-quick blows of their bills against the wood of a trunk or branch and not, as some ornithologists asserted, vocally.

Lodge's great ambition was to paint all the birds of Britain, and this was realised when he was commissioned by the ornithologist David Bannerman to produce all 385 colour plates to illustrate his twelve-volume *Birds of the British Isles* (1953–63). This was Lodge's crowning glory, and his boldly idiosyncratic style with the birds full of behaviour was well-suited to the equally unusual text, which went beyond the dry scientific descriptions of many other bird books and gave delightful word pictures of the birds' lives. Like Thorburn, Lodge worked right up to the end. He painted six extra plates of birds of prey in immature plumage for *Birds of the British Isles* at the age of ninety-one, with the same skill and finesse as always, despite the fact that he was almost without sight in one eye. Even though he was clearly better at painting some types of birds, especially birds of prey and gamebirds, than, for instance, some of the small songbirds, his total of 386 coloured plates for this work was a massive achievement. This was publicly recognised when an exhibition of some of the original watercolours was held in late 1953, only three months before his death, at the gallery of Rowland Ward in Piccadilly,

London, to coincide with the publication of the first volume.

One of the many illustrators who had a long association with the British Museum (Natural History) was Frederick William Frohawk (1861–1946). He was a man of varied interests and output, painting in watercolours and oils, and also producing wood engravings and lithographs. His best work was on butterflies, but he also depicted mammals, reptiles, amphibians, fish and other animals. Most of the illustrations he did for books, however, were of birds, although his work included drawings of amphibians, reptiles and birds for the ninth edition of *Encyclopaedia Britannica* (1875–89).

Like many other artist-naturalists working in the first half of the twentieth century, Frohawk shot birds to study and draw them more closely, as well as making patient observations of living birds. He discovered an important and interesting difference between the sexes in the Northern Lapwing (the male having very similar plumage but broader wingtips), and carefully studied the Manx Shearwaters on their nocturnal visits to their breeding burrows on Annet, one of the smallest of the Isles of Scilly.

Frohawk's first commission as a bird artist was to paint and lithograph the hand-coloured plates for a work on weaverbirds and finches by the entomologist and ornithologist Dr Arthur Gardiner Butler, assistant keeper of the Zoology Department of the British Museum from 1897 to 1901. Had the planned ninety-five parts of *A Monograph of the weaver-birds and arboreal and terrestrial finches* materialised, this would have been a huge achievement, but only five were published, with thirty-one plates, in 1888 and 1889. Although Butler abandoned this ambitious project, he did not do the same with its artist. He was sufficiently impressed with Frohawk's obvious talents to engage him to produce the illustrations of birds and eggs for his six-volume *British Birds with their Nests and Eggs*. Frohawk had to work fast on this title, producing 318 plates; three were done from mounted specimens, the remainder being drawn from skins but usually backed up by the artists' observations and knowledge of the living birds. Unfortunately, these were reproduced in black and white only, although the plates of eggs are in colour.

Other books on which Frohawk worked include a monograph on the birds of the Sandwich Islands (now known as Hawaii), written by two Cambridge ornithologists, Scott Wilson and A. H. Evans, which appeared

Sanderling 12·XI·07   Sampson Scilly?.
Shot by FWF

expanse 14¾ in.
length 7¼ in.
wing 5½ in.
wing ⅛ longer than tail.
ps. ⅜ longer than secs.
Weight 2 ozs 1 dram.
cul ⅞
Tarsus 1 in.

PLATE 186.
Sanderling *(winter plumage)*
Calidris alba

Frederick William Frohawk
1907. Watercolour and pencil.
178mm x 125mm
(7in x 5in)

Frohawk, like Charles Tunnicliffe some fifty years later, made studies showing the details of bills and feet of various birds to use as future reference, helping him to add veracity to his bird paintings. The species in this drawing is a little wader that breeds in the high Arctic but is seen by most birdwatchers in passage or, in winter, in small feeding flocks that scurry along the edges of sandy shores like clockwork toys, dodging the waves as they deliver the little worms, crustacea and other food on which they depend.

C. G. Finch-
19-

in eight parts between 1890 and 1899, and for which he was responsible for all sixty-four plates; and a book on the Old-World geese by the Russian ornithologist Prince Sergius Alferaky, containing twenty-four particularly handsome plates, again all by Frohawk.

One particularly unusual challenge for Frohawk was the commission from the great naturalist and collector Lord Walter Rothschild in the early 1900s to paint a series of reconstructions of extinct birds for a lecture at the International Ornithological Congress of 1905, including a life-size portrait of a giant moa. Frohawk had to work balancing on a ladder to complete this painting, which is some thirteen feet (four metres) tall and still hangs at Tring Museum, Rothschild having generously donated his collection and museum building on his death in 1937 to the British Museum (Natural History).

In contrast to many of the British artists described in this chapter, Claude Gibney Davies (1875–1920) found the subjects for all his bird paintings far from home, in Africa. Born in Delhi, India, he was the son of a senior British army officer, Major General Sir William Davies, who served as governor of the city for a short time. His mother, Lady E. Davies, was a keen amateur naturalist. Although she preferred studying the diversity of snakes found in India to birds, she was probably partly responsible for her son's passion for ornithology.

Like the offspring of so many highly placed colonial administrators, young Claude was shipped back to the home country to receive a 'proper' education, in his case at the tender age of six. His interest in illustrating birds was clearly already well-developed, as he sent bird paintings back to his older sister in India from his school in England.

A reluctant student, Davies went to South Africa in 1893, shortly after his eighteenth birthday, to enlist in the British Army, and remained there until his death at the early age of 45. His army career took him to many parts of Africa, and he was able to pursue his interest in observing, collecting and painting birds. His studies in pencil and watercolours are skilfully executed and beautifully coloured, and his rendition of lifelike plumage was outstanding.

In 1916, Davies married Aileen Finch. The serendipitous suitability of her surname did not go unnoticed by the bridegroom's friends who found it a splendid joke, while his wife's parents were adamant he should

PLATE 187.
Blacksmith Plover
Vanellus armatus

Claude Gibney Finch-Davies
1918. Watercolour & pencil.
178in x 255mm
(7in x 10in)

Finch-Davies' superbly drawn and coloured illustrations of many of the most attractive birds of South Africa appeared in various books and journals during the early twentieth century. This one, showing a boldly pied, long-legged plover of the lakes and marshes of eastern and southern Africa, is one of twenty-one paintings in the collections of the Natural History Museum. The odd name refers to the bird's harsh, metallic call, which resembles the sound of a blacksmith's hammer striking the anvil.

formally adopt it as part of his name. Finch-Davies, as he was now known, illustrated all the birds of prey, including the owls as well as the raptors known to occur in southern Africa at the beginning of the twentieth century; only eight more species have been recorded in southern Africa since then. He also painted at least sixty-eight watercolours of wildfowl and others of gamebirds and sandgrouse. Over his short lifetime, this part-time bird painter managed to illustrate almost half of all the bird species known to occur in South Africa.

Not long after Finch-Davies's impressive achievements, the Dutch painter and illustrator Marinus Adrianus Koekkoek (1873–1944) produced some of the finest of all plates intended to help identify birds. Although he also painted attractive studies in oils of farmyard scenes with poultry, his greatest achievement was to illustrate the five volumes of the great work by Eduard van Oort, *Ornithologia Neerlandica: The Birds of the Netherlands*, which illustrated all the birds known to occur in the Netherlands in 407 colour plates. Publication was irregular, in forty-six parts over the period 1922–35.

His work reached a far wider audience in Britain when many of these plates were used (along with a few others) by Frederick Frohawk, Roland Green, Henrik Grönvold, John Cyril Harrison, George Lodge, and Philip Rickman to illustrate *The Handbook of British Birds* (Witherby, Jourdain, Ticehurst and Tucker, 1938–41) which appeared in five volumes that, although not cheap, were affordable enough to be bought by many of the growing army of amateur ornithologists and birdwatchers; it became the standard work for almost the next forty years. Koekkoek's meticulous paintings showed the birds' plumage in clear detail; each plate depicted the male, female, young and seasonal or other variations of a single species. The birds were not only precise, but invested with a good deal of life within the constraints of the formulaic approach needed for comparisons between species. Koekkoek also integrated the birds skilfully with their background, paying great attention to the accurate portrayal of the habitat typical of each species.

Although book illustrations of the quality of those by Koekkoek were a great help to naturalists who wanted to identify unfamiliar species and unfamiliar plumages of common birds, they were, as they still often are to this day, idealised views in which the outlines and feathers of each bird are shown in great detail. A totally alternative approach, seen in the work of more recent practitioners, such as the outstanding pair of Eric Ennion and his protégé John Busby, is to make rapid but sure sketches in pencil, pen and/or watercolour of the living, often constantly moving birds. These sketches have minimal plumage detail, but when done by a skilled hand can instantly convey the unique character and salient features of each bird that distinguish it from other species – or to use the birder's term, its 'jizz'.

The first British artist to tread this adventurous and rewarding road was James Affleck Shepherd (1867–1946). A master of line and wash drawings with the plumage of the birds filled in as areas of colour rather than precisely delineated, he illustrated two bird volumes (bound as a single book) in the Bodley Head Natural History series. Published in 1913, this can be regarded as a forerunner to the modern field guide. Regrettably, although a third volume was planned, it was never published. In terms of conveying the features of each bird to a novice birdwatcher, these books were way ahead of their time.

Shepherd trained as a cartoonist, contributing to the famous satirical magazine *Punch* and other popular periodicals. This background shows in his work, with its wonderful economy of line and ability to convey instantly the essential personality of each bird, while at the same time avoiding the anthropomorphism of his humorous cartoons of birds and other animals.

Meanwhile, thousands of miles away, the most outstanding of all American bird painters since Audubon, Louis Agassiz Fuertes (1874–1927), was producing work of great originality and beauty. Born in Ithaca, New York State, Fuertes attended Cornell University, where his father Estevan was professor of civil engineering. Although Fuertes Senior named his son after one of America's greatest biologists, Louis Agassiz, who taught at Cornell as a visiting professor from Harvard and was a friend of the family, he did not think that painting birds was a sensible profession, and persuaded him to study architecture at the university instead. This did not stop the young Fuertes from following his real love, however, and his first published work – paintings for field guides – was done when he was still an undergraduate student at Cornell.

While still only a sophomore, Louis soon came to the attention of Elliott Coues, one of America's foremost ornithologists, through an introduction by a fellow student who was the great man's nephew. Coues

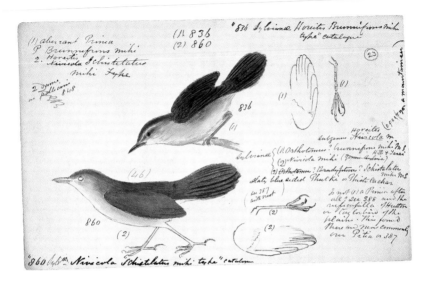

was fulsome in his praise of the budding young artist, showing his work to Audubon's granddaughters and writing in the journal *The Osprey* 'there is no one who can draw and paint birds as well as Mr Fuertes, and I do not forget Audubon himself when I add that America has not produced an ornithological artist of equal possibilities.' He also gave Fuertes his first commission, to produce 111 illustrations for *Citizen Bird*, a children's book he was co-writing with Mabel Wright. By the time he graduated from Cornell, Fuertes had illustrated three books.

He was a tireless bird collector, preparing his own skins for personal use and for museums with great skill. Like Audubon, he often used freshly shot birds arranged in lifelike postures as models for his studies. Above all, he spent much of his time drawing – if not on a sketch pad then on any other handy scrap of paper. But often he did not even need to do this to produce his lifelike paintings, for as important as his ability to sketch was the fact that

Fuertes had a photographic memory. After looking carefully at a bird, he could return to his studio and paint a brilliantly lifelike image. Perhaps because of this extremely powerful focus on the birds themselves, his backgrounds were rather skimpy, and at times even ill-conceived and unconvincing, but his genius at painting the main subject and investing it with character makes this less noticeable.

Fuertes was as energetic a traveller as he was as an artist, and the many places he visited on his expeditions included Mexico, the Caribbean and South America, as well as parts of North America. In summer 1927 he returned home from a long field trip to Abyssinia (now Ethiopia), in north-east Africa, with a superb collection of sketches that many regard as the best of all his work in watercolour. A short while later, on 22 August of the same year, Fuertes was driving home with his wife and many of the Abyssinian sketches. As he approached a railroad crossing, he attempted to overtake a hay wagon, when a train hit his automobile. His wife, though injured, recovered – and the paintings were saved by being thrown from the vehicle by the force of the impact – but Fuertes was killed immediately. Despite this tragic early death, Fuertes left not only a legacy of superb paintings but also provided inspiration for other American artists, both before and after his death.

Another important artist working in North America in the first half of the twentieth century was Allan Cyril Brooks (1869–1946). Like Fuertes, he had a characterful style very different from that of most of the artists working in Britain and Europe, and was an important influence on young artists who came after him, such as the Canadian Robert Bateman. Although he never had a single art lesson, he was a confident draughtsman, drawing the outlines of his birds with a single unbroken line, starting and ending at the bill. One of the first Canadians to make a profession out of wildlife art, Brooks was commissioned to paint an impressive number of plates of a wide range of birds for books, most of them published in the United States, as well as many paintings for North American museums.

Born in India to a British engineer father who collected birds for the British Museum and later took his family to Ontario, Canada when Allan was twelve years old, Brooks also achieved prominence as a soldier. For his bravery he won a Distinguished Service Order and was mentioned in dispatches three times while fighting in World War I for the British Army

PLATE 188.
Rufous-capped Bush-Warbler
Cettia brunnifrons

William Edwin Brooks

c.1865–75. Watercolour.
140mm x 229mm
(5½in x 9in)

The father of the better-known bird artist Allan Cyril Brooks, William Edwin Brooks (1828–99) was a civil engineer who emigrated from Newcastle-upon-Tyne, in north-east England, to India, to work on the East India Railway from 1868 until 1890. A keen ornithologist in his spare time, he collected birds for museums both here and in Canada, to which he retired in 1881. The Natural History Museum has eighty of his watercolour drawings of smaller Indian birds, including this detailed study of one of a group of warblers that present great difficulties in identification. It also shows the detailed notes and subsidiary pencil drawings he made to help untangle its true identity.

88
H
K

Merops albicollis of
true skin.

'60

C.E.Talbot Kelly.

and later for the Canadian Expeditionary Force, where he attained the rank of major. As well as becoming renowned in North America as a painter of birds and an ornithologist, he was a superb shot, both at international target-shooting competitions and, in the days before binoculars had replaced the gun as a way of studying birds, as a collector (and hunter) of birds. Hallmarks of Brooks's paintings are their rich colouring and the accuracy of plumage details of the birds, which are often set against dramatic skies with superb cloud effects.

Allen William Seaby (1867–1953) was not only a highly skilled artist, but also one of Britain's best teachers of art. His talents were recognised at an early age, when he was appointed as a pupil-teacher at the school he attended in rural Surrey. After studying at teacher-training college, he taught for a while at a school in Reading, Berkshire, and then, from the age of nineteen, spent the rest of his life there. After enrolling at the Reading School of Art, Seaby was greatly influenced by his teacher F. Morley Fletcher, who pioneered the use of Japanese woodcut colour printing in Britain, and learned to become an expert printmaker, using blocks of cherry wood and watercolours mixed with rice paste. In his turn, Seaby's grandson Robert Gillmor (B. 1936) who has for over forty years been one of Britain's best, best-known and busiest bird artists, learned much from his grandfather.

The work of Philip Charles Rickman (1891–1982) was very much in the tradition of Thorburn and Lodge, whom he greatly admired and from whom (especially Thorburn, who became a close friend) he learned much of his technique. Compared to their work, however, Rickman's was of much more variable quality, with some of his paintings being more decorative than arresting. Like Lodge, Rickman lived to paint into old age, his last book being published in 1979 when he was eighty-eight, and was eventually dubbed 'The Grand Old Man of British Bird Painting'.

A bird painter in a very different style was Richard Barrett Talbot Kelly (1896–1971). Greatly influenced by the bird art of China and of Ancient Egypt, Talbot Kelly had the ability to distil the essence of a bird to a few confidently drawn lines filled in with flat washes of colour, and to set it convincingly within a landscape that was often just suggested by skilfully drawn lines and colour. Often, by subtly exaggerating the features of a bird, he created an image that looked more lifelike than if it had been faithfully copied from life. Self-taught, Talbot Kelly began by drawing and

PLATE 189.
White-throated Bee-eater
Merops albicollis

Chloe Elizabeth Talbot Kelly
1960. Watercolour.
305mm x 228mm
(12in x 9in)

This painting by the daughter of the pioneering British bird artist Richard Talbot Kelly shows one of the most distinctive members of the bee-eater family, easily distinguished from all its relatives by its striking pied head pattern. It nests in large, loose colonies, digging its long nest burrows into sandy soil with its long sharp bill aided by the bicycling action of its feet. Each pair is usually assisted in the task of rearing the young by up to five related helpers. It breeds in a narrow belt of arid country spanning the African continent from Senegal to Somalia, and migrates to winter in a very different habitat, rainforest, savannah woodland and wooded farmland.

painting his impressions of people and landscapes he encountered during his time as a professional soldier in World War I, during which he was awarded the Military Cross and badly wounded. On his recovery, he became a specialist instructor in camouflage, an experience which contributed to his fascination about the effects of the environment and light on birds when he started to paint wildlife in earnest during post-war army service in India. In 1929, he resigned from the army and took up a teaching post as director of art at Rugby School, the famous public school that he had attended as a boy, and devoted his spare time to watching and painting birds and writing and illustrating books.

Another of the varied assortment of British bird artists born at the close of the nineteenth century, John Cyril Harrison (1898–1985), who showed a precocious artistic talent by the age of six, went on to study at the famous Slade School of Art in London. His best paintings of gamebirds and birds of prey rival those of Thorburn and Lodge for atmosphere and compositional skill.

Charles Frederick Tunnicliffe (1901–79) was undoubtedly one of the greatest of all British bird painters, and also justly renowned for his utterly convincing and superbly designed wood engravings of farming scenes, farm animals and country life generally. Raised on a farm in Cheshire, he had a deep understanding and love of the countryside. After a promising start at art school, he started his career not as a painter but in the difficult medium of wood engraving, that had largely fallen out of favour since the days of the great master, Thomas Bewick. He soon became a master of the craft with no equal in modern times. He made his name as a wildlife artist and book illustrator with his dramatic wood engravings for Henry Williamson's *Tarka the Otter* and his three other nature books. As he moved from engraving to painting, he went on to produce a huge body of work, producing pictures for cards issued with packets of tea, almost eighteen years' worth of Christmas cards, posters, magazine covers and other illustrations for the RSPB, and the illustrations for over seventy books and many other publications. He also wrote six himself, which included an excellent guide to drawing birds and a *Shorelands Summer Diary*, his paean to Shorelands, the house to which he happily moved in 1947 with his artist wife Winifred at Malltraeth, on the North Wales island of Anglesey, where he spent the rest of his life. Just as the famous eighteenth-century naturalist Gilbert White recorded his

PLATE 191.
Pallid Swift
Apus pallidus

**David Morrison
Reid-Henry**
c.1919–77. Ink line
drawing.
140mm x 125mm
(5½in x 5in)

*One of the finest of all
British bird artists of
the mid-twentieth century,
David Reid-Henry made
many superbly detailed
paintings of birds against
a meticulously detailed
habitat background, but
also simpler studies such
as this portrait of one
of over ninety species of
swift – a member of a
supremely aerial family
whose background is
usually the open sky.
His favourite birds were
birds of prey, but the
quality of his work was
remarkably consistent.*

precise and elegant observations of wildlife in and around his beloved parish of Selborne in his letters and journals, so Tunnicliffe created a visual diary of the birds he saw and studied in the equally beautiful world of his adopted home in Anglesey, a place he had fallen in love with and which meant so much to him.

For many years, Tunnicliffe submitted six big watercolour paintings annually to the Royal Academy in London. Some of his finished paintings appear rather tame – and at times over-designed – compared with his rough sketchbook drawings (he completed over fifty books of these in his long career) and the small paintings he made as records of every painting he sent off to a gallery or client for sale.

Eric Ennion (1900–81) was, in the opinion of many birdwatchers and wildlife painters, one of the greatest of all twentieth-century bird artists. He has certainly not been bettered at portraying the liveliness of his often restless subjects. A lack of formal training in art has never been a bar to the evolution of the best bird artists, and Ennion was no exception. The son of a doctor in the flat fenlands of rural Cambridgeshire, he took over his father's job and continued to serve his general practice until the age of forty-five; he did not exhibit any of his drawings before he was thirty. The birds in his superb watercolour and gouache drawings seem to spring off the page with life and motion, whether it is a group of Spotted Redshanks skittering across shallow water and dunking heads and necks underwater to catch fish fry at the famous RSPB bird reserve at Minsmere, Suffolk, which form the subjects of one of his most ambitious and unforgettable works, or three little vignettes of a Green Woodpecker painted as an exercise in portraying the colour changes as the bird moves from sunlight into shade.

Ennion seemed always to be drawing, whipping out his sketchbook while others were content merely to watch or talk – or if it was not to hand, drawing on an envelope or any other piece of paper. In this way he deftly fixed his interpretations of a constantly moving bird on to paper with astonishing speed and apparent ease. Ennion was able to complete one of his trademark rapid sketches in less time than it takes to sharpen a pencil.

His ability to capture that elusive quality of a bird – its personality, or 'jizz', which marks it out to a skilled observer as a member of its particular species – was astonishing. But it is not until recently that his work has been given the full acclaim it always deserved.

Ennion's major influences were Richard Talbot Kelly, with his similar, easy, fluid style and use of broad colour washes, and Frank Southgate (1872–1916), a fellow East Anglian, who unlike Talbot Kelly did not return from the horrors of World War I. Despite the limited time he had, Southgate produced – and sold – many fine watercolour paintings, mainly of wildfowl, gamebirds and waders. Thanks to his keen powers of observation and his deep understanding of the birds, gained by stalking them and watching them for days from a tent, there is a great authenticity about his portrayals, and he was particularly skilled at the difficult task of accurately painting birds in flight. Like most of his clients, but in striking contrast to Ennion, he was a keen shooter. Ennion learned from Southgate that it was not imperative to impose a pattern on a painting of a group of birds, but to remain faithful to what one observed, even if the birds were arranged haphazardly and moving in different directions.

Eric Ennion spent his life watching birds closely and imparting his knowledge and inspiring others to take up bird art. One of those who benefited greatly from his teaching, John Busby, put it well when he wrote in the introduction to the aptly named posthumous book celebrating Ennion's work, *The Living Birds of Eric Ennion* (1982), 'I doubt if any animal or bird painter has ever logged so many hours of watching'. Or as Ennion himself put it, in one of the eleven books which he both wrote and illustrated, '"How long," says the viewer, "did it take you to paint that picture?" The actual painting? – an hour maybe – plus fifty-odd years' experience'.

Sir Peter Markham Scott (1909–89) had a lot to live up to, being the son of the famous Antarctic explorer Captain Robert Falcon Scott; his mother was a noted sculptress, and his godfather was J. M. Barrie, the author of *Peter Pan*. His passion for natural history manifested itself at a very early age; as he wrote in his biography, 'by the time I was five years old, I was already a committed naturalist and a committed artist who spent long hours drawing.' In this the young Peter was helped by gentle encouragement from his mother. She was responding to the letter written to her by his father, a few days before his death on his heroic trek

back from the South Pole: 'Make the boy interested in Natural History. It is better than games. They encourage it at some schools …'

After reading natural sciences, zoology, botany, physiology, geology, art and architecture at Cambridge University, he studied painting at the Munich State Academy, Germany, and the Royal Academy Schools at Burlington House, London. By the early 1930s he was earning a living as a professional painter.

Much of Scott's work for book illustration was refreshingly new in spirit and different in appearance from the prevailing style at the time. Among the best examples are his clear, cleanly delineated plates for his own slim, very affordable and helpful *Coloured Key to the Wildfowl of the World* (1957), and those on flamingos, swans and geese for the first volume of the standard work in English on the birds of Europe and adjacent regions, *The Birds of the Western Palearctic*, which appeared in 1977. As with his paintings, these are notable for their strong sense of design.

A gifted communicator, Scott used this talent, together with his many contacts with famous and influential people worldwide, and his fame as an artist, to promote a great range of conservation initiatives. Much of his life was spent in this noble work, both as founder-director of the Severn Wildfowl Trust, and as an innovator of many other conservation initiatives. Together with the visionary ornithologist and conservationist Max Nicholson, he was the prime mover in the genesis of the World Wildlife Trust, and designed its famous Giant Panda logo. He received many honours over the years, including a knighthood for services to the conservation of wildlife and the environment.

David Reid Henry (1919–77) was born in Ceylon (now Sri Lanka), where his father George Morrison Reid-Henry (1891–1983) was a government entomologist and also a fine painter of wildlife. Like many other artists of the period, David was a great admirer of Thorburn and Lodge, and spent much time with the latter absorbing his vast knowledge of bird art and falconry when he was sent during the war to Sandhurst military academy near Lodge's Camberley home.

He developed into one of the most meticulously accurate of all bird illustrators working in the middle half of the last century, achieving this precision without making the bird static and lifeless, and setting his birds against an equally carefully painted background. Like Lodge, he learned much from his active interest in falconry and, again like his mentor, he

PLATE 192.
Northern Eagle Owl
Bubo bubo

Edward Julius Detmold

c.1930. Watercolour & pencil.
535mm x 445mm
(21in x 17½in)

The distinctive style adopted by the English wildlife painter and etcher Edward Detmold (1883–57) was the result of various influences, especially the woodcuts of the medieval artist Albrecht Dürer and Japanese art. This mysterious, menacing study of a huge Eagle Owl, its glowing orange eyes fixed on the flying Stag Beetle, is one of his most dramatic pictures. He and his twin brother, Charles Maurice, became well-known as animal painters during the Edwardian period, exhibiting their work and producing books together. Charles committed suicide when only twenty-four years old, and this deeply affected Edward, who shot himself after a long period of depression.

walked around with a bird of prey on his wrist, in his case not a falcon but a much bigger Crowned Hawk-eagle, which he had acquired on a painting trip to Rhodesia (now Zimbabwe). This powerful raptor, with its impressive double crest, created a spectacle wherever he went, and he became a popular subject for photographers in central London. His finest work appears in the many plates that were published in 1968 in the classic two-volume work on birds of prey *Eagles, Hawks and Falcons of the World* by two of the leading authorities on raptors, Leslie Brown and Dean Amadon.

Brought up by a Swedish father and a Slav mother in humble surroundings in Jamestown, upstate New York, Roger Tory Peterson (1908–96) is famous as the inventor of the modern field guide. Peterson has also often been referred to as the greatest populariser of ornithology in America since Audubon, and this is no idle accolade. While Audubon left a legacy that continues to inspire people today, over 150 years after his death, Peterson reached far more people in his lifetime than Audubon did in his, by virtue of the increasing army of amateur birdwatchers, the effectiveness of mass communication and the efficiency of the modern publishing industry. This meant that his books could be sold as cheaply as possible, while Audubon's were prohibitively expensive to all but the very wealthy.

Passionately interested in birds from childhood, Peterson spent much of his youth observing, drawing and painting them. Aided by his exceptionally keen eyesight and hearing, he became a very competent birdwatcher. After attending courses in 1927 and 1928 at the Art Students' League in New York, Peterson was accepted at the National Academy of Design where he honed his natural talent, and then went on to teach art and science at a school in a Boston suburb.

Soon he was busy working on his first field guide which, after being turned down by New York publishers, was cautiously accepted in 1934 by Boston publishers Houghton Mifflin. Peterson's genius lay in simplifying the complexities of each species' appearance into schematic, flat, side views that focused on their distinguishing shapes and plumage patterns. For ease of comparison, each plate showed a related group of birds all facing the same way. Although the illustrations were entirely black and white, they were so clear that they made it possible for the first time for beginners to become skilled at bird identification – a far cry from the images that had been available until then, which though often beautiful and inspiring, had celebrated the complexity and subtlety of a bird's feathering at the expense of clarity. In later editions, Peterson refined this approach by using colour and making the birds more solid with the use of light and shade. Most importantly, he introduced a system of arrows pointing to the key features of each species. Coming at the time it did, his inspired breakthrough played a major part in the revolution that saw the gun replaced by binoculars as a means of identifying birds.

Peterson is remembered mainly for his field guides and for popularising birdwatching in other ways, from writing to photography, but throughout his long and very full life he also painted fine, evocative studies of birds, many of which were reproduced as limited-edition prints. Most were done in watercolour and gouache and, in contrast to his field-guide plates, are finely detailed and in the tradition of Audubon.

Peterson worked tirelessly as an ambassador and educator for conservation, travelling the world to give lectures and speak up eloquently for the birds and other wildlife and wild places he loved. Again like Scott, he was rewarded by many honours, including America's highest, the Congressional Medal – and most of all by the knowledge that he had played a huge part in making birdwatching so popular, with perhaps approaching 100 million regular watchers in the USA alone.

Although photography may appear to pose a challenge to painting and drawing birds (Peterson himself said 'I prefer photography to painting … painting is so demanding. I do not do it easily …'), it is never likely to replace it. This is particularly true of illustrations designed for identification. Here the artist can build up a picture of a bird's features to create a composite image, with its most important distinguishing features emphasised. This is so much more useful than a photograph that shows a single pose under particular lighting conditions. But it is also generally true of other types of bird art. For while the best bird photographs can inspire, educate and create an emotional response equal to that gained from a great bird painting, most photographs represent moments frozen in time and reveal less about the bird – and its watcher – than the work of an accomplished artist.

PLATE 193.
Northern Cassowary
Casuarius unappendiculatus

Henrik Grönvold
1915. Watercolour.
990mm x 710mm
(39in x 28in)

*Cassowaries, from New
Guinea and Australia, are
powerful flightless birds
capable of killing animal
predators, and humans
when cornered, with a
running kick from their
powerful feet, each armed
with a huge razor-sharp
middle claw. The strange
casque on the head, of
uncertain function, was
thought to be a extension
of the skull but is now
known to be built around
a tough, elastic core.*

PLATE 194.
Atlantic Puffin *(male &
female)*
Fratercula arctica

Henrik Grönvold
c.1926. Watercolour.
115mm x 167 mm
(6⅛in x 4⅛in)

*The best-known of the
three puffin species, these
portly, boldly coloured,
comical-looking birds,
with their odd, clown-like
faces, nest deep within the
safety of long burrows.*

PL. 193.

PL. 194.

PLATE 195.
Yellow Wagtail *(male)*
Motacilla flava

Henrik Grönvold
1924–5. Watercolour.
115mm x 167mm
(4½in x 6½in)

*One of Grönvold's
paintings for the British
Museum's (Natural
History) book* British
Birds, Summer Visitors,
*this shows the aptly
named Yellow Wagtail,
which arrives from its
winter quarters in Africa*
*between late March and
mid-May, with the bright
yellow males returning
first. Grönvold has set his
male in a typical setting,
a marshy spot in a partly
waterlogged meadow,
where it can find plenty
of flies to eat among the
cowpats and cattle
hoofprints. Drainage and
loss of traditional
meadows have led to a
decline and a contraction
in the range of this lovely
bird in Britain.*

PLATE 196.
House Martin
Delichon urbica

Henrik Grönvold
1924–5. Watercolour.
167mm x 115mm (4½in
x 6½in)

*Another summer visitor
from Africa that depends
on muddy patches – in
this case to gather the
mud for its neat cup-
shaped nest beneath the
eaves of houses – is shown
in this plate from the
same book.*

PLATE 197.

Réunion Fody
'Foudia bruante'

George Edward Lodge
c.1905. Watercolour.
250mm x 333mm
(9¾in x 13in)

This illustration of a boldly coloured little member of the weaverbird family appears in Sir Walter Rothschild's book Extinct Birds *(1907), the author notes that no specimens of it are known to exist, only a description by the great French naturalist Buffon in the late eighteenth century.*

PLATE 198.

White-winged Sandpiper
Prosobonia leucoptera

George Edward Lodge
c.1905. Watercolour.
263mm x 365mm
(10¼in x 14⅜in)

This enigmatic wader was also painted by Lodge for Extinct Birds *(1907). Specimens were collected on the islands of Tahiti and Moorea in the South Pacific during Captain James Cook's famous voyages.*

Giant Moa
Dinornis novaezealandiae

**Frederick William
Frohawk**
c.1905. Watercolour.
317mm x 145mm
(12⅛in x 5¾in)

*Frohawk made this
painting of one of the
dozen or so species of
giant herbivorous
flightless birds of New
Zealand after examining
an 11½ feet (3.5m) tall
reconstructed skeleton of
the great bird, and
studying some preserved
feathers to work out the
plumage detail. The
painting was shown at the
Ornithological Congress
at Tring in 1905. Moas
became extinct, probably
about 400 years ago, as a
result of hunting by the
Maori colonisers of
the islands.*

PL. 200.

PLATE 200.
Hypothetical parrot
species
'Necropsittacus borbonicus'

Henrik Grönvold
1907. Watercolour.
221mm x 310mm
(8⅛in x 12¼in)

*Grönvold painted this
hypothetical, extinct,
species from descriptions
of a red-and-green parrot
described in sketchy
historical accounts by
visitors to the Indian
Ocean island of Réunion.
There is no evidence that
such a bird differed from
another now extinct*

*parrot that lived on
Rodrigues island, and it is
known only from further
early explorers' reports
and some fossil bones.*

PLATE 201.

European Robin
Erithacus rubecula

Paul Barruel
c.1970. Watercolour.
220mm x 145mm
(8¾in x 5¾in)

*This study of one of
Europe's commonest birds
by a great French bird
illustrator and sculptor is
deceptive in its apparent
simplicity. The plumage is
painted with little detail
but the colour work is
precise and accurate, and
the soft treatment makes
the feathers look very
lifelike, including the way
the bluish-grey feathers of
the breast side fluff out
slightly over the bend of
the wing.*

PLATE 202.

Blackcap *(male)*
Sylvia atricapilla

Paul Barruel
c.1970. Watercolour.
216mm x 142mm
(8½in x 5½in)

*This painting is of
another common European
species, whose name refers
to the most distinctive
feature of the male
shown here.*

Knot billed pigeon.
Ducula pacifica.
Pacific pigeon.

Long tailed dove
Rufous-bro
Mac

White throated pigeon.
*Columba
vitiensis*

PLATE 203.

Pacific Imperial Pigeon, Metallic Pigeon & Spot-breasted Dove
Ducula pacifica, Macropygia mackinlayi & Columba vitiensis

Thomas Theodore Barnard
1922. Watercolour.
178mm x 255mm
(7in x 10in)

PLATE 204.

Cardinal Honeyeater *(female & male)* & **Yellow-fronted White-eye**
Myzomela cardinalis & Zosterops flavifrons

Thomas Theodore Barnard
1922. Watercolour.
255mm x 178mm
(10in x 7in)

Thi splate shows two species of small songbirds from the island of Santa Maria (now usually called Gaua), in the south-west Pacific. Above is a pair of Cardinal Honeyeaters (female top, male centre); the scarlet in the male's bold plumage is among the most brilliant of all birds' colours. The other bird in this sketchbook study is one of eighty or so similar species of White-eye.

Shot at Benacre Suffolk nov. 30.1929 by R.L.S. Gooch.
Wild bred in 1927.

PLATE 205.

Common Pheasant
(male)
Phasianus colchicus

**Frederick William
Frohawk**
1930. Watercolour.
380mm x 540mm
(15in x 21¼in)

*Although the artist is
generally better known for
his illustrations of
butterflies and other
insects, this detailed and
carefully observed study of
a handsome, Common
Pheasant shows that he
could also produce fine
paintings of birds. As with
much of his work, the bird
in this portrait is very
much an individual rather
than just an average
example of the species.
Although it appears at
first glance that it could
show a largely albinistic
bird, which might have
been produced for Walter
Rothschild, who had a
great interest in aberrant
plumages and an extensive
collection of specimens to
prove it, it is more likely
that this is an
unfinished work.*

PLATE 206.

Northern Lapwing
Vanellus vanellus

Henry Payne
c.1920. Watercolour.
352mm x 250mm
(13¾in x 9⅞in)

Little is known of the artist who painted this delightful portrait of one of the most attractive European waders. He may be Henry A. Payne, a landscape and fresco painter as well as an artist in stained glass.

PLATE 207.

Schlegel's Francolin
Francolinus schlegeli

Henry Jones
c.1920. Watercolour.
255mm x 314mm
(10in x 12¼in)

Although one of the finest bird artists, Henry Jones (1838–1921) is little known today. After leaving the colonial army in India, Major Jones worked methodically through skins in the British Museum (Natural History), family by family. After completing work on the ducks and gamebirds, he made 120 paintings of the crow family before he died.

PL. 207.

Francolinus Schlegeli
Bongo Land (Stuttgart-Museum)
– Type –

PLATE 208.
Crested Shelduck
(female, left, & male)
Tadorna cristata
Shigeru Kobayashi
c.1920s. Watercolour.
346mm x 518 mm
(13⅝in x 20⅜in)

*At least three Japanese
bird artists bear the name
Kobayashi; this one is
distinguished by the
personal name Shigeru
and the pseudonym Kokei,
which he adopted when he
became an artist. His
great talent was apparent
at a very early age, and he
embarked on a study of
painting when just twelve
years old. He combined
the decorative, intuitive
approach of classical
Japanese painting with
the clear, scientifically
accurate style of the
modern Western
identification illustration,
to produce illustrations
reminiscent of the later
work of such painters as
Sir Peter Scott and Roger
Tory Peterson.*

PLATE 209.
Silvery-cheeked
Hornbill
Bycanistes brevis

**Claude Gibney
Finch-Davies**
1920. Watercolour
& pencil.
255mm x 178mm
(10in x 7in)

*The huge casque on top of
the head, much larger in
the male, is hollow with a
small opening into the
mouth, making it likely
that one function of this
strange appendage is to
serve, like the body of a
violin, as a resonator in
producing the bird's very
loud trumpeting calls .*

PLATE 210.
African Open-bill
Anastomus lamelligerus

**Claude Gibney
Finch-Davies**
1918. Watercolour
& pencil.
255mm x 178mm
(10in x 7in)

*This bird with sombre
plumage and an odd-
looking bill is a member
of the stork family. It
mainly haunts marshes
and other wetlands, where
it feeds on molluscs. Its
only other close relative
lives in Asia.*

C.G. Finch-Davies
30-6-18

PL. 212.

PLATE 211.

Kakapo
Strigops habroptilus

Angela Gladwell
1998. Watercolour.
570mm x 770mm
(22⅛in x 30¼in)

This modern artist is very gifted at rendering bird plumage convincingly, and at producing delicate effects of light and shade. The Kakapo is one of the world's rarest parrots, and a considerable conservation effort over many years has gone into ensuring that it still survives. It is instructive to compare this illustration of the species with that on page 262.

PLATE 212.

Brown Kiwi
Apteryx australis

Angela Gladwell
1997. Watercolour.
570mm x 770mm
(22⅛in x 30¼in)

In this sensitive portrait of a Brown Kiwi solicitously attending to its chick, the subtle range of colours of the birds' feathers is shown to great advantage. The strange plumage of the four species of kiwi is more like mammalian hair than feathers, and the wings are even smaller than in the other large flightless birds, or ratites, being reduced to mere stubs, hidden beneath their feathers.

A. Gladwell.
Strigops habroptilus

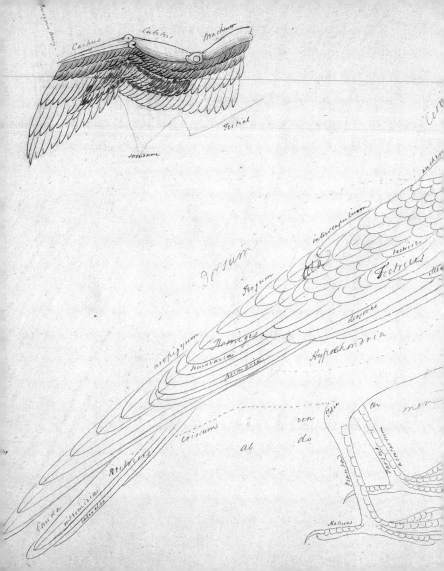

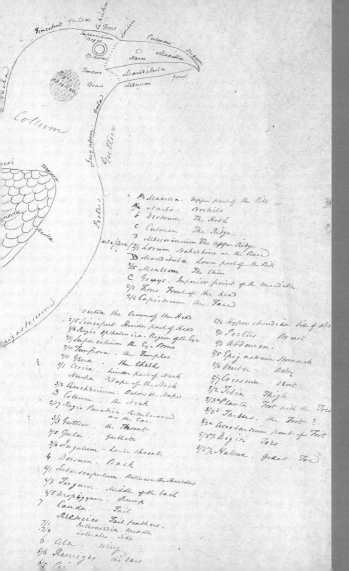

LIST OF ILLUSTRATIONS

the collection of Lady Mary Impey *(c.1780)*, watercolour, 345mm x 486mm (13½in x 19⅛in)

p114: Plate 77. Tern, *Sternidae* sp., by Sheik Zayn al-Din, drawing no.20 from the collection of Lady Mary Impey *(1781)*, watercolour, 614mm x 845mm (33¼in x 24¼in)

p115: Plate 78. Green Heron, *Butorides virescens*, William Bartram, drawing no. 17 from *Botanical and Zoological Drawings [1774]*, pen & ink & watercolour on paper, 377mm x 245mm (14¾in x 9¾in)

p116: Plate 79. Bobolink, *Dolichonyx oryzivorus*, William Bartram, drawing no. 24 from *Botanical and Zoological Drawings [1774–75]*, pen & ink & watercolour on paper, 256mm x 202mm (10in x 12½in)

p117: Plate 80. American Black vulture, *Coragyps atratus*, William Bartram, drawing no. 25 from *Botanical and Zoological Drawings (1756–88)*, pen & ink & watercolour on paper, 242mm x 319mm (10in x 12½in)

p118-9: Plate 81. Northern Cardinal, *Cardinalis cardinalis*, William Bartram, drawing no. 55 from *Botanical and Zoological Drawings (1772)*, pen & ink, 181mm x 304mm (7¼in x 12in)

p120-1: Endpaper from *The Natural History of Caroline, Florida and the Bahama Islands (1731)* by Mark Catesby

p123: Plate 82. Wild Turkey, *Meleagris gallopavo*, John James Audubon, plate 1 from *Birds of America*, original double elephant folio *(1829)*, hand-coloured aquatint, 970mm x 656mm (38¼in x 25¾in)

p126: Plate 83. Eggs of 1. Song Thrush; 2. Golden-crested Wren (now Goldcrest); 3. Chimney Swallow (now Barn Swallow); 4. Common Wren (now Northern Wren); 5. Jay (now Eurasian Jay); 6. Kingfisher (now Eurasian Kingfisher) 1. *Turdus philomelos*; 2. *Regulus regulus*; 3. *Hirundo rustica*; 4. *Troglodytes troglodytes*; 5. *Garrulus glandarius*; 6. *Alcedo atthis*; James Hope Stewart *(c.1835)*, watercolour, 106mm x 172mm (4⅛in x 6¾in)

p129: Plate 84. Purple Martin, *Progne subis*, John James Audubon, plate XXII from *Birds of America*, original double elephant folio *(1827–30)*, hand-coloured aquatint, 658mm x 525mm (26in x 20¾in)

p132: Plate 85. Carolina Parakeet, *Conuropsis carolinensis*, John James Audubon, plate XXVI from *Birds of America*, original double elephant folio *(1827–30)*, hand-coloured aquatint, 853mm x 600mm (33½in x 23½in)

p134: Plate 86. Golden Eagle, *Aquila chrysaetos*, John James Audubon, plate CLXXXI from *Birds of America*, original double elephant folio *(1833)*, hand-coloured aquatint, 970mm x 656mm (38¼in x 25¾in)

p137: Plate 87. Black-winged Stilt, *Himantopus himantopus*, anonymous Chinese artist, plate 62 from the John Reeves collection of Zoological Drawings from Canton, China *(1822–29)*, watercolour, 590mm x 477mm (23¼in x 18¾in)

p139: Plate 88. Black Guillemot, *Cepphus grylle*, John James Audubon, plate CCXIX from *Birds of America (1834)*, hand-coloured aquatint, 445mm x 518mm (17½in x 20⅜in)

p140: Plate 89. Channel-billed Toucan, *Ramphastos vitellinus*, Nicholas Aylward Vigors *(1831)*, oil on canvas, 340mm x 460mm (13½in x 18in)

p142: Plate 90. Peregrine Falcon, *Falco peregrinus*, William MacGillivray *(1839)*, watercolour, 750mm x 545mm (29½in x 21½in)

p144: Plate 91. Northern Raven, *Corvus Corax*, William MacGillivray *(1832)*, watercolour, 478mm x 683mm (18¾in x 27in)

p146: Plate 92. Grey Heron, *Ardea cinerea*, William MacGillivray *(c.1835)*, watercolour, 965mm x 735mm (38in x 29in)

p149: Plate 93. Long-billed Sunbird (male & young), *Cinnyris lotenius*, by Khuleeloddeen from the collection of Sir William Jardine *(c.1830–40)*, gouache, 122mm x 126mm (5in x 4½in)

p150: Plate 94. Beautiful Sunbird, *Cinnyris pulchellus*, William Swainson *(c.1835)*, watercolour, 164mm x 115mm (6½in x 4½in)

p153: Plate 95. Blue-bellied Roller, *Coracias cyanogaster*, William Swainson *(c.1835)*, watercolour, 170mm x 125mm (6¾in x 5in)

p155: Plate 96. African Grey Parrot, *Psittacus erithacus*, from the *Illustrations in Water-Colour of Indian Zoology and Botany* by Major-General Thomas Hardwicke and Mrs Duncan Campbell *(1822)*, watercolour, 435mm x 560mm (17¼in x 22in)

p156: Plate 97. Scarlet Ibis, *Eudocimus ruber*, John James Audubon, plate CCCXCVII from *Birds of America*, original double elephant folio *(1837)*, hand-coloured aquatint, 534mm x 740mm (21in x 29¼in)

p158: Plate 98. Savannah Sparrow, *Passerculus sandwichensis*, John James Audubon, plate CIX from *Birds of America*, original double elephant folio *(1831)*, hand-coloured aquatint, 496mm x 313mm (19½in x 12¼in)

p159: Plate 99. Barn Swallow, *Hirundo rustica*, John James Audubon, plate CLXXIII from *Birds of America*, original double elephant folio *(1833)*, hand-coloured aquatint, 493mm x 310mm (19½in x 12¼in)

p160: Plate 100. Rough-legged Hawk, *Buteo lagopus*, John James Audubon, plate CCCCXXII from *Birds of America*, original double elephant folio *(1838)*, hand-coloured aquatint, 725mm x 645mm (28½in x 25½in)

p161: Plate 101. Hairy Woodpecker & Three-toed Woodpecker, *Picoides villosus* & *Picoides tridactylus*, John James Audubon, plate CCCCXVII from *Birds of America*, original double elephant folio *(1838)*, hand-coloured aquatint, 770mm x 575mm (30¼in x 22¾in)

p162: Plate 102. Trumpeter Swan, *Cygnus buccinator*, John James Audubon, plate CCCCVI from *Birds of America*, original double elephant folio *(1838)*, hand-coloured aquatint, 656mm x 970mm (25¾in x 38¼in)

p163: Plate 103. Gull-billed Tern, *Sterna nilotica*, John James Audubon, plate CCCX from *Birds of America* original double elephant folio *(1838)*, hand-coloured aquatint, 495mm x 402mm (19½in x 15¾in)

p164: Plate 104. Magnificent Frigatebird, *Fregata magnificens*, John James Audubon, plate CCLXXI from *Birds of America*, original double elephant folio *(1835)*, hand-coloured aquatint, 970mm x 656mm (38¼in x 25¾in)

p165: Plate 105. American Swallow-tailed Kite, *Elanus forficatus*, John James Audubon, plate LXXII from *Birds of America*, original double elephant folio *(1829)*, hand-coloured aquatint, 524mm x 696mm (20¾in x 27½in)

p166-7: Plate 106. Leach's Storm Petrel, *Oceanodroma leucorhoa*, John James Audubon, plate XXII from *Birds of America*, original double elephant folio *(1835)*, hand-coloured aquatint, 313mm x 492mm (12¼in x 19¼in)

p168: Plate 107. Northern Gannet, *Morus bassanus*, William MacGillivray *(1831)*, watercolour, 810mm x 550mm (32in x 21¼in)

p169: Plate 108. Common Kestrel, *Falco Tinnunculus*, William MacGillivray *(1835)*, watercolour,

(1785) by Alexander Mondo

p213: Plate 149. Scarlet Macaw, *Ara Macao*, Edward Lear, plate 7 from *Illustrations of the family of Psittacidae or Parrots (1832)*, watercolour, 554mm x 365mm (21¾in x 14½in)

p215: Plate 150. Blue-and-Yellow Macaw, *Ara ararauna*, Edward Lear, plate 8 from *Illustrations of the family of Psittacidae or Parrots (1832)*, watercolour, 554mm x 365mm (21¾in x 14½in)

p217: Plate 151. 'Jacobine Pigeon', *Columba livia*, domestic variety, Edward Lear *(c.1835)*, watercolour, 155mm x 110mm (6in x 4¼in)

p218: Plate 152. Green Turaco, *Tauraco persa*, Edward Lear *(c.1835)*, watercolour, 231mm x 142mm (9¼in x 5½in)

p221: Plate 153. Marvellous Spatuletail, *Loddigesia mirabilis*, John Gould, plate 61 from *A Monograph of the Trochilidae or family of Humming-birds*, Vol. III *(c.1849–61)*, lithograph, 545mm x 365mm (21½in x 14½in)

p222: Plate 154. South American Painted Snipe, *Nycticryphes semicollaris*, by Elizabeth Gould *(c.1835)*, watercolour & pencil, 161mm x 227mm (6½in x 9in)

p225: Plate 155. Purple Cochoa, *Cochoa purpurea*, anonymous, plate 229 from the collection of birds and mammals of Nepal made by Brian Houghton Hodgson *(c.1850)*, watercolour, 280mm x 470mm (11in x 18½in)

p226: Plate 156. Pink-footed Goose, *Anser brachyrhynchus*, John Gould *(c.1865)*, watercolour & ink, 180mm x 133mm (7in x 5¼in)

p227: Plate 157. Pink-footed Goose (details), *Anser brachyrhynchus*, John Gould *(c.1865)*, watercolour & ink, 133mm x 180mm (5¼in x 7in)

p229: Plate 158. Eggs of various birds by Margaret Bushby Lascelles Cockburn *(1858)*, watercolour, 260mm x 202mm (10¼in x 8in)

p230: Plate 159. Snares Penguin & Fiordland Penguin, *Eudyptes robustus* & *Eudyptes pachyrhynchus*, John Gerrard Keulemans *(c.1887–1905)*, watercolour, 181mm x 176mm (7¼in x 7in)

p233: Plate 160. Buller's Albatross (upper) & Salvin's Albatross (lower), *Thalassarche bulleri* & *Thalassarche salvini* by John Gerrard Keulemans *(c.1887–1905)*, watercolour, 292mm x 232mm (11½in x 9¼in)

p234: Plate 161. Rufous-necked Hornbill, *Aceros nipalensis*, anonymous, from the Thomas Hardwick Collection *(c.1785–1820)*, watercolour, 271mm x 372mm (10¾in x 14¾in)

p238: Plate 162. Lady Amherst's Pheasant, *Chrysolophus amherstiae*, by Joseph Wolf, plate 14 from *A Monograph of the Phasianidae (1872)*, by Daniel Giraud Elliot, lithograph, 450mm x 592mm (17¾in x 23¼in)

p241: Plate 163. Wallace's Fruit-Dove, *Ptilinopus wallaci*, John Gould, plate 55 from *Birds of New Guinea*, Vol. V *(1875–88)*, hand-coloured lithograph, 548mm x 364mm (21½in x 14¼in)

p245: Plate 164. Yellow-casqued Wattled Hornbill, *Ceratogymna elata*, by John Gerrard Keulemans *(c.1876-82)*, watercolour & gouache, 357mm x 261mm (14in x 10¼in)

p248: Plate 165. Flame Bowerbird, *Sericulus aureus*, John Gould, plate 48 from *Birds of New Guinea*, Vol. I *(c.1875–88)*, hand-coloured lithograph, 548mm x 364mm (21½in x 14¼in)

p249: Plate 166. Resplendent Quetzal, *Pharomachrus moccino*, John Gould, from *A Monograph of the Trogonidae or Family of Trogons (1838)*, hand-coloured lithograph, 969mm x 347mm (38¼in x 13¾in)

p250: Plate 167. Koklass Pheasant, *Pucrasia macrolopha*, Rajman Singh *(c.1856–64)*, watercolour, 256mm x 367mm (10in x 14½in)

p251: Plate 168. Cheer Pheasant, *Catreus wallichii*, Rajman Singh *(c.1856–64)*, watercolour, 358mm x 256mm (14in x 10in)

p252: Plate 169. Fiordland Penguin, *Eudyptes pachyrhynchus*, Richard Laishley *(1863–88)*, watercolour & pencil, 254mm x 178mm (10in x 7in)

p253: Plate 170. Brown Kiwi, *Apteryx australis*, Richard Laishley *(c.1863–88)*, watercolour, 535mm x 425mm (21in x 16¾in)

p254-5: Plate 171. Long-billed Pipit, *Anthus similis*, Margaret Bushby Lascelles Cockburn *(1858)*, watercolour, 201mm x 254mm (8in x 10in)

p256: Plate 172. Asian Paradise-Flycatcher, *Terpsiphone paradisi*, by Margaret Bushby Lascelles Cockburn *(1858)*, watercolour, 254mm x 201mm (10in x 8in)

p257: Plate 173. Vernal Hanging-Parrot, *Loriculus vernalis*, Margaret Bushby Lascelles Cockburn *(1858)*, watercolour, 254mm x 201mm (10in x 8in)

p258: Plate 174. Spectacled Cormorant, *Phalacrocorax perspicillatus*, John Gerrard Keulemans *(c.1905)*, watercolour, 825mm x 620mm (32½in x 24½in)

p259: Plate 175. 'Oiseaux Bleu' ('Blue Bird'), *Apterornis coerulescens*, John Gerrard Keulemans *(c.1905)*, watercolour, 806mm x 621mm (31¾in x 24½in)

p260: Plate 176. Great Bustard, Little Bustard & Houbara Bustard, *Otis tarda, Tetrax tetrax & Chlamydotis undulata*, John Gerrard Keulemans *(c.1842–1912)*, oil on canvas, 1990mm x 2330mm (46¾in x 87¾in)

p261: Plate 177. Black-billed Magpie, *Pica pica*, John Gerrard Keulemans *(1896)*, watercolour & gouache, 635mm x 523mm (25in x 20½in)

p262: Plate 178. Kakapo, *Strigops habroptilus*, John Gerrard Keulemans *(c.1887–1905)*, watercolour, 295mm x 244mm (11½in x 9½in)

p263: Plate 179. Réunion Crested Starling, *Fregilupus varius*, John Gerrard Keulemans *(c.1905)*, watercolour, 385mm x 278mm (15¼in x 11in)

p264-5: Endpaper from *Voyage Autour du Monde sur la fregate La Venus (1846)* by M. Abel du Petit-Thouars

p267: Plate 180. Blue Tit (Canary Islands races), *Parus caeruleus*, subspecies (from top to bottom): *degener, teneriffae, palmensis, ambrosius*, Henrik Gronvold *(c.1920)*, watercolour, 260mm x 185mm (10¼in x 7¼in)

p268: Plate 181. Handsome Francolin (breast feathers), A. *Francolinus nobilis nobilis*; B. *Francolinus nobilis chapini*, Henrik Gronvold *(c.1934)*, watercolour, 139mm x 146mm (5½in x 5¾in)

p273: Plate 182. Brunnich's Guillemot & Guillemot, *Uria lomvia* & *Uria aalge* by Archibald Thorburn *(c.1885-97)*, watercolour, 247mm x 170mm (9¾in x 6¾in)

p274: Plate 183. Northern Raven, *Corvus corax*, Archibald Thorburn *(c.1885–97)*, watercolour, 150mm x 227mm (6in x 9in)

p277: Plate 184. Black-billed Magpie, *pica pica*, George Edward Lodge *(c.1930)*, chalk, 260mm x 208mm (10¼in x 9in)

p280: Plate 185. Green Woodpecker, *Picus viridis*, Frederick William Frohawk *(1920)*, pencil & monochrome wash, 228mm x 169mm (9in x 6¾in)

p283: Plate 186. Sanderling, *Calidris albus*, Frederick William

BIBLIOGRAPHY

Please note this is a select bibliography. For reasons of space, it does not include the many papers and articles in journals, magazines and specialist books that the author consulted during the writing of this book. Many of the books listed here are no longer in print, but they can be consulted in libraries or purchased second hand.

Allen, D. E. 1976. *The Naturalist in Britain: A Social History.* Penguin Books.

Anker, J. 1938. *Bird Books and Bird Art.* Munksgaard and Munksgaard, Copenhagen.

Bain, I. (Ed.) 1979. *Thomas Bewick Vignettes, being tail-pieces engraved principally for his General History of Quadrupeds & History of British Birds.* Scolar Press, London.

Bain, I. 1979. *Thomas Bewick: An Illustrated Record of His Life and Work.* Tyne and Wear County Council Museums, Newcastle-upon-Tyne.

Bannerman, D. 1954. Obituary of George Edward Lodge, in *Ibis,* 96, 474–6.

Bannerman, D. 1956. Tribute to George Edward Lodge in *The Birds of the British Isles, Volume 5,* Oliver & Boyd, London.

Barber, L. 1980. *The Heyday of Natural History 1820–1870.* Jonathan Cape, London.

Blaugrund, A. & Stebbins, T. E. Jr. (Eds.) 1993. *John James Audubon: The Watercolours for The Birds of America.* Villard Books/Random House & The New York Historical Society.

Boehme, S. E. 2000. *John James Audubon in the West: The Last Expedition.* Abrams, New York.

Buchanan, H. 1979. *Nature Into Art: A Treasury of Great Natural History Books.* Mayflower books, New York.

Cantwell, R. 1961. *Alexander Wilson, Naturalist and Pioneer.* Lippincott, Philadelphia.

Chalmers, J. 2003. *Audubon in Edinburgh: The Scottish Associates of John James Audubon.* NMS Enterprises, Edinburgh.

Chatfield, J. E. 1987. *EW Frohawk: his life and work.* Crowood Press, Marlborough.

Clark, K. 1977. *Animals and Men.* Thames and Hudson, London.

Cocker, M. and Inskipp, C. 1988. *A Himalayan Ornithologist: The Life and Work of Brian Houghton Hodgson.* Oxford University Press, Oxford.

Cusa, N. 1985. *Tunnicliffe's Birdlife.* Clive Holloway Books, London.

Datta, A. 1997. *John Gould in Australia: Letters and Drawings.* The Miegunyah Press, Victoria, Australia.

Ennion, E. (Introduction and Commentary by Busby, J.). 1982. *The Living Birds of Eric Ennion.* Gollancz, London.

Fisher, C. (Ed.) 2002. *A Passion for Natural History: The Life and Legacy of the 13th Earl of Derby.* National Museums & Galleries on Merseyside, Liverpool.

Fisher, J. 1966. *The Shell Bird Book.* Ebury Press and Michael Joseph, London.

Ford, Alice. 1964. *John James Audubon.* Oklahoma University Press, Norman, Oklahoma.

Foshay, E. M. 1997. *John James Audubon.* Abrams, New York.

Fuller, E. 1999. *The Great Auk.* Published by the author, Southborough, Kent.

Fuller, E. 2000. *Extinct Birds.* Oxford University Press, Oxford.

Fuller, E. 2002. *Dodo: from Extinction to Icon.* HarperCollins, London.

Gaskell, J. 2000. *Who Killed the Great Auk?* Oxford University Press, Oxford.

Gilbert, P. 1998. *John Abbot: Birds, Butterflies and Other Wonders.* Merrell Holberton and The Natural History Museum, London.

Glasier, P. 1963. *As the Falcon Her Bells.* William Heinemann, London.

Hammond, N. 1986. *Twentieth Century Wildlife Artists.* Croom Helm, Beckenham, Kent.

Hammond, N. 1998. *Modern Wildlife Painting.* Pica Press, Mountfield, East Sussex.

Hart-Davis, D. 2003. *Audubon's Elephant.* Weidenfeld & Nicolson, London.

Henry, B. 1986. *Highlight the Wild: The Art of the Reid-Henrys.* Palaquin Publishing, Hartley Wintney, Hants.

Hill, M. 1987. *Bruno Liljefors. The Peerless Eye.* Allen, Kingston upon Hull.

Huxley, E. 1993. *Peter Scott: Painter and Naturalist.* Faber & Faber, London.

Hyman, S. 1980. *Edward Lear's Birds.* The Wellfleet Press, Secaucus, New Jersey.

Jackson, C. E. 1975. *Bird Illustrators: Some artists in early lithography.* H. F. & G. Witherby, London.

Jackson, C. E. 1978. *Wood Engravings of Birds.* H. F. & G. Witherby, London.

Jackson, C. E. 1989. *Bird Etchings: the illustrators and their books 1655–1855.* Cornell University Press, Ithaca, New York.

Jackson, C. E. 1993. *Great Bird Paintings: Vol. 1: The Old Masters.* Antique Collectors' Club, Woodbridge.

Jackson, C. E. 1994. *Bird Painting: The Eighteenth Century.* Antique Collectors' Club, Woodbridge.

Jackson, C. E. 1998. *Sarah Stone: Natural curiosities from the New Worlds.* Merrell Holberton and The Natural History Museum, London.

Jackson, C. E. 1999. *Dictionary of Bird Artists of the World.* Antique Collectors' Club, Woodbridge.

Jonsson, L. 2002. *Birds and Light: The Art of Lars Jonsson.* Christopher Helm, London.

Kelly, R. B. T. 1955. *Birdlife and the Painter*. Studio Publications, London.

Keulemans, A. and Coldewey, J. 1982. *Feathers to Brush: The Victorian Bird Artist John Gerrard Keulemans 1842-1912*. Deventer, Netherlands.

Klingender, F. 1971. *Animals in art and thought to the end of the Middle Ages*. Routledge & Kegan Paul, London.

Knight, D. 1977. *Zoological Illustration: an essay towards a history of printed zoological pictures*. William Dawson, Folkestone and Archon Books, Hamden, Connecticut.

Lambourne, M. 1987. *John Gould: Bird Man*. Osberton Productions, Milton Keynes.

Lambourne, M. 1992. *Birds of the World: Over 400 of John Gould's Classic Bird Illustrations*. Rizzoli International, New York.

Lambourne, M. 2001. *The Art of Bird Illustration*, Quantum Publishing, London.

Lear, E. 1997. *The Family of Parrots Illustrations by Edward Lear*. Pomegranate Artbooks, San Francisco.

Lodge, G. E. 1946. *Memoirs of an Artist Naturalist*. Gurney and Jackson, London.

Lysaght, A. M. 1975. *The Book of Birds: Five Centuries of Bird Illustration*. Phaidon, London.

MacGillivray, W. S. 1910. *Life of William MacGillivray*. John Murray, London.

Marcham, F. G. 1971. *Louis Agassiz Fuertes and the Singular Beauty of Birds*. Harper Row, New York.

Mason, A. S. 1992. *George Edwards: The Bedell and His Birds*. Royal College of Physicians of London, London.

Mathews, G. M. 1931. 'John Latham

(1740-1837): an early English Ornithologist', *Ibis*, pp. 466-475.

McEvey, Allan. 1973. *John Gould's Contribution to British Art*. Sydney University Press, Sydney.

Mearns, B. & Mearns, R. 1988. *Biographies for Birdwatchers: The Lives of Those Commemorated in Western Palaearctic Bird Names*. Academic Press, London.

Mearns, B. & Mearns, R. 1988. *The Bird Collectors*. Academic Press, London.

Mearns, B. & Mearns, R. 1992. *Audubon to Xántus; The Lives of Those Commemorated in North American Bird Names*. Academic Press, London.

Moyal, A. 1986. *'A Bright and Savage Land': Science in Colonial Australia*. Collins, Sydney.

Niall, I. 1980. *Portrait of a Country Artist: Charles F. Tunnicliffe, RA, 1901-1979*. Gollancz, London.

Niall, I. 1983. *Tunnicliffe's Countryside*. Clive Holloway Books, London.

Noakes, V. 1979. *Edward Lear: The Life of a Wanderer*. Fontana/Collins, London.

Noakes, V. 1985. *Edward Lear 1812-1888*. Royal Academy of Arts Exhibition Catalogue, London.

Norst, M. 1989. *Ferdinand Bauer: Australian Natural History Drawings*. The Natural History Museum, London.

Palmer, A. H. 1895. *The Life of Joseph Wolf, Animal Painter*. Longmans, Green and Company, London.

Peck, R. M. 1982. *A Celebration of Birds: the Life and Art of Louis Agassiz Fuertes*. Walker, New York.

Peterson, R. T. 1980. *Audubon Birds*. Abbeville Press, New York.

Peterson, R. T. 1994. *Roger Tory Peterson: The Art and Photography of the World's Foremost Birder*. Houghton Mifflin, Boston, Massachusetts.

Rajnai, M. 1989. Biography of Jakob Bogdani, in introduction to catalogue of an exhibition of his paintings at the Richard Green Gallery, London.

Ralph, R. 1999. *William MacGillivray: Creatures of Air, Land and Sea*. Merrell Holberton and The Natural History Museum, London.

Rice, T. 2000. *Voyages of Discovery: Three Centuries of Natural History Exploration*. The Natural History Museum/ Scriptum Editions, London.

Sauer, G. 1982. *John Gould the Bird Man, a Chronology and Bibliography*. Lansdowne, Melbourne.

Schneider, N. 2003. *Still Life: Still Life Painting in the Early Modern Period*. Taschen, Cologne.

Scott, P. 1961. *The Eye of the Wind: an Autobiography*. Hodder and Stoughton, London.

Scott, P. 1992. *The Art of Peter Scott: Images from a Lifetime*, Sinclair Stevenson, London.

Shackleton, K. 1986. *Wildlife and Wilderness. An Artist's World*. Clive Holloway Books, London.

Sitwell, S., Buchanan, H. and Fisher, J. 1990. *Fine Bird Books, 1700-1900*. H. F. & G. Witherby, London.

Southern, J. 1981. *Thorburn's Landscape: The Major Natural History Paintings*. Elm Tree Books, London.

Stresemann, E. 1975. *Ornithology from Aristotle to the Present*. Harvard University Press Cambridge, Massachusetts.

Thackray, J. & Press, B. 2004. *The Natural History Museum: Nature's Treasurehouse*. The Natural History Museum, London.

Thorburn, A., Fisher, J. and Parslow, J. 1985. *Thorburn's Birds*. Bounty Books, London.

Thorburn, A. 1990. *Thorburn's Birds of Prey*. Hyperion Books, New York

Trapnell, D. 1991. *Nature in Art: A Celebration of 300 Years of Wildlife Paintings*. David & Charles, Newton Abbot.

Tree, I. 2003. *The Bird Man: The Extraordinary Story of John Gould*. Ebury Press, London.

Tunnicliffe, C. F. 1945. *Bird Portraiture*. The Studio, London and New York.

Tunnicliffe, C. F. (Ed. Gillmor, R.) 1981. *Sketches of Bird Life*. Gollancz, London.

Tunnicliffe, C. F. (introduction and commentary by Cusa, N.) 1984. *Tunnicliffe's Birds. Measured drawings by C. F. Tunnicliffe*. R.A. Gollancz, London.

Tunnicliffe, C. F. 1984. *Shorelands Summer Diary*. Clive Holloway Books, London.

Walters, M. 2003. *A Concise History of Ornithology: the lives and works of its founding figures*. Christopher Helm, London.

Yapp, B. 1981. *Birds in Medieval Manuscripts*. The British Library, London.

INDEX

ACKNOWLEDGEMENTS

A book such as this one represents the fruit of many labourers. At my publishers, I owe a huge debt of gratitude to my editor, David Shannon, whose wise counsel, unflagging patience, enthusiasm and good humour have been of immense help throughout the creation of this book; to the designer, David Mackintosh, whose skills are apparent on looking at any one of its beautiful pages, and to Ruth Deary and Pritti Ramjee for their assistance. I also owe a great debt to my redoubtable agent, Pat White.

At the Natural History Museum, I must first thank Trudy Brannan, the Editorial Manager of NHM Publishing, with whom I have been privileged to work as an editor on a variety of Natural History Museum titles over the last five years, for it was she who first suggested that I write this book, and also Beverley Ager, Lynn Millhouse and Hillary Smith. For help with tracking down information, and for reading the text, checking facts and suggesting valuable improvements, I am greatly indebted to the following NHM staff: Paul Cooper, Ann Datta, Christopher Mills and others in the Zoology Library, South Kensington, and at Tring: Jo Cooper, Katrina Cook, Alison Harding, and for his delightful Foreword, Robert Prys-Jones, Head of Bird Group. I also thank the many others from other libraries, museums and art galleries who shared their time and knowledge, especially Ann Sylph, Michael Palmer and Marie Monaghan at the Zoological Society of London Library, and Clemency Fisher, Curator of Birds and Mammals at the Liverpool Museum, who made valuable contributions to chapter three and also enlisted help from Lesley Overstreet and Bob Peck in the USA.

I must also mention by name my very good friend, the fine ornithologist and writer Mark Cocker, for our many stimulating discussions and for his constructive criticisms and constant encouragement throughout; and also his partner Mary Muir and daughters Rachael and Miriam for their hospitality on my escapes from my London desk to his Norfolk home. I also owe a debt to a host of others – ornithologists, bird artists and various friends and relatives – for sparing valuable time to write and talk to me, provide accommodation or help me in other ways.

They will, I hope, understand that the lack of space prohibits individual mention.

Writers are often not the easiest people with whom to share one's life and home, but I am fortunate indeed to be blessed with a very understanding family; as ever, I thank you, Melanie, Becky, Alys and Tom, for putting up with both the long periods when I was shut away in my library and my occasional longer absences from the breakfast, lunch and dinner tables (and in Becky's case, the telephone). I couldn't have done it without you.

Finally, I must not forget my debt to all the bird artists, both past and present, whose labours have made my own so fulfilling and fascinating.

Original artworks photographed by the Natural History Museum's Photographic Unit.
NHM Picture library website: http://piclib.nhm.ac.uk/